SERVANTS and FOOLS

Praise for *Servants and Fools*

"We pastors and church leaders have been buffeted about in the past couple of decades by hundreds of books on leadership. We are accused of being ineffective leaders, are charged with neglecting the fascinating insights of business and organizational leadership, and are given ten surefire, always effective principles for fail-safe leadership. Arthur Boers has written the book we have sorely needed, a book that is destined to become the main text in my seminary courses in church leadership, a book that is sure to be enthusiastically received by thousands of contemporary Christian leaders. Boers underscores the joyful peculiarity of specifically Christian leadership. His book is unique: a biblically based, christologically grounded defense of leadership in the name of Christ."

—Will Willimon, Professor of the Practice of Christian Ministry, Duke Divinity School, Durham, NC; United Methodist Bishop, retired; author of *Pastor: The Theology and Practice of Ordained Ministry*

"Arthur Boers in this book punctures all pretensions, unveils delightful discoveries, and exhibits perceptive insights. This is necessary when there are so many less-than-Christian publications vying for renown in an overcrowded field. Truly *Servants and Fools* is the most potent book on Christian leadership!"

—Marva J. Dawn, theologian, author, speaker

"Leadership is a trendy topic, but Boers digs deep to discover what God has been saying all along. Apparently we are not the first generation to survey the shallow waters and ask God for something more. Beyond motivational speeches, success seminars, and the reminiscences of the rich and famous, there is a subversive strain of scripture just waiting to be rediscovered."

—Lillian Daniel, author of *When "Spiritual But Not Religious" Is Not Enough: Seeing God in Surprising Places, Even the Church*

"*Servants and Fools* is a brilliant and essential contribution to any serious study of leadership: robust, faithful, insightful biblical teaching. Plus judicious, knowledgeable harvesting of the best contributions of leadership and management theorists and practitioners. Plus humor, in-the-trenches experiences, and practical applications. I cannot imagine ever teaching another class on leadership without assigning and discussing Arthur Boers's book!"

—David W. Gill, Mockler-Phillips Professor of Workplace Theology and Business Ethics, Gordon-Conwell Theological Seminary, South Hampton, MA

"All of society, including the church, requires leadership in order to function. In *Servants and Fools*, Arthur Boers searches for biblical and theological meanings and purposes of leadership. In so doing, he expands our understanding of how to lead."

—Brian C. Stiller, Global Ambassador, The World Evangelical Alliance

"In *Servants and Fools: A Biblical Theology of Leadership*, Arthur Boers deconstructs the contemporary cult of 'leadership' and serves up a refreshingly biblical alternative. He reviews all the evangelical community's usual suspects when it comes to great leadership models in the Bible and finds most of them wanting. *Servants and Fools* makes for a great cautionary tale for today's churches, seminaries, and Christian nonprofits. At the same time, his reconstruction of what leadership could be offers great insight for secular organizations and leaders as well. In the end Boers roots his own positive reflections in the prophetic tradition, in Jesus's teachings, and counter-intuitive stories of great biblical leaders who were, at least by the standards of contemporary leadership literature, often amazing failures too. I wish I had read this book years ago when I was starting my career as a pastor, professor, and Christian graduate school president. I would have relaxed when it came to my day-to-day striving to succeed, and I might have enjoyed working out my ideals more."

—John Suk, author, former editor-in-chief of *The Banner*, and pastor of Lawrence Park Community Church, Toronto, Canada

Arthur Boers

SERVANTS and FOOLS

Foreword by Eugene Peterson

A Biblical Theology of Leadership

Abingdon Press
Nashville

SERVANTS AND FOOLS:
A BIBLICAL THEOLOGY OF LEADERSHIP

This book is printed on acid-free paper.

Library of Congress Cataloging-in-Publication Data

Boers, Arthur P. (Arthur Paul), 1957-
Servants and fools : a biblical theology of leadership / Arthur Boers.—First [edition].
pages cm
Includes bibliographical references.
ISBN 978-1-4267-9978-5 (binding: soft back) 1. Christian leadership. 2. Leadership—Religious aspects—Christianity. I. Title.
BV652.1.B64 2015
253—dc23

2015019014

Disclaimer: All names and significant details have been changed by the author to protect the identities of the persons mentioned in this book.

15 16 17 18 19 20 21 22 23 24—10 9 8 7 6 5 4 3 2 1
MANUFACTURED IN THE UNITED STATES OF AMERICA

I dedicate this to Kevin Abma,
my lifelong friend,
closer than a brother.

Contents

Foreword

It is not easy for Christians to acquire a vocational identity these days. The society is long gone in which virtually everyone in the community more or less knew, even if vaguely, what Christian leaders do, much as they did physicians and lawyers and pharmacists and the blacksmith. But as our society has secularized, the leaders in affairs of faith and church are now understood through the filters of a secular culture and are now understood variously as a religious CEO, a community organizer, a therapist, a chaplain to a religious club, or a religious entertainer. Moses, David, Jesus, and Paul have been elbowed to the sidelines by Marx, Darwin, and Freud.

So those of us who have the responsibilities of leadership in the Christian community are hard pressed to maintain a vocational imagination adequate for preserving and nurturing our distinctive way of life in a media and Internet culture that "knew not Joseph."

It took me by surprise when I first encountered it. It was in Minneapolis in 1962 at a gathering of new church pastors convened by my denomination. I had recently been ordained and selected to organize a new congregation in a fast-growing suburb near Baltimore. The primary speaker at the gathering quickly caught my attention by announcing, "The size of your congregation will be determined far more by the size of your parking lot than by any biblical text from which you will preach." He said a lot more than that over the next three days but not anything very different.

On returning to Baltimore I reported to my supervisor. "I know you are upset, Eugene, but he is right. You can only motivate Americans, maybe especially suburban Americans, if you give them a goal that they can see, get their hands around. Believe me, the people you are attempting to attract have to see it before they believe it. We call it 'vision casting.' "

So what was I to do? The forty people who were my congregation at the time were worshipping in the basement of our house with exposed cement block walls. The few young people attending had taken to calling it "Catacombs Presbyterian Church" after overhearing one of them saying to me while leaving worship, "Oh pastor, I love worshipping here. It always reminds me of the early Christians worshipping in the catacombs." And the only parking available was on-street parking that the neighbors were getting pretty tired of.

I decided that the first thing to do was what *not* to do—I was *not* going to cultivate a "parking-lot imagination."

+++

What I wouldn't have given then to be in conversation or correspondence with Arthur Boers. We are not quite the same age but a few years after we became friends we found that we were both appalled by the secularization of the pastoral vocation in North America and had been doing our best to write articles and books to recover a biblical and theological imagination for ourselves, our colleagues, and our denominations. It was lonely work. But it was worth it. His most recent book, *Servants and Fools: A Biblical Theology of Leadership*, is the evidence.

The book is the product of years of working out an understanding and practice of Christian leadership handed to us by our respective ecclesial cultures (Canadian and American). As a tenured professor in the R. J. Bernardo Family Chair of Leadership for six years at Tyndale Seminary in Toronto, the conditions for the researching and writing of the book were particularly propitious. In those years he carefully examined most if not all the writings on Christian leadership in the context of the biblical text and found them wanting. This book that you hold in your hands is the most definitive response and challenge to the secularization that has emptied virtually all biblical and vocational considerations from the practice of leadership in our churches and seminaries.

But while critical of what he has discerned, there is nothing combative in his approach and counsel. The tone is irenic throughout, carefully examining the current "leadership culture" though the lenses of the biblical text.

+++

We Christians have been at this pastor/leadership business for 2,000 years, working with men and women to bring "every thought captive to obey Christ" (2 Cor 10:5), to present our "bodies as a living sacrifice" (Rom 12:1; 6:13). Minds and bodies, thinking and behaving, as one person formed in both the way and the truth of Jesus in order to live the life of Jesus. But for the last 300 years, under the influence of the Enlightenment project and industrialization, there has been a silent tectonic shift under our feet. We have become fascinated with learning and doing on a large scale with a corresponding erosion of life lived locally and in the ordinary to the glory of God. And now, all of a sudden it seems, many church leaders and their congregations are looking around and at themselves and saying, "I don't want to live like this." It is gratifying to have so many people interested and curious, ready for a life congruent with the conditions in which we live, attentive to the invisible realities that go into the making of us as followers of Jesus who identified himself as "the way, the truth, and the life" (John 14:6 CEB).

+++

Arthur Boers, a pastor, professor, and writer all of his adult life, has discerned that all is not well in our church culture in matters of leadership. He has written this book in an attempt to recover the core nature of leadership in a culture that seems to not be doing so well at it. His words: "Jesus never explicitly said that we are to be leaders but commanded us all—specifically in contrast to the leaders and rulers of this age—to be *servants*. This servanthood instruction may be his *most important* term when speaking of leadership."

He supports his statement by entering into a detailed, explicit, exegetical treatment of virtually every passage in the Old and New Testaments that has to do with what so many today are calling leadership. Arthur's words again: "But for Christians, the first priority is *followership*. Some people define leadership very simply as 'having followers.' Yet in the Christian perspective, since we are followers, it can faithfully and truthfully be said that only Jesus is the leader."

His conclusion, and given the extent of his exegetical work on the actual passages in which "leaders" have a role, is simply this: "Much—actually *most*—of what the Bible says about leaders is negative." He reads the biblical text in a way intended to recover the actual ways in which our biblical "leaders" performed their tasks as prophets, kings, priests, and apostles. He calls us to *reimagine* what we so glibly define as "leadership" as a way of life radically redefined and replaced by Jesus and along the way to exorcise anything narcissistic or arrogant in the ways any of us in the church—pastors, elders, bishops, laity, professors, executives, administrators—carry out our assigned vocations.

This is by far the best treatment that I have ever come across on this much-discussed feature of church life in these changing times. Arthur is both generous and discerning, having lived deeply and well what he is writing for us.

+++

Two things basic to what defines the Christian way of life are radically counter to most things North American. First, the Christian way is not about us; it is about God. The Christian way of life is not a life project for becoming a better person. We are in on it, to be sure. But we are not the subject. Nor are we the action. We get included by means of a few prepositions: God-with-us (Matt 1:23), Christ-in-me (Gal 2:20), God-for-us (Rom 8:31). *With*... *in*... *for*... powerful, connecting, relation-forming words, but none of them naming us as either subject or predicate. We are the tag end of a prepositional phrase.

The great weakness of North American spirituality is that it is all about *us*: fulfilling our potential, getting in on the blessings of God, expanding our influence, finding our gifts, getting a handle on principles by which we can get an edge on the competition. But the more there is of us, the less there is of God.

It is true that sooner or later we are invited or commanded to do something. But in that doing, we never become the subject of the Christian life nor do we perform the action of the Christian life. What we are invited or commanded into is what I want to call prepositional-participation. The prepositions that join us to God and his action in us and in the world—the *with*, the *in*, the *for*—are very important but they are essentially a matter of the ways and means of participating in what God is doing.

And second, these ways and means are also counter to most things North American. Ways and means must be appropriate to the ends. We cannot participate in God's work but then insist on doing it our own way. We cannot participate in building God's kingdom but then use the devil's methods and tools. Christ is the *way* as well as the truth and the life. When we don't do it his way, we mess up the truth and we miss out on the life.

+++

My Montana neighbor, philosopher Albert Borgmann, whom I have gotten to know in the last few years, is our most eloquent and also most important spokesman in these matters, exposing the dangers of letting technology determine the way we live our lives, dictate the means by which we, in his phrase, "take up with the world." It doesn't take long while in his company, whether personally or through his books, to realize that the methods that we use today have plunged us into a major crisis, a crisis in the *way* we live. Dr. Borgmann is head of the philosophy department at the University of Montana and has given a lifetime of sustained attention to understanding and discerning the ways technology affects the way we live, how the ways and means by which we do things (technology), if used unthinkingly or inappropriately, corrupt or destroy the very things we set out to do. Borgmann is not antitechnology; in fact he is very respectful of it. He just doesn't want it to ruin us—and it is ruining us. In great and thoughtful detail he is answering the question posed so brilliantly and insistently by Walker Percy in his several novels: "How does it happen that we know so much and can do so much and live so badly?"

This is the concern right at the core of the work of giving leadership to the church: to focus attention on the *way* we live the Christian life, the *means* that we employ to embody the reality and carry out the commands of Jesus who became flesh among us. In other words, nothing impersonal, nothing nonrelational, nothing "unfleshed."

+++

Meanwhile, and this has been going on for a long time now, our culture has become steadily depersonalized. And that has gradually over the last century developed into a consumer enterprise. We North Americans have developed a culture of acquisition, an economy that is dependent on wanting more, *requiring* more. We have a huge advertising industry designed to stir up appetites we didn't even know we had. We are insatiable.

It didn't take long for some of our colleagues to develop consumer congregations. If we have a nation of consumers, obviously the quickest and most effective way to get them into our congregations is to identify what they want and offer it to them, satisfy their fantasies, promise them the moon, recast the gospel into consumer terms—entertainment, satisfaction, excitement, adventure, problem solving, whatever. This is the language Americans grow up on, the language we understand. We are the world's champion consumers, so why shouldn't we have state-of-the-art consumer churches?

Given the conditions prevailing in our culture, it's the best and most effective way that has ever been devised for gathering large and prosperous congregations. Americans lead the world in showing how to do it. There is only one thing wrong: this is not the *way* in which God brings us into conformity with the life of Jesus; this is not the *way* in which we become less and Jesus becomes more; this is not the *way* in which our sacrificed lives become available to others in justice and service and resurrection. The consumer mentality is the antithesis of a sacrificial, "deny-yourself" congregation. A consumer church is an antichrist church.

Human life is endlessly complex, intricate, mysterious. There are no shortcuts to becoming the persons we are created to be. We can't pump up the Christian life by taking steroids. But patience is a difficult word to introduce into a technology-saturated, consumption-obsessed society that is contemptuous of slowness. The result is that the faster we move and the more we get, the more we are, ironically, diminished.

To discuss the life of Christ and a Christian vocation under American conditions sometimes seems just absurd. The primary concerns of those of us who are called to provide leadership to the community of the faithful don't rank high in the American stereotype of an effective leader. In this culture of arrogant leadership, pushing and shoving, insatiable consumerism, they appear to most to be fragile, inefficient, and ineffective. And yet.

And yet Jesus tells us to do it this way. Arthur Boers has provided us with an adequate imagination to embrace it.

Eugene H. Peterson
Professor Emeritus of Spiritual Theology
Regent College, Vancouver, Canada

Acknowledgments

I continue to be upheld, inspired, and challenged by exemplary pastors who are also key collegial conversation partners: Bishop Patrick Yu and Bishop Peter Fenty, Frs. Dean Mercer and Theadore Hunt, and the Rev. Annette Brownlee all apprenticed me into a new ecclesial context; Kenny Benge is hands-down the best-read pastor I have ever known; Glenn McCullough is my favorite conversationalist; Eugene Peterson and philosopher Albert Borgmann continually call me to the good life; Peter Roebbelen (now of the Charis Foundation) has prayed with and for me for over two decades and is a particular supporter of this project; John Suk's life and ministry so parallel mine; David Wood keeps pressing me on to higher ground. I am also particularly grateful to Doreen Harvey and Jonathan Wilson, who consistently show discerning wisdom as they reflect carefully on leadership in spheres largely unfamiliar to me.

While I have had many inspirational teachers over the years, the one who has spoken good and unexpected words to me in every phase of my life is Rae Struthers.

I happily acknowledge how students at Anabaptist Mennonite Biblical Seminary and Tyndale Seminary helped me hone my ideas on leadership. I have been especially blessed in these last years by the collegial support of Rebecca Idestrom, Dennis Ngien, Bob Shaughnessy, Paul Scuse, Victor Shepherd, and Yau Man Siew. Jim Beverley offered helpful book-writing tips.

I am indebted to the late Bob and Leslie Bernardo and their legacy; they modeled extraordinary generosity and it was a privilege to know them. My appointment to the RJ Bernardo Family Chair of Leadership, an endowed position named in their honor, enabled me to engage in two unexpected but fruitful challenges: teaching seminarians about leadership and pondering the state of Christian leadership understandings today.

I am grateful to Steven Purcell, Tim Blanks, and so many others at Laity Lodge for graciously and hospitably providing me with an ideal writing space at a critical juncture in this project. I thank David Rylaarsdam and Calvin Theological Seminary for including me in the "Leadership and Christian Formation in the Early Church" seminar (July 2014). The timing of this great learning experience could not have been more providential.

I treasure Lorna McDougall, the love of my life all these many years, who patiently absorbs the twists-and-turns of my explorations, who makes hospitable space for my writing, who understands me better than anyone, and who loves me nevertheless.

I dedicate this book to my significant friend, Kevin Abma. This friendship has lasted decades. What it means to me cannot be described or repaid.

Arthur Boers
Toronto, Canada

Introduction

Omnipresent Leadership

Everywhere I turn, people talk perpetually and perplexingly about leadership. I'm never entirely sure what they mean. I'm not even sure *they* know what they mean. Many commentators do not define leadership, but that does not, however, prevent preoccupation with the topic—in front-page headlines, business-section news, or Christian periodicals for that matter. Our era cannot stop mulling over leadership.

When my wife and I returned to Canada and moved to Toronto, our country's largest city was embroiled in a garbage strike. The press kept criticizing the mayor for this "leadership issue." (This was the administration immediately prior to the mayor who would oh-so-charmingly make international headlines for public intoxication and admitted crack cocaine use.)

North American election coverage of the last decades repeatedly pondered the concept of leadership. In one Canadian campaign, nasty political ads showed photos of then Prime Minister Jean Chretien, suggesting that he did not *look* like a leader—whatever that means. Actually the ads appeared to mock a facial defect of Chretien's. One might ask what kind of *leadership* was behind those kinds of ads.

When a friend became pastor of a troubled congregation, he told me that the previous pastor showed a "failure of leadership."

These scenarios suggest that with the right leadership in place, things would not go wrong or would at least go more smoothly. There would not be labor strikes, heads-of-state would look the part, and churches would sail along. Leadership becomes an ultimate panacea; in it we rest messianic hopes.

Following the Leader Fads

Leadership drives much contemporary agenda. Universities and seminaries endow leadership chairs. Schools offer leadership education, development, and training. Leadership degree programs are on the rise. One can pursue doctorates, PhDs and DMins, in leadership. While explicit curricular focus on leadership is recent, one could argue that graduate schools always were about forming leaders even if they did not explicitly use that terminology.

Barbara Kellerman, James MacGregor Burns Lecturer in Public Leadership at Harvard University, writes disparagingly of "the burgeoning . . . leadership industry with its . . . countless centers, institutes, programs, courses, seminars, workshops, experiences, teachers, trainers, books, blogs, articles, websites, webinars, videos, conferences, consultants, and coaches, which all claim to teach people how to lead."[1]

Ironically, leadership is faddish; one might expect *leadership* to be about creativity, initiative, and setting new directions rather than joining bandwagons. Publishers snap up leadership books; there are usually several on best-seller lists. Numerous volumes are of the self-help, how-to-succeed, or motivational genre, descendants of *How to Win Friends and Influence People.* Many a time those leadership tomes are written by those whose spectacular business achievements led to lucrative careers and who now give highly paid addresses to corporate executives, colleges, universities, and pastors' gatherings. Anne Applebaum notes that the offerings are virtually interchangeable: "These are the words of successful people . . . trying to sell the secrets of their success to others. In order to do so, they have tailored their language to appeal to the widest possible audience." She describes this kind of literature as "'how to succeed in business' motivational" books, even referring to them as "motivational tract[s]." Their "inspiring but generic suggestions . . . could have equally come from a fortune cookie." Applebaum believes "motivational slogans . . . are almost always useless in real-life situations." Determining action in a particular context is at best improvisational. What worked for Lee Iacocca at Chrysler, Steve Jobs at Apple, or Bill Hybels at Willow Creek may not have meaningful application for other locales and situations. Applebaum continues, "Sometimes it makes sense . . . to leap at opportunities. Sometimes it's foolish. Some risks are worth taking and others are not."[2] In other words, leadership guru literature is of limited practical usefulness or application. Scott Cormode argues that we can learn more from failure:

1. Barbara Kellerman, "Leadership: Learning to Lead the Old-Fashioned Way," *Strategy and Business* 65 (Winter 2011): 71.

2. Anne Applebaum, "How to Succeed in Business," *New York Review of Books*, June 6, 2013, 12, 14.

> There is a strong sentiment among many organizational scholars that copying the success of others... *cannot* work. They argue that so many factors have to come together for a program to work that it is all but impossible for an outside observer (or even for an insider) to determine which of the factors contributed most to the success of the program. These scholars believe, by contrast, that less-than-successful endeavors are more educational because we... point to the moment when things started to go wrong. Their point is that eliminating known mistakes is often a far more effective way to improve than emulating perceived successes.[3]

It is all very well to hear extraordinary stories of legendary corporate titans—Richard Branson, Bill Gates—who apparently shape their own realities, but one needs to wonder how realistic, applicable, or helpful these examples are. Even the most impressively "self-made" geniuses have had all kinds of aid, supports, and opportunities along the way. Moreover, how can strikingly exceptional people meaningfully speak to regular folks with limited opportunities? One sad memory is a university friend who was impressed by Ayn Rand's grandiose ideas about the possibilities of individualistic greatness. His subsequent life—dropping out of college, an unsatisfying job, alcohol abuse, a broken family—look all the sadder because of those lofty Randian pretensions.

Besides, even many major business "leaders"—people that Bruce Cockburn describes as "faceless kings of corporations"[4]— may have little agency. Terry Tempest Williams reported a conversation with a successful Procter & Gamble executive who loved his exorbitant salary and lavish lifestyle. The P & G officer celebrated his corporation's power but recognized a momentum, a culture that cannot be reined in: "I'm telling you, it's out of control." Williams inquired why he does not make changes.

> "It's out of our hands."
>
> "What do you mean it's out of your hands? Your hands are the ones creating it, aren't they?" [asked Williams].
>
> "You don't understand, the corporation is its own entity. Nobody sitting around the boardroom believes any one of them can change things. Even we who run Procter & Gamble speak of 'it' as though it is something outside ourselves."[5]

3. D. Scott Cormode, *Making Spiritual Sense: Christian Leaders as Spiritual Interpreters* (Eugene, OR: Wipf and Stock, 2013), 61n57.

4. Bruce Cockburn, "Feast of Fools," *Further Adventures Of (*Toronto: True North Records, 1978).

5. Terry Tempest Williams, *Leap* (New York: Vintage Books, 2001), 76–77.

This powerful "leader's" startling admission is a troubling confession about both the momentum of corporations and the despairing sense that not much can be done. Here is a story that ought to unsettle anyone pondering leadership.

This book is not a comprehensive exploration of all the biblical points of view regarding leadership. Clearly there are many different perspectives in the scriptures. Nevertheless there are key strands: criticizing and contesting prevailing models of leadership and de-emphasizing and dethroning power, powers, and the powerful while experimenting with leadership styles. All those emphases are in the service of doing justice, loving kindness, and walking humbly with God (Mic 6.8).

This volume explores particular scriptural themes—especially countercultural strains and the ongoing experimental and improvisational nature of Christian leadership on behalf of God's priorities of justice and compassion. This exploration is required for a coherent biblical theology of leadership that needs and deserves to be part of wider church conversations. You will undoubtedly detect my biases—shaped as I am by being the eldest son of immigrants and entrepreneurs; having an ecclesiastical journey that led me to join a Mennonite church as a teen and eventually move to Anglicanism (from "Anglican Mennonite to Mennonite Anglican" as I like to think of it); having served for years in two countries, varied settings (inner city, urban, rural), and three denominations (United Methodist, Mennonite, Anglican); and possessing strong convictions about social justice issues and priorities.

For most of my adult life, I have been either a pastor or seminary professor. Thus my perspectives are inevitably church-oriented and theological. Along the way I have known business executives, military officers, denominational officials, coaches, and consultants; all taught me their take on leadership. I value their teaching, but mostly what I know I learned in local congregations and seminary classrooms.

Part One

Christians and Contemporary Leadership Fascinations

So let no one boast about human leaders.

(1 Cor 3:21)

Chapter One

Dispelling Leadership Delusions

From Faddish Fascination to Critical Appreciation and Redemption

But What about Me?

I seldom speak about this, one of my greatest moments of pastoral failure. I am still haunted by the memory of how many mistakes I made in this one incident.

Our congregation was embroiled in conflict. Much of the turmoil circled around a congregational leader who was frustrated with me. I grew worn down by his behavior (which I preferred to label "antics"). I was not alone; congregants frequently complained about him. Yet I should have been cautious about "victims" triangling me. More significantly, I had not yet learned enough about self-examination and self-awareness.

One day, I was complaining bitterly about this antagonist to a senior stalwart in the church. A gentle, dedicated soul, he had quietly served our congregation over the years and was a model of Christian patience and faithfulness. I did not always agree with him, but I knew him to be wise. Rather than learn from him this time, however, I tried to recruit him to be on "my side" in the disputes.

I speculated about how to rein in the troublesome congregant, and the wise member said: "Arthur, we have to be gentle with our brother." I exploded, raising my voice: "But what about me?" Feeling sorry for myself, I wanted someone to look after me. My angry outburst stunned the elder into silence. Our conversation ended. I apologized later but our relationship was never quite the same again.

That unfortunate moment marked a turning point. I realized that I had become too bound up in the conflict. I began recognizing that while it is important to pay attention to—and take care of—your own needs, the organization you serve will not necessarily do this for you.

I have been ambivalent about leadership. I did not want to be "lonely at the top"; I longed to be "just one of the gang," as casual in clothing and commitments as everyone else. I wanted the right to sound off without representing a group or institution. In *Mudwoman*, a novel by Joyce Carol Oates, the main character goes from an impoverished childhood to being an Ivy League school president, discovering that she is not free to say all she believes. A "public position" means that "the first freedom you surrender is the freedom to speak impulsively, from the heart."[1] Like that frustrated president, I did not appreciate needing to act mature and calm even when I did not feel it. I identified with Bruce Cockburn, who "cried out glad and cried out sad / With every voice but mine."[2]

I tired of being the one responsible to suggest ideas, launch initiatives, keep things moving, challenge "we've-always-done-it-this-way" inertia. I wearied of being carefully alert to relational issues and wondering and worrying about whom I could befriend and who merited cautious distance. I wanted to "take on" those who disagreed with me and found it difficult to acknowledge the sincerity and even wisdom in opposing viewpoints. I did not enjoy facing up to how my own wounded neediness sometimes drove my exercise of leadership. I got fed up with the fact that being a leader means that I will be challenged to change and grow and stretch.

Christian Leadership Fascinations

Leadership is a primary quality people expect of pastors, even if no one is precisely sure what leadership actually is.

On the first day at an excellent weeklong leadership workshop, the teacher asked whether any of us—mostly Anglican clergy—admired George Herbert. (Herbert was a prayerful Anglican priest in the seventeenth century; he cared for a small congregation and wrote poetry. Centuries later Simone Weil was converted by reading one of his poems; if his work accomplished nothing else, surely that alone is more than enough.) In response to the question, a few of us raised hands. The teacher quickly responded: "Herbert is not what the church needs today. We need change agents, leaders." I stayed for the week but still admire George Herbert. And still question what people mean by "leadership."

1. Joyce Carol Oates, *Mudwoman* (New York: Ecco, 2012), 132.

2. Bruce Cockburn, "One Day I Walk," *High Winds White Sky* (Toronto: True North Records, 1971).

Harvard theologian and Anglican priest Sarah Coakley is concerned:

> Sometimes I fear that English Anglicanism has given up on holiness. . . . I note now that many, even most, advertisements for new Anglican incumbents seek a minister who is gifted in 'leadership,' or one who is 'energetic' and 'efficient'. Rarely do they ask for one who is 'prayerful' . . . But this ecclesiastical trend towards secular models of personal efficacy is odd; for if ever an age yearned for authentic sanctity, it is surely ours. Think of the magnetism of John Paul II, of Mother Teresa, of 'Father Joe'.[3]

Surely this is not a problem for Anglicans alone. Seminary faculty colleagues commonly lament how our understanding of pastoring and church life is malformed by expectations inappropriately derived from business models.

It is important to get clarity about all of this.

Sometimes "leadership" is its own justification, used by rogues and scoundrels to excuse questionable behavior. A major "Christian" institution where a friend worked got caught in a public relations nightmare. Ill-advised and questionable decisions received national publicity. A key administrator thanked employees who supportively understood "the challenges of leadership," as if leadership equals standing firm behind poor choices. That message certainly came out of the 2003 invasion of Iraq; "leadership" was shown by "deciders" who moved resolutely, never mind whether or not their actions were ethically justifiable.

Too many times we have only the leader's perspective on what is accomplished, not hearing the actual costs and consequences of choices and policies. In a powerful scene in the film *Lines of Wellington* (2013), the Duke of Wellington commissions a painting of one of his victorious, but bloody, battles. Disturbed by an artist's graphically honest portrayal, Wellington disdainfully tosses the painting aside, saying: "We need more heroes. Fewer corpses. Less dead." Having heroes can come at the expense of the truth.

Some "leaders" are enveloped in hagiographical mystique: their laudably commendable achievements are the only lens through which we view them, while we disregard other facts about them. A friend worked for years with a famous pastor. My friend was thrilled—at first—as that pastor was a pioneering soul, one of the first women ordained in her denomination. But my friend gradually came to see that, locally, the denominationally trailblazing lead pastor was authoritarian and controlling. When the groundbreak-

3. Sarah Coakley, "Introduction: Prayer, Place and the Poor," in *Praying for England: Priestly Presence in Contemporary Culture*, ed. Samuel Wells and Sarah Coakley (New York: Continuum, 2008), 7.

ing minister retired, the wounded church took years, more than one pastor, and pricey consultants before it was stable. This is not to downplay the pioneering pastor's impressive accomplishments, but it does remind us that "leaders" are human and their records often deeply mixed.

North American evangelicals are preoccupied with leadership. Evangelicals describe the process of winning conversions as "*leading* someone to Christ." Numerous parachurch ministries are named after founders, sometimes fostering personality cults. Evangelicalism frequently "focuses on individual personalities and rallies around charismatic leaders, who often need and seek out acclamation."[4]

Evangelical publishers offer numerous leadership books, frequently boasting specific surefire steps to success: *9 Things You Simply Must Do to Succeed in Love and Life*; *The Shaping of an Effective Leader: Eight Formative Principles of Leadership*; or *Practicing Greatness: 7 Disciplines of Extraordinary Spiritual Leaders*. The most famous is *The 21 Irrefutable Laws of Leadership* (subtitled *Follow Them and People Will Follow You*).[5] One friend likes to joke that he can refute each of those laws. Even more unsettling is the extraordinary quantity of books that purport to offer "secrets" to success or effectiveness. ("Leadership secrets" generated 144,000 Google hits.)

A seminary I know well hosts visiting speakers, celebrated graduates, and distinguished guests who may even receive honorary doctorates. Almost invariably, these folks are lauded as "leaders," apparently the highest praise. I do not recall anyone commended for being a "disciple" or "faithful follower of Jesus." It happens, I am sure. Just not nearly as much as I hear the more cherished "leader" accolade.

It is probably human nature to admire the famous and the powerful, to look for heroes who perform deeds of might, and to adulate "stars," those up front, in the know, and holding the reins.[6] Yet there are problems when

4. Beau Underwood, "The Self-Destruction of Mark Driscoll: Churches—Like Everyone Else—Need Accountability," *Sojourners* (November 2014), 11.

5. Henry Cloud, *9 Things You Simply Must Do to Succeed in Love and Life: A Psychologist Learns from His Patients What Really Works and What Doesn't* (Nashville: Thomas Nelson, 2007); Gayle D. Beebe, *The Shaping of an Effective Leader: Eight Formative Principles of Leadership* (Downers Grove, IL: InterVarsity, 2011); Reggie McNeal, *Practicing Greatness: 7 Disciplines of Extraordinary Spiritual Leaders* (San Franscisco: Jossey-Bass, 2006); John C. Maxwell, *The 21 Irrefutable Laws of Leadership: Follow Them and People Will Follow You* (Nashville: Thomas Nelson, 1998).

6. Mark van Vugt and Anjana Ahuja, *Naturally Selected: The Evolutionary Science of Leadership* (Toronto: HarperCollins, 2011); Leo Braudy, *The Frenzy of Renown: Fame and Its History* (New York: Oxford University Press, 1986).

Even secular France has a long tradition of "panthéonizacion," dramatic nationally

Christians unduly emphasize leadership. As Luke recounts events leading up to Jesus's birth, he deliberately names luminaries of his day—Emperor Augustus, King Herod, Governor Quirinius. Yet he startlingly shifts focus to unimportant, unlikely folks—Zechariah, Elizabeth, Mary, Joseph—who are in fact the unexpected channels of God's work, the *real* sphere of God's transforming activity. Augustus, Herod, and Quirinius made the *news*. But *good news* is consistently discerned and found elsewhere. As Albert Schweitzer observed, public noteworthies are not where the greatest changes and most important events happen; acknowledged public leaders, people at the front of organizations or on top of pyramids, are merely "like the foam on the waves of a deep ocean."[7]

Lew Parks argues that how the church appropriates leadership ideas leaves much to be desired: "We need . . . church leadership that risks a robust correlation of its scripture and theology with the very best that secular leadership studies can offer. What we get is church leadership that congratulates itself for dabbling in secular leadership studies twice borrowed, church leadership with a preference for simplistic formulas, catchy buzz words, and inane parables." Such "Church Leadership Lite" is both "short on biblical and theological integrity and oblivious to serious leadership study."[8]

Much leadership literature—even from "Christian" publishers—dwells on executives or "stars" in big businesses, professional sports, and the military. Frequent are the celebrations of leadership in Disney, Apple, Southwest Airlines, or Shell. While there are things to be learned, caution is also appropriate. These kinds of books reinforce the interests and perspectives of the status quo.[9] Many corporations earn success by questionable ethical practices, too frequently *externalizing* real costs, polluting the environment, or oppressing overseas labor. Staggering profits may come from exploita-

---

broadcast ceremonies of moving the remains of French heroes from their graves to France's Pantheon. Julian Jackson and Matthew Cobb, "Magical Incantation," *Times Literary Supplement* (December 12, 2014): 14–15.

7. Albert Schweitzer, *Out of My Life and Thought: An Autobiography*, trans. Antje Bultmann Lemke (Baltimore: John Hopkins University Press, 1998), 90.

8. Lew Parks, "Envy: A Study in Church Leadership from an Alternative, Biblical Vision," *Journal of Religious Leadership*, 2, no. 1 (Spring 2003): 88.

9. Stephen Preskill and Stephen D. Brookfield, *Learning as a Way of Leading* (San Francisco: Jossey-Bass, 2009), 2.

Two exceptions are: Michel Villette and Catherine Vuillermot, *From Predators to Icons: Exposing the Myth of the Business Hero,* trans. George Holoch (Ithaca, NY: Cornell University Press, 2009), and Nassir Ghaemi, *A First-Rate Madness: Uncovering the Links Between Leadership and Mental Illness* (New York: Penguin, 2011).

tion, therefore we need to be cautious about turning business leaders into heroes. A Presbyterian pastor cites a prominent example:

> About a year before I'm writing this, the entrepreneurial co-founder of Apple computers died. As a businessman, Steve Jobs did a great deal to change the way we communicate with one another and helped Apple amass an incredible fortune, but Jobs had many personal failings and used immoral employment practices in China. In spite of all that, in the last months, instead of ministers decrying the abuses in the workplace, I have read articles, posts, and sermons imploring pastors to be like Steve Jobs and the church like Apple computers.[10]

Others notice that "romanticizing" leadership can lead to CEO cults of celebrity; North Americans especially are fascinated with heroes and exceptional leaders.[11]

Leadership literature promotes envy with false promises. Casinos and lotteries encourage gambling with two messages: first, you, too, can win buckets of money, and, second, this is only possible if you gamble. Most gamblers and lottery ticket consumers do not win but lose. The truth is: "You can be a loser too."[12] When leadership books dwell on five-star generals, corporation executives, metropolis mayors, and megachurch CEOs, the implicit promise is like gambling: you can only win if you enter the game, and you, too, might hit the big time. But the majority of people, no matter how talented, motivated, and connected, will never be generals, executives, mayors, or megachurch pastors.

Exceptional, extraordinary people may fascinate us, but there is no need to aspire to lofty heights. Eugene Peterson and Wendell Berry have reminded us for a long time of the blessing of serving patiently and humbly on behalf of God's reign in human-sized localities. Most North American churches are small, and I am not convinced that that is bad. Taking celebrity

---

10. Carol Howard Merritt, "Leadership and the Christianity and Culture Dance," in *Pastoral Work: Engagements with the Vision of Eugene Peterson*, ed. Jason Byassee and L. Roger Owens (Eugene, OR: Cascade, 2014), 96–97.

11. Brad Jackson and Ken Parry, *A Very Short, Fairly Interesting and Reasonably Cheap Book about Studying Leadership* (Thousand Oaks, CA: Sage, 2011), 55, 77.

12. This idea was derived from Pico Iyer's review of *Darling: A Spiritual Autobiography* by Richard Rodriguez (Viking/Penguin); Iyer reports that the book "notes that Vegas is a city that lives off the sorrows of others, less a vindication of the American belief that everyone can become a millionaire than a monumental reminder that the majority of gamblers are failures." Pico Iyer, "An Unknown America of the Mind," *New York Review of Books* (August 14, 2014): 77.

leadership too seriously risks downplaying the actual challenges that God puts before us.

Redeeming Leadership Emphases

I am not claiming that *nothing* can be learned from leadership literature, emphases, and studies or from spheres and disciplines that rely heavily on those kinds of perspectives, for example, the occasionally maligned "business world."

William Stringfellow was once invited to lecture in two locations near to each other, Harvard Business School and Harvard Divinity School.[13] He presented essentially the same content in both places, biblical and theological reflections on the powers and principalities (e.g., Eph 6:12; Col 1:16). He was unsure about how he would be received at the business school. A Stringfellow aficionado reports: "The business school students . . . engaged him thoroughly, bending his ear long past the hour appointed, with numerous examples from their own experience of corporate dominance and possession by the commercial powers."[14] But the theological students made a marked contrast; they reacted with disbelief, rejection, and mockery. Put simply, business students comprehended and were able to apply and integrate Stringfellow's theological reflections; theology students could not.

Yes, there is much to learn from the business world, even matters we had *better* learn. Brian McClaren makes a good point: "'The church doesn't need to be run like a business,' a mentor once told me, 'but it surely shouldn't be run like a bad business.'"[15] Nevertheless, caution is in order. Bottom line concerns about profits, shareholder interests, and value-added priorities do not necessarily add up in God's economy.

Reviewing Sheryl Sandberg's best-selling *Lean In: Women, Work, and the Will to Lead*, Betty Smartt Carter raises critical issues. Sandberg, COO of Facebook, wrote about how women can shatter corporate glass ceilings and the implications of those choices on family life and priorities. Carter acknowledges attractiveness in Sandberg's ideas, but asks:

---

13. Stringfellow's account of this incident is found in William Stringfellow, *Free in Obedience* (New York: Seabury, 1954), 50–51.

14. Bill Wylie Kellermann, *Seasons of Faith and Conscience: Kairos, Confession, Liturgy* (Eugene, OR: Wipf and Stock, 2008), 71–72. Stringfellow argued that the powers and principalities were at work in "images" (e.g. Marilyn Monroe), institutions, and ideologies (*Free in Obedience*, 52–59).

15. Brian McLaren, "Read This First," review of *The E-Myth Revisited*, by Michael Gerber, *Christian Century* (April 30 2014): 11.

> What ends justify such sacrifices of ordinary family life...? If the pay-offs were a cure for cancer and a solution to global warming, that would be one thing; but the benefits of so much corporate busy-ness usually don't amount to much... Phones get smarter, packaged food travels farther, and more people in India can like each other's statuses.[16]

These critiques are not just ethical.

L. Roger Owens argues that much leadership literature promotes "functional atheism": working from "the unconscious assumption that if I don't make something good happen here it never will."[17] Relying on techniques and best practices, we may forego reliance on God; we act like atheists. We effectively deny God's existence or efficacy. Walter Brueggemann portrays three faithful priorities that differ from common values encountered today: "YHWH is not a workaholic," "YHWH is not anxious about the full functioning of creation," and "the well-being of creation does not depend on endless work."[18]

How do conscientious believers faithfully challenge where worldly emphases—including faddish leadership preoccupations—take us off course? Scriptures warn against getting caught up in the wrong values:

> The LORD proclaims:
> the learned should not boast of their *knowledge*,
> nor warriors boast of their *might*,
> nor the rich boast of their *wealth*.
>
> No, those who boast should boast in this:
> that they understand and know me.
> I am the LORD who acts with kindness,
> justice, and righteousness in the world,
> and I delight in these things,
> declares the LORD. (Jer 9:23-24 CEB; emphasis added)

Jeremiah's attention here to wisdom and knowledge, power and might, wealth and affluence specifically responds to the reign of Solomon, the

16. Betty Smartt Carter, "Look Before You Lean," *Books and Culture* (January/February 2014): 8.

17. L. Roger Owens, "Staying with God: Eugene Peterson and John Chapman on Contemplation," in *Pastoral Work: Engagements with the Vision of Eugene Peterson* (Eugene OR: Cascade, 2014), 132. He has more to say on this theme on p. 142.

18. Walter Brueggemann, *Sabbath as Resistance: Saying No to the Culture of Now* (Louisville, KY: Westminster John Knox, 2014), 6.

greatest Jewish king, one of Israel's most famous leaders.[19] Rather than honoring worldly priorities, we are to imitate God, who puts "kindness, justice, and righteousness" at the top of the agenda.

Pondering how the church engages the newly emerging discipline of leadership, I see a parallel challenge from not so long ago. Since the late nineteenth century, Christians have struggled with the emergence of another relatively new discipline, psychology (Freud, Jung, James, and so on). At first, several broad trends were evident. Some Christians rejected psychology, insisting that faithfulness was enough; serious problems were to be met with prayer and would be conquered with sufficient faith. Others, advocating "biblical counseling," insisted that the Bible itself offered alternative psychological agenda. Still others embraced the "triumph of the therapeutic," displacing classic soul care. (Therapeutic emphases hijacked understandings of worship, spiritual direction, church discipline, pastoral identity, and so on.)

In the 1970s, however, substantive theological engagement began between theologians and psychology in the work of University of Chicago's Don Browning and impressive literature from the Lilly-sponsored Religion, Culture, and Family Project. These examples show that it is possible to approach a new emerging discipline in ways that are both *appreciative* (without naively embracing a theory wholesale) and *critical* (without dismissing or writing off completely).

We now have a parallel challenge of *critically and appreciatively appropriating* leadership studies. Leadership has implications for church life and how we relate to workplaces and society. We need to learn from others and to examine underlying assumptions. We also must speak forthrightly where Christian faith has different priorities. We settle for neither uncritical embrace nor wholesale rejection; we can opt for redemption.

Redemption implies both that something requires redeeming and is *worth* redeeming. Leadership studies have significant insights. But there also needs to be caution and criticism in our reception.

Michael Walzer asks, "How much room for politics can there be when God is the ultimate ruler?"[20] Christians might echo, "How much room can there be for leadership when Jesus is Lord of all?" The church needs to be deliberate and discerning in these considerations.

---

19. Walter Brueggemann, *Truth Speaks to Power* (Louisville, KY: Westminster John Knox, 2013), 76.

20. Michael Walzer, *In God's Shadow: Politics in the Hebrew Bible* (New Haven, CT: Yale University Press, 2012), xi.

Chapter Two

Navigating the Ambiguity

Christian Challenges of Teaching Leadership

Leadership Fascinations as New Clericalism?

As teens in the 1970s, my Christian friends were deeply affected by the charismatic renewal. Our big controversy was about being "baptized in the Spirit." Fellow believers asserted that people who spoke in tongues were spiritually superior. Many of us without that ability felt like second-class citizens of God's kingdom. For years I prayed daily for this gift, something that was never granted. Now I imagine that people might petition God for the gift of "leadership" (a gift that gets even less attention in the Bible than the gift of tongues, as it happens). It is human nature to divide and rank people.

The church has frequently struggled with clericalism, overemphasizing the importance of clergy or ordained persons. We gave too many privileges to official ministers and downplayed the contributions and giftedness of others.

There have been periods in some church traditions where priority was given to "full time ministry." Or making exorbitant heroes of overseas missionaries so that domestic Christians felt that their own commitment was substandard. We neglected the kingdom-advancing service of those who raised families, labored in the workplace, created in the marketplace, prayed in their homes, and promoted justice in the public square.

Current leadership fascination verges on a new form of clericalism. Recently a student timidly asked whether I might allow her to take a leadership course. She e-mailed me: "I am not a leader and feel no calling to leadership.

Would this disqualify me from the class?" Her inquiry saddened me because unseemly prioritizing of leadership made her feel inferior. I welcomed her to the course, where her contributions were enormously worthwhile.

Leadership Never Was What It Used to Be

Barbara Kellerman, having taught, researched, and written about the subject for decades, is obviously deeply committed to fostering leadership, but she also raises important issues from *within* that discipline. She bemoans the fact that the leadership industry has become a "big business" promoting overly optimistic ideas about how easy it is to foster good leadership. She notes that only recently have theorists spent so much attention on regarding leadership positively.[1]

She also scathingly observes that while the leadership industry has thrived for some time, "leaders by and large are performing poorly, worse in many ways than before, miserably disappointing in any case to those among us who once believed the experts held the keys to the kingdom."[2] Leadership is not all that it's cracked up to be.

In *The End of Leadership* she asserts that leadership is being emphasized less and less. Movements like "Occupy Wall Street" and "Tea Party" are essentially leaderless; the same is true of "Idle No More" and various "Arab Spring" manifestations. She warns against overvaluing leaders in a world where leaders' roles are devolving. Twenty-first-century leadership preoccupation "flies in the face of the obvious—that leaders now have less power, authority, and influence than they did before." (Moses Naim makes similar points in *The End of Power.*)[3]

With these realities in mind, it grows difficult to make a case for emphasizing leadership. Think of the huge crises of recent decades—Watergate, the Vietnam War, the 2008 financial meltdown, astonishing patterns of pedophile abuse and cover-ups in Roman Catholic communities, fallen evangelical televangelists, "weapons of mass destruction" deceptions leading to war. Are these "failures of leadership"? Or are these tragedies inevitable and *intrinsic* to leadership? Some question whether we truly need leaders

1. Barbara Kellerman, *Bad Leadership: What It Is, How It Happens, Why It Matters* (Boston: Harvard School Business Press, 2004), 3–5.

2. Barbara Kellerman, *The End of Leadership* (New York: Harper Collins, 2012), xv.

3. Kellerman, *The End of Leadership,* 154–55. Moses Naim, T*he End of Power: From Boardrooms to Battlefields and Churches to States, Why Being in Charge Isn't What It Used to Be* (New York: Basic Books, 2013).

when the costs are so high. F. G. Bailey pessimistically asserts that leadership always and inevitably involves compromise, evil choices, and villainy.[4] None of this should surprise biblically informed Christians. A prevailing bias of scriptures is suspicion of leaders, as we shall see.

With a clear-eyed view, the faddish focus on leadership raises difficulties. For example, a connection between leadership and narcissism is frequently noted. Many celebrated leadership qualities correlate to this disorder: confidence about success, influencing others, assertiveness, savoring authority, optimism about being great, viewing oneself as extraordinarily special, enjoying being the focus of attention, expecting much from others, wanting power, trusting the world is better under one's own leadership.

There are other concerns. The distressing truth is that toxic leadership can be highly effective (many dictators, for example).[5] Some disconcertingly note a frequent connection between leadership and mental illness. "Psychopaths can easily look like ideal leaders: smooth, polished, charming."[6] We might want to exercise caution in encouraging people to be leaders: after all, a number of people are not ruined so much by failure as by success.[7]

Historically, many Christian leaders that we retrospectively regard as great died tragically, apparent failures. Their fruitfulness came only long afterwards. I taught at a seminary named after William Tyndale. This remarkable man was executed in ignominy; only long after his death did his vernacular Bible translation bear fruit. Christians measure greatness or effectiveness well past when the respective leaders perished. At the end of their lives, their accomplishments looked meager and dubious. Yet we can say of them what is written of Abel: "Though he died, he's still speaking through faith" (Heb 11:4b CEB).

We do not of course completely dismiss the importance of leadership. The aforementioned "leaderless" movements—Occupy, Idle No More, Tea Party, Arab Spring—have not yet demonstrated staying power, and one dynamic might be lack of clear leadership. I am particularly inspired by the twentieth-century civil rights movement and how that involved incredible—usually alternative—forms of leadership. Many of its central figures

4. F. G. Bailey, *Humbuggery and Manipulation: The Art of Leadership* (Ithaca, NY: Cornell University Press, 1988).

5. Thomas E. Cronin and Michael A. Genovese, *Leadership Matters: Unleashing the Power of Paradox* (Boulder, CO: Paradigm, 2012), 262, 266.

6. Adrian Furnham, *The Elephant in the Boardroom* (New York: Palgrave Macmillan, 2010), 109.

7. Nassir Ghaemi, *A First-Rate Madness: Uncovering the Links between Leadership and Mental Illness* (New York: Penguin, 2011), 55, 56.

learned skills and instincts in the church, especially as they may not have had access to other institutions for their own development and growth.

Yes, leadership is important. But the agenda of the church (like that of the civil rights movement) is different from the leadership agenda of "the world" or "powers that be." The church may call forth and create leaders to accomplish changes that the status quo prefers to repress. Throughout history the church and its believers frequently threatened the establishments of their day. We dare not abandon commitment to creating leaders on behalf of God's disruptive agenda.

The civil rights movement embodied God's priorities of justice and liberation. Results came from dedicated efforts of low status people who many a time had little education. Nevertheless their voices were heard. These overturnings resemble the startling surprises that Mary (like Hannah long before her) celebrates:

> He has shown strength with his arm.
> He has scattered those with arrogant thoughts and proud inclinations.
> He has pulled the powerful down from their thrones
> and lifted up the lowly.
> He has filled the hungry with good things
> and sent the rich away empty-handed. (Luke 1:51-53 CEB)

While history focuses on victors and the powerful, people at the top and in charge, the Bible pays an astonishing amount of attention to regular, normal folks who are nevertheless the unexpected means of God's dramatic work.

Christians have countercultural and counterintuitive leadership perspectives.

Teaching Leadership in Seminary

I understand why it is important to teach *leadership* in seminary. I get it. I really do. As people prepare to take up reins of responsibility, it is vital for them to reflect on what that means—for them personally, for the skills of that work, for reasons to accept this kind of charge.

Teaching a basic mandatory course on leadership development, I heard from a range of students. I encountered different stories and was exposed to an array of leadership motivations and attitudes. I regularly ran into two groups that concerned me.

First, there were those who emphatically said something like, "I am a leader," "God called me to be a leader," "I am very eager to be in charge of a church." Many students who spoke this way were young men, more often than not in their mid-twenties. They had a clear sense of what was amiss in local churches or inadequate in leadership offered by those in charge there, and these students wanted to put things right. They were people of determination and energy.

I admire their conviction, passion, drive, and motivation. I had some of that also as a young adult convinced that I could change the world. Earlier, as a rural secondary school student, my debating skills and my passion for politics led fellow students to predict that I might some day be nothing less than Canada's prime minister. It was easy to think of myself as a leader. Those who resolutely declare themselves leaders may "go far." Yet they also leave me hesitant.

Biblically, Old Testament kings who eagerly accepted or usurped crown and throne frequently went awry. There are well-meaning New Testament characters wanting to charge forward in God's service: James and John long to sit on Jesus's right and left in the kingdom, Saul (later "Paul") determinedly eliminating believers, Peter impetuously rushing ahead of Jesus time and time again (and once called "Satan" because of that). In each case, those enthusiastic servants of God are urged to slow down, reconsider, change direction, be reoriented.

Young zealots who want the reins, who want to reign, sometimes need a corrective, to be reined in. They do not necessarily grasp how complicated it is to oversee a group. They may not fully appreciate the history and culture that form their congregations, factors that shape a local church that they may think they know well enough already. They might not be aware of how hard it is to win a group over to change or how slowly change can happen. They might not see that there could be good reasons for others having different ideas, positions, and values.

Perhaps most important, they have not necessarily wrestled with *why* they feel called to lead. Is it purely and simply God's idea? Or do they have a need to be needed? To rescue? Do they enjoy solving problems and reinforcing the dependence of others? Do they have a touch of messiah complex? Is their ego stroked by being up front? Does family formation adversely affect how they lead? Becoming a healthy, whole leader requires rigorous self-awareness.

There was a second group that equally concerned me. These students told me—sometimes bashfully, sometimes with embarrassment—that they are not leaders and not called to be leaders. They were unsure why they should study "leadership." This second cadre might say something like "I only intend to do spiritual direction," "I am only going to be a pastoral counselor," "I am only a stay-at-home parent." As if parenting, counseling, or caregiving are not worth commending; as if those practices *are not* leadership. They cited absent abilities: being up front, leading a group, public speaking, socializing, making small talk, extraversion. This group was disproportionately composed of women (all further complicated if their church traditions opposed ordaining women).

I admire and respect the reticence. I marvel when I encounter humility. As an introvert, I understand the urge to stay away from the front, from the podium, from the spotlight. Yet these students might also be surprised at how well they could lead with the gifts they already had.

With them I worked on several levels. Many leaders in the Bible—Moses, Jeremiah, Jonah—hesitated to embrace tasks and responsibilities that came their way. In each case, God and circumstances had to lure them into leadership. I spoke theologically of the Pentecost event where the Spirit was poured out on "all flesh" and Paul's conviction of each believer having (or even being) gifts. I reminded them that Jesus said that we *are* (not that we should be or could be) salt and light. I spoke of why situations, groups, and organizations demand a range of leadership styles. I coaxed introverts to risk opinions. I pointed out that even the gentlest ministries—pastoral counseling, spiritual direction—are forms of leadership. Besides, leadership is not necessarily even about formal recognized positions.

One of the most influential, effective, and inspirational leaders I ever knew was a seminary receptionist; she impacted the ethos of an entire institution. Her desk was near the front door. No one could enter without passing her and being greeted by her. She was warm, welcoming, and friendly to all comers. Her hospitality affected the mood of the place. She was not paid much, not elevated in any hierarchy, nor was she formally recognized for her contributions, but she was vital to the school. She was a leader and a good one. She inspires me still.

Peculiar People and Other Unlikely Leaders

> And hath made us kings and priests unto God and his Father; to him be glory and dominion for ever and ever. Amen. (Rev 1:6 KJV)

> But ye are a chosen generation, a royal priesthood, an holy nation, a peculiar people; that ye should shew forth the praises of him who hath called you out of darkness into his marvelous light. (1 Pet 2:9 KJV)

New Testament authors struggle with how to describe the citizens of God's new reign. Various metaphors are applied in the verses cited above. My favorite is the King James Version phrase, "a peculiar people" (also in Titus 2:14). Intriguingly, several terms here relate to offices that we associate with leaders—kings, priests. I link these sorts of ideas with the popular idea of getting crowns in heaven, suggesting that in God's eyes all of us are royalty. These texts connect to Exodus 19:6 (CEB): "You will be a kingdom of priests for me and a holy nation." That ancient passage has "a radical meaning. God promises a social transformation and a novel politics: a kingdom without kings, a universal priesthood."[8]

When Christians talk about leadership or ministry, we reflect on what God calls us to do, who God calls us to be, how God calls us to act and behave. Our identity and vocation are rooted in God first of all. Our identity and vocation have everything to do with how we relate and respond to this God. Both verses cited above move from metaphors about Christian believers to praise of God. And so it should be. We were created to give God honor and glory and called to direct attention—ours and others'—to God who is worthy of all worship.

This is a challenge for Christians trying to reflect seriously and deliberately on "leadership." It seems impossible to settle on a common definition. As I teach this subject, read many books on the matter, and pay attention to the term's use in media, I find that views of leadership suggest several possibilities:

- forceful charismatic personalities who move groups or institutions to action
- having influence and followers
- getting things done
- possessing vision

I do not deny the promising potential value of these characteristics but am reluctant to esteem them too highly. These qualifications are not specifically Christian. They could describe many kinds of leaders, ethical and nonethical, from Martin Luther King Jr. and Nelson Mandela to Adolf Hitler and Joseph Stalin. Even more troublesome, these definitions at times contradict intrinsic insights about what it means to be Christian.

8. Michael Walzer, *In God's Shadow: Politics in the Hebrew Bible* (New Haven, CT: Yale University Press, 2012), 126.

You will look long, hard, and fruitlessly for scriptural testimony commending forcefully winsome personalities, having followers, or needing to accomplish great deeds or possess lofty visions. A Christian is primarily rooted in and devoted to God and this raises questions about those leadership generalizations. First, true motivation, change, transformation, and action (whether by individuals or groups) is accomplished by the Holy Spirit whose movements cannot be tracked or predicted (John 3:8). Second, we are not called to have followers but to *be* followers of Jesus Christ. Third, "getting things done" is rarely a biblical priority; we are encouraged rather to cooperate in God's purposes and rely on God for fruitful results. A few people in the Bible accomplish great things in their lifetime but most do not: "All these people didn't receive what was promised, though they were given approval for their faith" (Heb 11:39 CEB). Fourth, while we may have visions (see Acts 2), those require weighing and discernment. Christians do not have their own visions—or "cast" visions, a popular cliché—they are invited to be channels of someone else's vision and purposes, namely God's.

Too much leadership talk adulates talented, strong-willed individuals who emerge as the head of groups, at the top of hierarchies, in front of meetings and organizations. These kinds of people, though important, are never all-important, not in God's scheme of things, not in God's economy. All gifts of believers are vital when they serve God's purposes and priorities. No one gift or bearer of a particular gift is more significant than another. "Instead, the parts of the body that people think are the weakest are the most necessary" (1 Cor 12:22 CEB).

There are Christian traditions that are suspicious of hierarchy, verging at times toward egalitarianism that looks like anarchism: Quakers, Plymouth Brethren, many Anabaptists. These groups honor the verses from Revelation and 1 Peter, suggesting that all Christians are "priests." Traditions suspicious of clergy have a deep-seated conviction that God's kingdom has no hierarchy. As an ordained clergyperson (some people actually call me "Father"!), I do not embrace that most radical possible interpretation of "the priesthood of all believers." But their critiques caution me against clinging too tightly to titles, mine or anyone else's. More important, they remind me that my responsibility always is to promote and uphold the gifts of others, not to exhibit my particular talents or agenda.

Christian faithfulness does not overemphasize the few who appear to have the greatest promise and potential, the so-called best and brightest. In the Bible, the most interesting leaders are usually those who do not look the part.

Christians are all kings or queens, royal priests, a holy nation. This may not make much sense in the wider world. But then we are a peculiar people.

The Mother and the Provocateur

Mother Teresa is easy for discussing leadership. When I present her as a case study, everyone knows who she is and not much explanation is required for students to have opinions about her. On top of that she is almost universally admired. Evaluating Mother Teresa is a lot like discussing motherhood.

I like to read to students a two-page summary of her life, witness, and ministry. Then I ask questions: Was Mother Teresa a leader? If so, how do you evaluate her leadership? Usually people conclude that she was a leader and a good one too. Each discussion produces a number of points about her:

- vision
- courage and determination
- having followers
- dedicated to her faith
- making a difference and achieving results
- prophetic challenger of ideas and norms
- worldwide attention and influence
- love of God and compassion for others
- responding to God's call and challenge
- holding firm in the face of obstacles
- integrity and consistency in living out her values

The term "leader" usually implies positive evaluation. If we say a person is "not a leader," we usually mean that they are *poor leaders*; thus they do not deserve to be elected or that is why their ministry did not succeed. If we say a person is "a leader," we usually mean that they are *good leaders. Leadership* courses presumably teach *good* leadership, just as *parenting* classes are for forming *good* parents.

Other languages are ambivalent about this terminology. *Fuhrer* is the German word for "leader." (This in itself should caution against overly emphasizing leadership.) Seminaries do not offer fuhrership development classes. (I am told by friends abroad that leadership is a particularly North American preoccupation and not emphasized in education elsewhere.) But when students agree that Mother Teresa was a leader, they usually consider her a *good* one.

There is little or no controversy so far. Even though our student body represents forty plus denominations and Christian traditions and even though some of our students fiercely oppose Catholicism, it is easy to achieve near consensus on these matters. (One student did say that clearly Mother Teresa is going to hell as a heretic; but his was a mercifully rare opinion.)

Then I describe someone else who was famous, another person that most had heard about. This pastor became internationally notorious. World leaders talked about him and pleaded with him. He directly affected world events. Terry Jones pastored a small church in Florida but his threat to burn a Qur'an got noticed and produced consequences, including massive protests and even deaths. He made national and international news. There were demonstrations in the United States and fatal riots abroad. Leading political and military figures appealed to him. A lot of attention was focused on him and on what he would or would not do. While Jones is closer theologically to many of my students, he provokes division and controversy among them. Some are sympathetic to his goals; others loathe what he stood for and what he's done.

Curiously, Jones exemplifies many characteristics that lead people to conclude that Mother Teresa was a leader and a good one: vision, courage and determination, having followers, dedicated to faith, making a difference, achieving results, being a prophetic challenge, receiving worldwide attention, loving God, passionate commitment to God's priorities, changing how people think, holding steady in the face of opposition, remaining consistent to his values, and trying to do what one understands as best for others.

Yet students are generally dissatisfied with this analysis. They sense it is wrong to equate Mother Teresa and Terry Jones, both famous influential Christians. Many perceive Jones as divisive and judgmental. Furthermore, his results—possibly even ones he wanted—polarized people, and individuals died.

The conversation gets dicier when we ask whether he was a *good* leader. Do we mean ethically good? Do we agree with his deeds? On those counts, we could argue for a long time.

In talking about *leadership* we need something more. We need a way to evaluate the *spirit* and *fruits* of leadership. This is an aspect of what the

Roman Catholic Church does when it tests whether or not to canonize a "saint." Mother Teresa may be canonized; I doubt many would want to canonize Terry Jones even if fundamentalists did canonizations. I do not find much to like about him but believe that he is a Christian, deeply committed to his passionate convictions. Yet his spirit seems wanting. While he is good at staging dramas—he appears to enjoy the attention—his actions fan fires of division. Mother Teresa over and again stressed love and compassion. She was a source of healing and support for many; a lot of people are still inspired by her and imitate her good works.

In teaching leadership, I hoped to encourage the formation of saints. It is conceivable that some had potential to be like either Mother Teresa or Terry Jones. Is it our responsibility to equip both, trying to make both more effective, enjoining them to employ "best practices" in whatever enterprise and endeavor they undertake?

Some would say yes. But I disagree. Seminaries do not teach any kind of leadership. It needs to be leadership that honors the priorities of God's reign—reconciliation and redemption, justice and healing. It must discern between faithful and unfaithful pursuit of priorities. By my reading, Terry Jones is a disaster for the Christian gospel and, not coincidentally, disastrous for peace and reconciliation too.

We should form faithful and fruitful Christian leaders. While I would be honored to work with a potential Mother Teresa, I hope that seminary formation would dissuade if not derail a possible Terry Jones.

I was shocked when a student said that we should not discuss Mother Teresa: "She is a heretic and obviously going to hell." I was also shocked at the end of the semester when I realized that this same student's major paper was heavily plagiarized. I called him to my office to discuss this. He agreed that the material was stolen. He indicated that he understood the concept of plagiarism and that he had done it before and done so deliberately. What bothered me most was his matter-of-fact remorselessness. While I find it deeply painful to give poor grades, in this rare instance my duty was clear.

Good Christian leadership does involve, after all, discerning what is good and worthwhile from what is not.

Part Two

Reflecting Biblically on Leadership

*"These people who have been turning the world upside down
have come here also. . . .
They are all acting contrary to the decrees of the emperor,
saying that there is another king named Jesus."*

(Acts 17:6-7)

Chapter Three

Not Quite Biblical

Inadequate Christian Approaches to the "Gift of Leadership"

Still Riding My Shirttails

Returning to a retreat center where I had been a speaker five years earlier, I was delighted to meet retreat participants that I remembered from my prior visit and had not seen since. It was a pleasure to get caught up on each other's lives.

A repeat retreater brought notes from my previous presentation. On a page in his journal he showed me one word in tall capitals, *SHIRTTAIL.* Apparently my shirt had been regularly untucked; this made such an impression on him that he not only wrote about it then but also needed to tell me about it all these years later. Whether he remembered anything of what I said, I haven't a clue. He didn't say, nor did I dare ask. For the rest of the retreat, I kept checking the back of my shirt.

This amusingly reminded me that when offering leadership, we're not necessarily credited or affirmed for what we think is our legacy or accomplishment.

After serving my last church for over nine years, I was invited to teach in our denomination's seminary. Before I left for my new position, the congregation hosted a lovely lunch on my final Sunday. As part of the program, people talked about what they especially appreciated during my tenure.

The compliments were humbling. I was given undue credit for fulfilling my responsibilities. (After all, visiting people in the hospital was part of the job description.) But I was also surprised at what I felt was missing. I regarded preaching as one of my major contributions. I worked hard, trying to produce insightful, relevant sermons. I put lots of time into research and crafting what I said. I felt that preaching was among *the* most important things that I did, one of my strengths as a pastor. Yet not a soul mentioned sermons, let alone commended the quality of my preaching. Again, another reminder that what I think I contribute is not necessarily what is noticed or appreciated.

In leadership roles, expectations can frequently be confused. People might want actions from us that we do not regard as our responsibility. Folks might be angry over decisions that are not necessarily our doing. Bad deeds might occasionally be overlooked. Good deeds may go unrewarded or unobserved.

Mismatched Terminology

In contemporary leadership discussions we sometimes ask scriptures to address and answer issues that were not of actual interest to biblical authors. Nowhere does the Bible think of *leadership* as we use that term today. Interest in leadership is recent and viewing leadership positively even more so.

Thus we must be careful when exploring leadership terminology from a biblical perspective. Culture shapes our understanding of these terms; for us "authority is circumscribed" by checks-and-balances, legislation, shareholders, and so on.[1] What people in biblical times understood by *leader* is not necessarily what we understand. Just as mid-twentieth-century Germans though of *fuhrer* uniquely: before Hitler it meant "leader"; during Hitler's reign it became larger-than-life and messianic; since then it has connotations of mass delusion and barbaric dictatorship. This need not surprise biblically informed Christians.

My Kingdom for a Decent Leader

After all, from Moses versus Pharaoh; to prophetic critiques of kings (at home and abroad); to the contrast of Jesus with Herod, Pilate, and Caesar; to apocalyptic Lamb versus Beast battles, the scriptures say much about leadership, and it is usually negative. From its earliest chapters in Genesis to the book of Revelation there is deep-seated hostility to rulers.

The Bible emphasizes over and again that earthly leaders do not just fail to measure up to God's standards. More than that, they all too regularly and usually, almost invariably, actively *oppose* and degrade God's priorities.

"Good" rulers are rare. Whether Israelite, Judean, or foreign kings in the Old Testament or political rulers (governors, emperors, kings) and

1. Andrew D. Clarke, *Serve the Community of the Church: Christians as Leaders and Ministers* (Grand Rapids: Eerdmans, 2000), 233.

religious authorities in the New, most not only fail to measure up but also contravene God's purposes. The psalmist warns: "Don't trust leaders; / don't trust human beings— / there's no saving help with them!" (Ps 146:3 CEB). Or: "It's far better to take refuge in the LORD / than to trust any human leader" (Ps 118:9 CEB). Most kings are problematic, perpetually thwarting God's purposes:

> The earth's rulers take their stand;
>   the leaders scheme together
>   against the LORD and
>   against his anointed one. (Ps 2:2 CEB)

Much—actually *most*—of what the Bible says about leaders is negative. Isaiah laments: "My people—your leaders mislead you and confuse your paths" (Isa 3:12b CEB). Frequent are the warnings about faithless leadership—or about how even faithful leaders go awry. There are cautions against desiring power.

> Don't seek political power from the Lord
>   or a seat of honor from the king.
> Don't justify yourself
> in the Lord's presence,
>   and don't make a show of your wisdom
>   with a king.
> Don't aspire to become a judge;
>   you might not be strong enough
>   to get rid of injustice.
>   Perhaps you will be too cautious
>   in the presence of a powerful person
>   and bring a scandal on your good name. (Sir 7:4-6)

We are counseled against believing that any of us could do much better in power. A prevailing scriptural bias is unremitting suspicion of leaders.

As good leadership is an outlier, an exception, God frequently opposes kings and their agenda.

> Let all around him pay tribute to the One who strikes terror,
> who cuts short the breath of princes,
> who strikes terror in the kings of the earth. (Ps 76:12b-13)[2]

2. *The Revised Grail Psalms: A Liturgical Psalter* (Chicago: GIA, 2010), 161.

Suspicious observation does not justify writing leaders off or dismissing them. Scriptures advocate respect and prayer for and obedience to rulers (Rom 13:1-5; Titus 3:1; 1 Pet 2:13-15). God can work through them, even through *evil* ones. In Jeremiah 25:9, King Nebuchadnezzar, an enemy military ruler, is called God's "*servant*" in the "horror" and "disgrace" he will bring.

In the New Testament also, religious officials, provincial rulers, emperors, and governors are seen as problematic. Jesus had little time or patience for them. Authorities of the day are responsible for his death and the subsequent persecution of Christians. Christ overcame and ultimately defeated leaders and leadership: "When he disarmed the rulers and authorities, he exposed them to public disgrace by leading them in a triumphal parade" (Col 2:15).

A distinctive "strand of biblical imagination, in both Testaments, distrusts the managers of official power and dismisses them from center stage."[3] This is not merely a matter of "good guys" versus "bad guys"; something deeper is at work. This is not only about whether the *right leader* prevails (Pharaoh or Moses, Herod or the magi, Pilate or Jesus) but also calls into question each and every contemporary view and model of leadership. Leadership is problematic as it so often deeply contravenes the way God would have matters ordered. Biblical faith regards leadership counterculturally, but this is easily overlooked by superficial scripture readings.

What about Paul's "Gift" of Leadership?

One evening in my living room, seminary professors contemplated a which-came-first-chicken-or-egg question: Are leaders born or made? A scripture scholar brought the discussion to a merciful if misguided halt by saying: "It's obvious. Paul told us that leadership is a gift." I was glad to move on to other issues but perplexed by this claim.

Paul names "leadership skills" (*kybernēsis*) as a spiritual gift (1 Cor 12:28 CEB). The term's ambiguity is shown by the fact that it is variously translated as "administration" (NAB), "governments" (KJV), "guidance" (NIV), "administrating" (ESV), and "organizers" (*THE MESSAGE*). Wayne Meeks employs the term "guidances."[4] This text and Romans 12:8 (see below) are popularly cited by my leadership students. Intriguingly, I never see anyone

3. Walter Brueggemann, *Truth Speaks to Power* (Louisville, KY: Westminster John Knox, 2013), 89.

4. Wayne A. Meeks, *The First Urban Christians: The Social World of the Apostle Paul* (New Haven, CT: Yale University Press, 1983), 135.

quote something else Paul says about leadership: "So let no one boast about human leaders" (1 Cor 3:21).

First Corinthians 12:28 is of limited significance, showing that the "chief forms of service"[5] in order of importance are "first apostles, second prophets, third teachers" and not "leadership" itself (CEB). This in itself is intriguing as much current discussion emphasizes leadership's primary importance. Churches seeking pastors are prone to put this quality near the top of their job description. For Paul, however, *leadership* is less important than "gifts of healing" and "ability to help others"; it only has a higher rank than "different kinds of tongues," the last item listed. *Leadership skills*, whatever that term actually means, is a second to last priority.

The word *kybernēsis* seldom occurs in the New Testament. It usually means "acts of administration"; variants suggesting "shipmaster" or "pilot" are found in Acts 27:11 and Revelation 18:17. Neither "administrator" nor "pilot" has quite the lofty implications of one evangelical term for leadership: "vision caster." Many respectable commentaries do not even bother translating the 1 Corinthians 12:28 use of *kybernēsis*, presumably because it has a low priority for Paul's theology and his ecclesiology.

Romans 12:7-8 speaks of "the leader [*proistēmi*], in diligence" (in parallel with "the teacher, in teaching; the exhorter, in exhortation; the giver, in generosity"). KJV translates this "ruleth"; NAB says "he who rules should exercise his authority with care"; *The Message* sees it as "put in charge." The term *proistēmi* may mean "to put over or above" but also connotes patronage. This ambiguous terminology could refer to a group of people "who are exceptionally generous."[6] Meeks argues that "patron or protector" is the most likely interpretation; this kind of patronage may have included the responsibility to "admonish."[7]

Many early Christian communities relied on patrons for funds and food. These were affluent members whose homes were used for gatherings.

---

5. Hans Conzelmann, *1 Corinthians: A Commentary on the First Epistle to the Corinthians,* trans. James W. Leitch, Hermeneia (Philadelphia: Fortress, 1975). 215.

6. Alistair C. Stewart, *The Original Bishops: Office and Order in the First Christian Communities* (Grand Rapids: Baker Academic, 2014), 164. See also pp. 82–84.

7. Meeks, *The First Urban Christians,* 134–35, 234n75. On the admonishment observation, see pp. 134, 146. Similar terminology is also used in 1 Tim 3:4, 5, 12; 5:17; 1 Thess 5:12, 17; Titus 3:8, 14. Benjamin L. Merkle, "The Pattern of Leadership in Acts and Paul's Letters to Churches," in *Shepherding God's Flock: Biblical Leadership in the New Testament and Beyond,* ed. Benjamin L. Merkle and Thomas R. Schreiner (Grand Rapids: Kregel, 2014), 73–74.

Inevitably, they were of a higher status, both because they were wealthy and because the community felt indebted for their generosity.

Pastors know that affluent members can have strong and complicated influence. In churches, a minority of households typically give substantially and proportionately more than others. As a pastor, I never knew the actual giving of individuals but had suspicions. (A pastor friend is glad *not* to know congregant giving, not because he would kowtow to large donors but because he would resent people who gave far below their means.) Occasionally I was aware in sensitive discussions by congregational leaders that an underlying dynamic was the fact that some stakeholders were major donors. Patronage can go awry. In one church a wealthy individual occasionally got upset and then withheld donations for a time. If we had trouble meeting our budget he made clear what would encourage him to donate again. It was healthy for our church when he tired of ultimatums and left.

Whether or not Paul referred to patrons, he seldom used *proistēmi*. As it is infrequent, we need to be careful about attributing too much importance to it, let alone deriving an entire theology of leadership from it. This is one gift of a number mentioned. Paul's intention is a matter-of-fact reference to people with authority, perhaps for no other reason than the reality that they financially support the congregation. There is no sense here of what "leadership" connotes in our culture: charismatic, entrepreneurial, innovative initiators that win followers and make good things happen. Furthermore, Paul is giving counsel on how this kind of leadership is to be offered, with the virtue of "diligence." The virtue of diligence is the priority here, not the gift itself.

Paul never spoke of *leadership* as we employ the term. New Testament scholar Andrew Clarke shows that Paul did not use the most common terminology of his day for "leader" or refer to usual understandings of leadership.[8]

It is more accurate to regard all the gifts Paul names as forms or *aspects* of what we understand to be leadership. There is not one all-encompassing leadership gift apart from—or above—teaching or healing or giving or prophecy or ministry or what have you. All of them reflect ways that different forms of leadership are exercised.

Just because biblical authors did not explicitly address the topic of leadership does not mean that there is nothing to be gleaned about leadership from the Bible. But it certainly does indicate that we need to exercise careful discernment in our explorations.

8. Clarke, *Serve the Community of the Church*, 250.

Of the Making of Biblical Leadership Case Studies There Is No End

Christian leadership literature has an affinity for deriving leadership "principles" or *secrets* from Bible characters. When I asked students to reflect biblically and theologically on leadership, many wrote about the usual suspects: Moses, David, Nehemiah, and, of course, Jesus (who, students routinely told me, was the "perfect leader"). They are in good company; many Christian authors do the same thing. Lewis Parks and Old Testament scholar Bruce Birch write scathingly about

> devotional exercises praising Jesus' executive abilities: how he keeps in contact with his boss (prays), how he delegates responsibility (teaches disciples); how he gives his disciples inspiring keepsakes (the Lord's Meal). There are lists of leadership principles allegedly derived from... Moses, Esther, or Paul—principles that... have little to do with these figures as presented in the canon of scripture but say a lot about some contemporary fad of self-help.[9]

I have read papers beyond number (and heard even more sermons) over the years on Moses acquiring the art of delegation from his wise father-in-law. One author contends that Moses learned "to avoid the mistakes that are common among leaders today," including the micromanaging temptation.[10] Seriously, do we truly think that God's Spirit inspired Exodus 18 to deliver a twenty-first-century leadership management lesson? Exodus 18 is fascinating in many respects. Jethro is a foreign priest, a Gentile. Yet he is tuned in to God's ways and *instructs* his son-in-law Moses, the exemplary man-of-God. That in itself is astonishing, as it guards against restricting God's grace and revelation to within one's own community. This theme of God working through outsiders pops up throughout scriptures: Melchizedek, Rahab, Ruth, magi. Another startling Exodus 18 revelation is that all power need not reside in one person. Actually, the contention goes further: all power *ought not* reside in one person. Jethro chides Moses: "What you are doing isn't good" (Exod 18:17 CEB). Here is another surprising yet

9. Lewis A. Parks and Bruce C. Birch, *Ducking Spears, Dancing Madly: A Biblical Model of Church Leadership* (Nashville: Abingdon, 2004), 9.

10. Roy E. Gane, "The Pentateuch," in *Servants and Friends: A Biblical Theology of Leadership*, ed. Skip Bell (Berrien Springs, MI: Andrews University Press, 2014), 57.

persistent scriptural theme, one especially pertinent to leadership questions: aversion to centralized power, instead favoring devolution of power.

I grow increasingly uncomfortable with deriving effective leadership "principles" from biblical accounts and narratives. Deeper readings are required.

One cautionary note with character studies is that we need to pay attention to larger contexts. Practical principles or "best practices" drawn from Moses leading people from slavery through the wilderness do not transfer neatly to what it takes to manage a nonprofit organization or pastor a congregation large or small, let alone run a corporation or launch a business or manage a store. Nehemiah's rebuilding of Jerusalem's walls is inspiring to be sure, but again this one-time historical event might not translate into the challenges of North American inner-city community organizing or energizing dying churches in post-Christendom.

It also must be said that many biblical characters are so decidedly mixed that it is difficult to tease out positive values from their lives.[11] While King David was "a man after God's own heart (1 Sam 13:14; 16:12) and the exemplar king (2 Kings 14:3),"[12] he also committed adultery, covering that up with murder. His fatherhood skills left much to be desired, as shown by rebellions of various sons. The picture is not prettier at the end of his life. In 1 Kings 2, he first preached piously to his successor son Solomon (2:2-4). But then, in his final words, he advised retaliatory assassinations. Daniel Berrigan observes, "David dies intemperate, transfusing his venom into the veins of his son."[13] As Yoram Hazony says, "Many of the best-known biblical stories are fraught with moral ambiguity, carefully balancing multiple reasons for approving of what has been done against a no less impressive arsenal of reasons for reaching the opposite conclusion."[14]

"Biblical" leadership character studies give partial pictures. Noteworthy innovators and trailblazers are frequently glaring failures. There is far more tragedy than triumph. Martin Buber noted this in his "Biblical Leadership" essay; David and Moses were not permitted to complete their

11. This problem is helpfully explored in A. J. Culp, *Puzzling Portraits: Seeing the Old Testament's Confusing Characters as Ethical Models* (Eugene, OR: Wipf and Stock, 2013).

12. Ibid., 38–39.

13. Daniel Berrigan, *The Kings and Their Gods: The Pathology of Power* (Grand Rapids: Eerdmans, 2008), 17.

14. Yoram Hazony, *The Philosophy of Hebrew Scripture* (New York: Cambridge University Press, 2012), 80.

greatest tasks. God forbade David from building the temple and Moses was not allowed in the promised land.[15]

A great deal of David's life was a failure. Much of the time he was in flight—first from Saul, later from a son. Even when achieving something commendable—bringing the ark to Jerusalem—he was shamed by his wife. Buber sees a repeated "glorification of failure" in the experience of prophets, judges, and kings—three preeminent Old Testament leadership types.[16] Let us pay closer attention to Moses.

Moses as Exemplary Leader?

Moses might be the greatest Old Testament leadership figure. He led the people out of captivity, through decades in the wilderness, to the promised land's boundaries. He delivered the Ten Commandments; four books (Exodus, Numbers, Leviticus, and Deuteronomy) are preoccupied with him, his life, and his ministry. His achievements were stunning. No leader before or after matched him. He blended elements of king, revolutionary, military commander, priest, prophet, and sage—all roles that later are separate and distinct. Subsequent Hebrew leaders are wan imitations of him and his achievements. Yet his story, for all his accomplishments, is not an unambiguously positive leadership narrative.

Moses's role was not merely to succeed or replace Pharaoh but to be an entirely different kind of leader, to undermine presumptions of a pharaonic style of leadership. Moses was an "antiking"; his life contrasted with usual monarchs:

> His birth narrative... brings his role as an antiking into sharp focus. He became a prince in Egypt only after he was born a slave. When he went to the wilderness, therein was the presence of God to be found, not in the palaces or the temples of the urban centers.[17]

Brueggemann puts this even more forcefully, suggesting that the work of Moses "is nothing less than an assault on the consciousness of the empire, aimed at nothing less than the dismantling of the empire both in its social

15. Martin Buber, "Biblical Leadership," in *On the Bible: Eighteen Studies*, ed. Nahum N. Glatzer (Syracuse, NY: Syracuse University Press, 2000), 140–41.

16. Ibid., 143–44, 146, 147.

17. Robert Gnuse, *No Tolerance for Tyrants: The Biblical Assault on Kings and Kingship* (Collegeville, MN: Liturgical, 2011), 39.

practices and in its mythic pretensions."[18] God, through Moses, aimed at overthrowing oppressively hierarchical ideas, arrangements, priorities, and presuppositions.

Moses resembled a king (proclaiming laws, leading people), but his was an alternative kingship:

> His kingdom was one of slaves, he led no worship in a beautiful temple, he had no palace, he wore no regalia, he possessed no wealth, and his retainers were few and humble in origin—Aaron, Miriam, and Joshua. His temple was a craggy mountain in the wilderness, and therein was the true God to be found, not in the posh palaces or ornate temples of settled society. Moses was not a real king by the world's standards; he was an antiking. . . . Moses became the ultimate indictment of kings and rulers in this world and Yahweh provided that indictment.[19]

While definitely a leader, what does he teach us about leadership and how would we apply that to our experience? There the picture grows murkier.

For one, as we saw, Moses's story ended in tragedy, not triumph. While scholars disagree on *why* he was denied the promised land, this judgment proves that even Moses, for all his accomplishments, must not be revered too highly: "Leaders are not gods. The Hebrew people must not deify their leaders."[20]

Buber concludes:

> The Bible knows nothing of this intrinsic value of success. On the contrary, when it announces a successful deed, it is duty bound to announce in complete detail the failure involved in the success. When we consider . . . Moses, we see how much failure is mingled in the one great successful action, so much so that when we set the individual events that make up his history side by side, we see that his life consists of one failure after another, through which runs the thread of his success. True, Moses brought the people out of Egypt; but each stage of this leadership is a failure. Whenever he comes to deal with this people, he is defeated by them.[21]

18. Walter Brueggemann, *The Prophetic Imagination,* 2nd ed. (Minneapolis: Augsburg Fortress, 2001), 9.

19. Gnuse, *No Tolerance for Tyrants,* 52–53.

20. Aaron Wildavsky, *Moses as Political Leader* (New York: Shalem, 2005), 182.

21. Buber, "Biblical Leadership," 142–43.

This sad, sorrowful sense is pronounced in Deuteronomy's final chapters. In chapter 30, Moses delivered a rousing exhortation to faithfulness—promising prosperity if people obey God and great hazards if they do not. Then Moses was reminded that he will die soon, without reaching the promised land. God told him that, by the way, the Israelites are not going to heed his counsel: "The people will rise up and act unfaithfully, going after strange gods of the land they are entering. They will abandon me, breaking my covenant that I made with them" (Deut 31:16b CEB). Quite a note upon which to end one's leadership and one's life. Bruce Feiler says: "Moses is as much a model of disappointment as he is of achievement."[22]

There are further cautions when considering Moses as a leadership model. He did not have the drive to achieve that so many times is commended by leadership teachers. When he tried to intervene in a dispute between two Hebrew slaves, one directly challenged his presumption to leadership, "Who made you a ruler and judge over us?" (Exod 2:14a). Moses was fearful of Pharaoh's wrath and shortly thereafter fled to the desert and became a shepherd. When God called him, he suggested reasons why he was not a good candidate. He frequently showed ambivalence about tasks set before him. That is understandable given the stubborn ingratitude, regular complaining, and outright rebellions of his "followers." Elie Wiesel summarizes this way:

> Moses was the greatest legislator and the commander in chief of perhaps the first liberation army. He was a prophet, God's representative to the people and the people's representative to God. And he never had a good day in his life. Either the people were against him, or God was against him.[23]

We frequently define leaders as people who help followers achieve goals. But Moses at times did the opposite. Wildavsky observes "(at the Golden Calf and again just outside the Promised Land) he prevented his followers from going where they wanted to go—back to slavery in Egypt." Wildavsky continues that Aaron was better at helping people get what they wanted, for example, the golden calf. [24]

---

22. Bruce Feiler, *America's Prophet: Moses and the American Story* (New York: William Morrow, 2009), 31.

23. Elie Wiesel, "10 Questions for Elie Wiesel," by Jeff Chu, *TIME,* January 22, 2006.

24. Wildavsky, *Moses as Political Leader*, 209.

Even when Moses triumphed at the Red Sea, his "credit" from the Israelites for this achievement lasted only a few days.[25] Perhaps all this is not surprising.

> Moses is not a charismatic leader. On the contrary, he begins by questioning his own competence. He continues to doubt himself. Whatever authority Moses does possess is challenged by practically everyone. Popular acclamation, to say the least, is lacking. . . . Charisma, indeed! If there is such a thing as an anticharismatic force, . . . Moses is it.[26]

None of this suggests that Moses was not in many ways admirable and exceptional. It does, however, mean that we must be restrained in trying to claim him as someone whose leadership example we want to closely emulate.

> Moses is not meant to be a paradigm of leadership. Are future leaders . . . to try wriggling out of responsibility (as Moses does at the burning bush), or to encourage followers to take a heavy responsibility in abiding by a covenant for which they are ill-prepared? Are future leaders supposed to kill off a significant part of the people or to delay their maturity until a generation has died off?[27]

Buber says it is "an impossible undertaking" to derive "so-called character sketches of biblical leaders."[28] To understand leadership, we need to look further.

This Can't End Well: Biblical Failure Studies

While biblical character case studies are intended to teach successful leadership principles, a deeper reading of scriptures warn those of us foolhardy enough to pursue leadership that surely suffering and sorrow lie ahead.

The Bible dwells more on leadership *failures* than *successes*. This is not a popular approach in our culture. Reams of books are published by well-known personalities who were astonishingly successful and now share their leadership principles. Yet failure may be the best teacher.

Political scientist Aaron Wildavsky contends that errors and failure are *better* for reflecting on leadership, but "learning from success is more

25. Ibid., 210.

26. Ibid., 234.

27. Ibid., 238.

28. Buber, "Biblical Leadership," 137.

difficult and less appropriate." A favorable outcome generally relies on "many elements outside of one's own actions" but also "breeds the temptation to repeat the same actions in a less appropriate context."[29] Triumphal leadership gurus—whether corporation executives, military officers, megachurch pastors, athletes—are not necessarily in the best position to teach generic or general leadership lessons. Excellent athletes, for example, are not always good coaches; they may not understand how hard it is for less gifted athletes to perform and develop; what worked for stars or prodigies does not necessarily apply to others.

Scripture's Surprising Insights about Leadership

I am not claiming that the Bible has nothing to say about leadership. As it has much to present on Christian formation and what it means to follow Jesus, we can be sure that it will be filled with implications for leadership too.

In fact, once I began paying attention to leadership, I read familiar texts in unexpected ways and gained new insights into well-known passages.

Let's consider a few familiar examples from Luke, ones that we might not immediately regard as "leadership texts."

Parable of the Good Samaritan (Luke 10:25-37)

An outcast famously acted with compassion toward a wounded Jew. He behaved as a leader: took initiative, claimed agency, assisted, recruited help. But here's the thing, two *official* leaders, a priest and a Levite, "crossed over to the other side" and did nothing (v. 31 CEB). This story not only commends emulating the marginal outsider but also specifically rebukes prominent classes of leaders.

Solomon's Glory and the Gloriously Clothed Lilies (Luke 12:27-28)

Jesus contrasted Solomon, the most successful of all Hebrew kings (known for wisdom and wealth), unfavorably with lilies. His "glory" was far surpassed by flowers that "neither toil nor spin."[30]

29. Wildavsky, *Moses as Political Leader*, 9.

30. Walter Brueggemann connects this teaching with the preceding parable of the rich fool and sees that also as a negative commentary on Solomon. Brugge-

Parable of the Prodigal (Luke 15:11-32)

One could interpret this story as three kinds of leadership. The younger son decided to go his own way, live his own life, and reject family obligations. He took initiative and ventured into new possibilities. The father released his son but kept faith with him when he returned, offering not only compassion but celebration too. The older son, a likely "caricature of the religious leaders" of Jesus's time, remained loyal to family and tradition but wanted to withhold mercy from his brother.[31]

The Widow's Offering (Luke 21:1-4)

Jesus watched affluent people and a poor widow give offerings. Just before this (20:45-47 CEB), he cautioned the disciples about whom they admire and emulate: those who are "greeted with honor in the markets . . . [and] long for the places of honor in the synagogues and at banquets." He explicitly criticized contemporary leaders and commended the widow as the model to follow. She "from her hopeless poverty has given everything she had to live on" (21:4 CEB). Although anonymous, her example has spoken to us for two millennia.

Leadership themes are implicit in these passages.

Looking more broadly at the Bible, we recognize that a number of consistent leadership motifs emerge. One of the most important here—and one of most neglected in so much leadership literature—is the fact that at all times rulers and their responsibility need to be treated circumspectly. When it comes to talking about leaders, the Bible is especially cautionary.

---

mann, *Truth Speaks to Power: The Countercultural Nature of Scripture* (Louisville, KY: Westminster John Knox, 2013), 153–54.

31. Timothy S. Laniak, *Shepherds After My Own Heart: Pastoral Traditions and Leadership in the Bible* (Downers Grove, IL: InterVarsity, 2006), 205. Laniak shows that all three Luke 15 parables (lost sheep, lost coin, lost son) critique contemporary leaders, "shepherds" who did not measure up.

Chapter Four

What's the Bible Got to Do with It?

Challenges of Discovering Christian Perspectives on Leadership

St. Peter's Rump? Really?

Years ago, on retreat at the famous Abbey of Gethsemane, I was startled when the guestmaster informed me that it was the Feast of the *Seat* of St. Peter. Even as an appreciative observer of matters liturgical, I had trouble understanding why Peter's *seat* was worth celebrating. I worried that *seat* was a euphemism for a body part (taking the cult of relics a little too far). I lived in suspense until I was told that this day honored the *chair* or *throne* of Peter, in other words, the establishment of the papacy. I was a little disappointed, as by then I was mischievously savoring the idea of some bizarre religious observance.

This memory was a cautionary note years later when I was granted an endowed chair—in leadership of all things. Christians need to be careful about honors coming our way. Jesus warned against religious *leaders* who "love to have the place of honor... and the best *seats*" (Matt 23:6; emphasis added). Or endowed chairs I suppose.

Preparing for that new role, I studied leadership literature and discovered a curious fact: it is difficult to settle on a succinct leadership definition. Just as I was vague on the religious significance of Peter's "seat," many are unclear on the meaning of "leadership." Joseph Rost argues that most leadership literature does not even define the term and just takes it for granted. Warren Bennis encountered 350 definitions. Kellerman counts higher; she knows of 1,500 versions.[1] An indicator of the ambiguity or inadequacy of the term is the diverse adjectives applied to it, especially in book titles on my shelves: adaptive, authentic, bad, biblical, boundary, Christ-centered, connective, contrarian, courageous, cross-cultural, cross-shaped, effective, empowered, ethical, heroic, incarnate, inspirational, introverted, intuitive, missional, organizational, primal, quiet, real, reflective, relational, resonant, servant, shepherd, spiritual, steward, strategic, strengths-based, toxic, transforming, upside-down, visionary.

Because of this confusing array of ideas, when strangers asked what I taught, I sometimes responded, "Leadership." Then, after waiting a bit, added, "Whatever that is." Documents and archives about the chair did not offer a definition either.

I interviewed key people (faculty, board members, administrators, constituency representatives) who were instrumental in dreaming about and launching the chair. I asked for a definition of leadership and heard a range of responses: taking responsibility; facilitating the fulfillment of the purposes of persons, groups, or organizations; being a person of influence; helping people see reality and inspire them to move to possibility; understanding and discerning one's time and context; suggesting or setting a vision and moving a group to long-term results and human satisfaction; exercising authority in managing resources to accomplish common good; influencing people to do what is needed; stewarding influence; and so on.

These definitions posed by intelligent Christians said nothing explicitly *Christian*. They described dynamics of *any* commendable leadership, whether in churches, parachurch agencies, nonprofits, social service organizations, corporations, businesses small and large, or sports teams. When Christians discuss leadership, do we simply articulate capacities and priorities that any leadership advocates would promote for all settings? Not one person that I interviewed offered a specifically Christian view of leadership without my prompting.

When I pressed subjects for something uniquely *Christian*, there was regularly hesitation. One person noted that we must lead as Christ led. Another that Christian leaders "serve the purposes of God for his people in time." These clarifications remind us that Christian leadership is not just about having or influencing people to achieve goals. Rather, this kind of

1. Joseph C. Rost, *Leadership for the Twenty-First Century* (Westport, CT: Praeger, 1993), 7. Warren Bennis is cited in Wesley Granberg-Michaelson, *Leadership from Inside Out: Spirituality and Organizational Change* (New York: Crossroad, 2004), 128. Barbara A. Kellerman, *The End of Leadership* (New York: Harper, 2012), xxi.

leadership must always have a certain orientation. "From a Christian point of view, it is only when the direction and the method are in line with God's purposes, character, and ways of operating that godly leadership takes place."[2]

I heard Stanley Hauerwas lecture on end-of-life issues at Toronto's Regis College (November 2011). As important as the medical sciences are, he noted, Christians have alternative perspectives on wholeness, health, life, and death; he called this "the Christian difference." Surely, Christian leadership approaches also ought to have a "Christian difference." In his autobiography, Hauerwas speaks of living a life that is unintelligible if God did not exist.[3] Is there a form of leadership that is incoherent without God? I certainly hope so.

Vague understandings similar to what many people—including non-Christians—regard as leadership do not offer much clarification. "Christianized" takes merely advance leadership with a little Christian icing: concepts that may or may not be worthy of our affirmation. If unclear about teaching *Christian* leadership, then we end up not being substantially different than any MBA. I do not disparage MBAs, but church or seminary settings should not merely be MBA-lite imitators. We must have unique leadership perspectives, ones not necessarily covered in business schools.

Another problem with across-the-board definitions of "leadership principles" is expecting them to fit anywhere. Ros Tennyson notes that three different spheres—public sector, businesses, and civil society—have strikingly varying "priorities, values and attributes." The public sector is concerned with rights and stability; business with profits, entrepreneurialism, productivity; and civil society (including nonprofits, e.g., churches) with values that are "responsive, vocal, inclusive and imaginative."[4] It is a mistake to assume that what qualifies as commendable leadership in one sphere is fitting for another. Christian leadership ought to be unique. We need a Christian difference.

Competing Biblical Perspectives on Leadership

The most prominent leaders in scriptures are political leaders of Israel, religious leaders (Old Testament priests and prophets; New Testament

2. Robert Banks and Bernice M. Ledbetter, *Reviewing Leadership: A Christian Evaluation of Current Approaches* (Grand Rapids: Baker, 2004), 17.

3. Stanley Hauerwas, *Hannah's Child: A Theologian's Memoir* (Grand Rapids: Eerdmans, 2012), x.

4. Ros Tennyson, *The Partnering Toolbook,* 4th ed. (London: The International Business Leaders Forum, 2011), 5.

disciples, apostles, and so on), and "outside" political leaders (especially from occupying empires). These require much of our attention, both because they figure so largely in the Bible and because these are the kinds of roles that most people first think of when they ponder leadership.

Several things are worth noting.

We today take the separation of church and state as a given and assume that spiritual and secular are distinguishable, but those distinctions were not understood in biblical eras. Kings in those cultures had religious functions and prophets impacted political realities.

While there were specified leadership roles, there was little attention to the *idea* of a leader or the *concept* of leadership, especially as we use those terms. There was no sense of entrepreneurial, winsome, charismatic innovators who influence people, win followers, and achieve impressive accomplishments. "Leadership" is not explicitly and directly explored in the Bible. There are narratives on people we regard as leaders, counsel on what it means to faithfully lead a country or church, and cautionary tales about unfaithful leaders (far more of the latter). So we certainly expect scriptures to give important resources.

Yet we do so carefully. We find people who organize movements, command armies, govern nations, administer justice, but leaders in the Bible generally bear little resemblance to the polished, powerful, educated mandarins heading today's corporations, not-for-profits, nongovernmental organizations, or megachurches. Therefore, we need to be cautious about comparisons and applications.

How we draw on scriptures is also important. Too many Christian books quickly leap from superficial readings to contemporary applications. As if the Bible is a text on management, sociology, psychology, or business administration. At best, God's word can be in meaningful dialogue with those disciplines.

Many biblical examples are explicitly *political*, and thus in this book we examine how the Bible's political ideas and stories help us extrapolate potential applications for our own day. Eminent theologian Oliver O'Donovan writes:

> Almost the whole vocabulary of salvation in the New Testament has a political pre-history of some kind: 'salvation'... (*y*^{e}*shūāh*), 'justification' (*ts*^{e}*dāqāh*), 'peace' (*shālōm*), 'faithfulness' (*hesed*), 'faith' (^{e}*mūnāh*), and above all the Kingdom of God. Israel's knowledge of God's blessings was, from beginning to end, a political knowledge.[5]

5. Oliver O'Donovan, *The Desire of the Nations: Rediscovering the Roots of Political Theology* (New York: Cambridge University Press, 1996), 22–23.

To interpret leadership in the Bible, it is more helpful to turn to *political* theology than to rely on business literature or management theory.

Politics is not only about running governments and electing officials. Modern corporations resemble what we formerly regarded as governments, states, or empires. Terry Tempest Williams recounts a conversation with a highly placed Procter & Gamble executive who matter-of-factly discussed how his company operated in China with no environmental standards: "The air is appalling and the rivers are filthy. We're just giving the people what they deserve, what they need to elevate their lifestyle and create a higher quality of life." He also described how P & G broke the Mediterranean "siesta culture." Both accomplishments he deemed "progress." Corporations are political in at least two ways, both in relating to governments and in the fact that they also rework countries and cultures.[6]

Elusive Unifying Themes

It is impossible to derive a single, coherent attitude toward leadership in the Bible. The scriptures are a collection of voices from different directions. Some celebrate the establishment of a monarchy, while others see kingship as a major turning point for the worst, in fact, a serious downfall for Israel.

Consider three stories that at first appear to have much in common: Joseph in Pharaoh's court, Esther married to the Persian king, and Daniel as a high-placed minister in succeeding regimes. In each situation, a Jew occupied a position of responsibility and power in a foreign government. (In two cases, the regime held the Jewish people in captivity or exile.) For anyone advocating ethical purity at all costs, it is hard to imagine that this could be faithful. (Some Christians—for example, the Amish—argue against holding any political office at all, regardless of political system.) Yet Joseph, Esther, and Daniel achieved impressive results for their people. Joseph's family was spared starvation. Esther's intervention averted the genocide of Persian Jews. Daniel triumphed for Jewish observance and against idolatrous temptations. On the surface these three leadership stories could be interpreted as employing power to benefit the vulnerable.

But look a little closer. What do they really show?

While Joseph successfully rescued and fed his clan, his managerial efficacy was also responsible for putting into place distressing policies that helped Pharaoh and his successors become more and more oppressive toward the entire kingdom and toward the Jews. "The cunning food admin-

6. Terry Tempest Williams, *Leap* (New York: Pantheon Books, 2000), 71–77.

istration plans of Joseph... created for Pharaoh a peasant underclass of very cheap labor."[7] The Hebrews eventually suffer the brunt of the consequences with "no rights, no protectors or guarantors; they are completely vulnerable to the unchecked power of Pharaoh."[8] Joseph unknowingly set the stage for a subsequent regime that God would need to overcome and overthrow.

Daniel is a portrait of unmitigated faithfulness—in what he ate or abstained from, not bending the knee to an idol, keeping threefold Jewish prayer. He showed that "faith in God is virtually all one needs to gain political salvation."[9] His fidelity had no adverse consequences. He witnessed and predicted the downfall of regimes.

Esther was part of a harem before replacing a murdered queen by marrying the murderous king. Through clever use of her position, she intervened and successfully saved fellow Jews. Nevertheless this book "comes closer to the view that in politics God tends to help those who help themselves."[10] In fact, God is never mentioned in the entire book, perhaps more of that "functional atheism." Her bravery saved the Jewish people, but this story has a very different feel than the others.

These three accounts, at first glance so similar, all point in varying directions. The Bible does not give one clear teaching on leadership. Voices appear to contradict and conflict with each other. Some texts prioritize hierarchies, but others suggest an implicit egalitarianism, what certain Protestants call the "priesthood of all believers." Particular passages commend obedience to rulers, but others celebrate resistance and disobedience to tyranny and injustice. What chief rabbi of the United Hebrew Congregations of the Commonwealth Jonathan Sacks says is also applicable to the entire Bible (including the New Testament) on leadership: "The book's stories, messages, and political arrangements are... too diverse to fit under any unified theory of government. In fact, they give credence to many." He later

7. Walter Brueggemann, *Truth Speaks to Power* (Louisville, KY: Westminster John Knox, 2013), 18.

8. Ibid., 20. "The bitter ironies of this tale reflect the conflict that is at the heart of the biblical ethics: Yes, mankind might have perished were it not for the successes of the Egyptian state; and a young Israelite can save his people... by building up the might of the greatest empire of them all. But what kind of salvation is it to return to the house of bondage, to serve it, to build it that others may serve it and so increase the suffering and idolatry in the world?" Yoram Hazony, *The Philosophy of Hebrew Scripture* (New York: Cambridge University Press, 2012), 124.

9. Hazony, *The Philosophy of Hebrew Scripture*, 41.

10. Ibid.

adds "the Hebrew Bible is deliberately structured not as a consistent system of thought but as a field of tensions."[11]

I celebrate the highly differing points of view. Hearing varying perspectives is like listening to all the conflicting opinions in each and every church of which I have ever been a part. I trust that needed truths emerge in the dialogue—and even in intense tensions and disagreements. On this side of eternity, there are numerous questions we can never hope to resolve fully. Thus this book is *a* biblical theology of leadership; it is impossible to land on *the* biblical theology of leadership. There is not one consistent point of view.

All the same, there are steady, countercultural, interrelated cautionary themes that are frequently overlooked in Christian leadership discussions. We explore three voices: suspicion about leadership; ongoing leadership innovation and leadership devolving in unexpected directions; and prioritizing the goals and means of doing justice, loving kindness, and walking humbly with God (Mic 6:8).

The *first* voice repeatedly criticizes dominant leadership models of the day and questions their priority, significance, even their basic justice. When it comes to leadership, a prevailing scriptural sense is subversive suspicion about powers-that-be and rulers of this age (no matter which age is being discussed), the "Establishment" as I heard it spoken of when I was a teenager.

The *second* voice shows that God's people continually tinker and *experiment* with models. We see a succession of leadership types—judges, kings, wise ones, itinerant teachers, disciples, apostles, deacons. Different forms responded to something missing or not working well in other leadership modes of the day. Thus ongoing experimentation is in order. God's people are flexible, inventive, and improvisational when it comes to those in charge, up front, or at the top. The innovation frequently involves *devolution of power*. Over and again, God empowers unlikely prospects, giving agency to individuals who were normally marginalized and excluded and commending odd images for would-be leaders: servants and fools. The Spirit consistently aims to widen the circle of those empowered by God: "In the last days, God says, / I will pour out my Spirit on all people" (Acts 2:17 CEB).

The *third* scriptural voice needs repeated emphasis, namely that leadership is never about power for the sake of power or being on the "winning,"

11. Jonathan Sacks, "God's Politics: The Lessons of the Hebrew Bible," review of *In God's Shadow: Politics in the Hebrew Bible,* by Michael Walzer, *Foreign Affairs,* vol. 91, no. 6 (November/December 2012): 123, 124.

most influential, side. Rather it is about emphasizing and honoring God's priorities, moving toward that great day when:

> They won't harm or destroy anywhere on my holy mountain.
> The earth will surely be filled with the knowledge of the LORD,
> just as the water covers the sea. (Isa 11:9 CEB)

These three themes are encapsulated in a few words from Acts. Paul and Silas were embroiled in a local uproar. Those two missionaries, and local supporters, were dragged before city authorities. The complaint against them said much about leadership:

> These people who have been turning the world upside down have come here also.... They are all acting contrary to the decrees of the emperor, saying that there is another king named Jesus. (Acts 17:6-7)

There you have it. Cultural values are being overturned, upset. No one is safe; they "have come here also." For one, they violated the emperor's rules. For another, his followers created a new kind of order, "turning the world upside down." The surprise at unexpected reversals was articulated earlier by authorities in Jerusalem: "Now when they saw the boldness of Peter and John and realized that they were *uneducated* and *ordinary men*, they were amazed" (Acts 4:13; emphasis added). Finally, the followers gave allegiance to "another king named Jesus," undermining current power arrangements and making way for a new reign to emerge in support of subversive priorities.

Leadership in the Wilderness

Intriguingly, these themes and their criticism of—even rebellion against—established modes of power, the palaces of the day, frequently involve movement to or from the wilderness.

Moses escaped there from Pharaoh's wrath but returned from it to demand liberation of the Hebrews. In the wilderness, he and his people learned lessons preparing them for the promised land. Elijah, frightened by Jezebel's threats, headed for the wilderness. David fled murderous King Saul and assembled a band of social rejects there. When King Nebuchadnezzar broke down, he dwelled in the wilderness, "driven away from other humans" (Dan 4:33 CEB). Prophets, including John the Baptist, spoke in that sphere: "The voice of one shouting in the wilderness" (Matt 3:3 CEB). When Jesus learned of Herod's execution of John at a palatial party, he retired to a "deserted place" (Mark 6:32 CEB). After his dramatic conversion, Paul went to Arabia for a spell.

Timothy Laniak demonstrates that a key biblical leadership metaphor of "shepherd" plays out in wilderness: "Jeremiah, like Isaiah and Ezekiel, finds in the ancient Sinai desert a symbolic setting for the divine . . . work of provision, protection and guidance."[12] The wilderness represents a primary place where Israel learned about God and God's leadership. And it was vital whenever Israelite leaders needed to ponder and recalibrate.

Wilderness stands in tension over and again with the agenda of palaces and the powers-that-be. The centrality of wilderness, especially in contrast to palaces, is especially inescapable when we ponder biblical views of leadership.

The wilderness was the place to defy and rebuke palatial politics and to rework understandings of power and authority. It was a key location for leadership experimentation, and unlikely excluded leaders were formed there. It was the location for envisioning God's new realities and putting them into practice. No wonder then that later on many Christians, desert fathers and mothers, lived out critiques of affluent Roman Christianity by heading to the outskirts of civilization.

12. Timothy S. Laniak, *Shepherds After My Own Heart: Pastoral Traditions and Leadership in the Bible* (Downers Grove, IL: InterVarsity, 2006), 22–23.

Chapter Five

The Plattered Head and Five Smooth Loaves

Competing Kingdoms

A Tale of Palace Versus Wilderness

After forty years, I still have not forgotten one of my most unexpected Bible lessons. When I left home to attend a public university, I was astonished that I could study the Bible for academic credit. I immediately signed up to do just that.

Our professor was a nun. A young die-hard sectarian Protestant, I was not confident of what to expect from this devout Roman Catholic. Most challenging of all, I felt threatened by her introduction of critical tools of scripture study. Yet her love of the Bible won me over, even as she patiently reworked many of my ideas.

One assignment proved particularly difficult. She required us to analyze Matthew 14:1-21. I was baffled by the two different stories—John the Baptist's execution and a miraculous feeding. I understood interpreting one story or the other but could not conceive of analyzing both at once. I asked for help. "Look," my professor explained, "both stories are about a meal."

Then the pieces began to fall into place.

What still strikes me is that I have never encountered anyone else who suggested that these passages were beside each other for a reason. Yet in the parallel versions—Mark 6 and Luke 9—they are also lined up that way. This suggests purposeful arrangement, not merely happenstance. These two stories contrast deeply in mood, setting, action, consequences, and implication. They encapsulate important biblical insights on vexing leadership questions.

Herod's Murderous Banquet and the Feeding of the Five Thousand in Three Versions

First of all, it is worth considering the texts in their entirety.

Matthew 14:1-21

At that time Herod the ruler heard reports about Jesus; and he said to his servants, "This is John the Baptist; he has been raised from the dead, and for this reason these powers are at work in him." For Herod had arrested John, bound him, and put him in prison on account of Herodias, his brother Philip's wife, because John had been telling him, "It is not lawful for you to have her." Though Herod wanted to put him to death, he feared the crowd, because they regarded him as a prophet. But when Herod's birthday came, the daughter of Herodias danced before the company, and she pleased Herod so much that he promised on oath to grant her whatever she might ask. Prompted by her mother, she said, "Give me the head of John the Baptist here on a platter." The king was grieved, yet out of regard for his oaths and for the guests, he commanded it to be given; he sent and had John beheaded in the prison. The head was brought on a platter and given to the girl, who brought it to her mother. His disciples came and took the body and buried it; then they went and told Jesus.

Now when Jesus heard this, he withdrew from there in a boat to a deserted place by himself. But when the crowds heard it, they followed him on foot from the towns. When he went ashore, he saw a great crowd; and he had compassion for them and cured their sick. When it was evening, the disciples came to him and said, "This is a deserted place, and the hour is now late; send the crowds away so that they may go into the villages and buy food for themselves." Jesus said to them, "They need not go away; you give them something to eat." They replied, "We have nothing here but five loaves and two fish." And he said, "Bring them here to me." Then he ordered the crowds to sit down on the grass. Taking the five loaves and the two fish, he looked up to heaven, and blessed and broke the loaves, and gave them to the disciples, and the disciples gave them to the crowds. And all ate and were filled; and they took up what was left over of the broken pieces, twelve baskets full.

Mark 6:14-44

King Herod heard of it, for Jesus' name had become known. Some were saying, "John the baptizer has been raised from the dead; and for this reason these powers are at work in him." But others said, "It is Elijah." And others said, "It is a prophet, like one of the prophets of old." But when Herod heard of it, he said, "John, whom I beheaded, has been raised."

For Herod himself had sent men who arrested John, bound him, and put him in prison on account of Herodias, his brother Philip's wife, because Herod had married her. For John had been telling Herod, "It is not lawful for you to have your brother's wife." And Herodias had a grudge against him, and wanted to kill him. But she could not, for Herod feared John, knowing that he was a righteous and holy man, and he protected him. When he heard him, he was greatly perplexed; and yet he liked to listen to him. But an opportunity came when Herod on his birthday gave a banquet for his for his courtiers and officers and for the leaders of Galilee. When his daughter Herodias came in and danced, she pleased Herod and his guests; and the king said to the girl, "Ask me for whatever you wish, and I will give it." And he solemnly swore to her, "Whatever you ask me, I will give you, even half of my kingdom." She went out and said to her mother, "What should I ask for?" She replied, "The head of John the baptizer." Immediately she rushed back to the king and requested, "I want you to give me at once the head of John the Baptist on a platter." The king was deeply grieved; yet out of regard for his oaths and for the guests, he did not want to refuse her. Immediately the king sent a soldier of the guard with orders to bring John's head. He went and beheaded him in the prison, brought his head on a platter, and gave it to the girl. Then the girl gave it to her mother. When his disciples heard about it, they came and took his body, and laid it in a tomb.

The apostles gathered around Jesus, and told him all that they had done and taught. He said to them, "Come away to a deserted place all by yourselves and rest a while." For many were coming and going, and they had no leisure even to eat. And they went away in the boat to a deserted place by themselves. Now many saw them going and recognized them, and they hurried there on foot from all the towns and arrived ahead of them. As he went ashore, he saw a great crowd; and he had compassion for them, because they were like sheep without a shepherd; and he began to teach them many things. When it grew late, his disciples came to him and said, "This is a deserted place, and the hour is now very late; send them away so that they may go into the surrounding country and villages and buy something for themselves to eat." But he answered them, "You give them something to eat." They said to him, "Are we to go and buy two hundred denarii worth of bread, and give it to them to eat?" And he said to them, "How many loaves have you? Go and see." When they had found out, they said, "Five, and two fish." Then he ordered them to get all the people to sit down in groups on the green grass. So they sat down in groups of hundreds and of fifties. Taking the five loaves and the two fish, he looked up to heaven, and blessed and broke the loaves, and gave them to his disciples to set before the people; and he divided the two fish among them all. And all ate and were filled; and they took up twelve baskets full of broken pieces and of the fish. Those who had eaten the loaves numbered five thousand men.

Luke 9:7-17

Now Herod the ruler heard about all that had taken place, and he was perplexed, because it was said by some that John had been raised from the dead, by some that Elijah had appeared, and by others that one of the ancient prophets had arisen. Herod said, "John I beheaded; but who is this about whom I hear such things?" And he tried to see him.

On their return the apostles told Jesus all they had done. He took them with him and withdrew privately to a city called Bethsaida. When the crowds found out about it, they followed him; and he welcomed them, and spoke to them about the kingdom of God, and healed those who needed to be cured.

The day was drawing to a close, and the twelve came to him and said, "Send the crowd away, so that they may go into the surrounding villages and countryside, to lodge and get provisions; for we are here in a deserted place." But he said to them, "You give them something to eat." They said, "We have no more than five loaves and two fish—unless we are to go and buy food for all these people." For there were about five thousand men. And he said to his disciples, "Make them sit down in groups of about fifty each." They did so and made them all sit down. And taking the five loaves and the two fish, he looked up to heaven, and blessed and broke them, and gave them to the disciples to set before the crowd. And all ate and were filled. What was left over was gathered up, twelve baskets of broken pieces.

Contrasting the Banquets

Let us examine parallels and contrasts.

Herod's Banquet: Brutal Murder Amidst Luxury	Jesus's Banquet: Lavishness in a Desolate Place
Location/Setting	
royal festivity	teaching "crowds"
royal setting, possibly palace and prison	"deserted place" (Matt 14:13)

	"solitary place" (Matt 14:13 NIV)
	"quiet place" (Mark 6:31 NIV)
	"out-of-the-way place" (Mark 6:31 NAB)
	"desolate place" (Matt 14:13, 15 ESV)
	"desert place" (Matt 14:13, 15; Mark 6:31, 32, 35; Luke 9:10 KJV)
Protagonist	
Herod, "ruler" "king" (Matt 14:1, 9), tetrarch (Matt 14:1 NIV)	Jesus, no title given, but early on speculation about his identity
Protagonist's Character and Emotion	
fear, perplexed, torn, misgivings	desiring solitude—grief? (Matt 14:13)
pleased by step-daughter's dance impulsively makes rash promise worried about what others think (Matt 14:9)	compassion, curing sick (Matt 14:14) welcoming and ministering to crowd, deciding to feed multitude trusting God's miraculous abundance
acts because of reputation	acts with integrity
Vices and Virtues	
lust, greed, hatred	compassion, concern, hospitality
Methods Employed	
coercive power	weakness, vulnerability—relying on others

Participants	
elite of the day	needy, hungry crowds—"five thousand men, besides women and children" (Matt 14:21)
Herod's "courtiers and officers and . . . the leaders of Galilee" (Mark 6:21)	
Meal	
lavish, decadent (note the dance)	ample but simple meal, fish and loaves
things get out of hand: dance, rash promise, execution	meal done in orderly fashion
	allusion to Communion—taking, blessing, breaking, giving
Consequences	
death of "righteous and holy" person (Mark 6:20)	"all ate and were filled" (Mark 6:42)
distress, grief, sorrow	
bitter regret (Mark 6:26 NAB)	satisfaction

Emerging Leadership Themes

These two narratives pose stark contrasts. Herod's story began with a reference to John's and Jesus's "powers" or "miraculous powers" (NIV) and moved to death; Jesus's story started with John's death and ended with a stunning miracle. Herod was full of ambivalence: curiosity about Jesus, angrily begrudging of John but enjoying listening to him, fearful of others' opinions, distress at being manipulated into killing John. Jesus acted with clarity and certainty. Even when his plans for a retreat were interrupted, he extended ministry, healing, and feeding.

Mark's version, the longest, has the most details. Luke's rendering, the shortest, tells little about the circumstances of John's execution.

Nevertheless, all versions begin with speculation about Jesus's identity; move through Herod's mixed feelings about John, perplexity about Jesus, and John's execution; turn to Jesus and the disciples attempting a retreat but giving hospitable ministry; and end with an orderly, miraculous feeding that evokes (take-bless-break-give) Eucharist.

A major and significant contrast is in the locations.

In the Bible, palaces, royal lodgings, official headquarters—places of privilege and prestige—are generally bad news. People flee from them to the wilderness or "deserted," "solitary," or "out-of-the-way" places. Prophets come from the wilderness—or other marginal locations—to bring God's needed word. In palaces, royal lodgings, and official headquarters, plots, schemes, and conspiracies are planned, hatched and launched. Lusts and other base instincts are gratified. One might rework Nathanael's question: Can anything good come from a palace? And the biblical response would be: usually not much.

The meal accounts portray contrasting visions of strikingly different kingdoms or kinds of leadership. One resorts to power, hierarchy, coercion, threat. The other relies on prayerfulness, compassion, generosity. One ends in death; the other leads to life.

This two-storied passage thoroughly encapsulates what the Bible teaches about leadership.

First, over and again scriptures suggest that the "kingdoms of this world" or "rulers of this age" are in deadly competition with God's reign; there is ongoing *suspicion* about leadership. The rivalry is physical (people die under Herod) and moral (drastically varying priorities of the two kingdoms). Worldly leadership prioritizes power and coercion; violence and fear play a large role. Jesus's kingdom is characterized by compassion, hospitality, healing.

Furthermore, scriptures show that what the world rates as triumphs are ultimately vain. Victory and success in worldly kingdoms mean conquering, defeating, and eliminating enemies. But in God's kingdom, faithfulness may mean martyrdom (as for John). Suffering is more likely than success. Persecution and misunderstanding are expected. Ministry frequently ends in tragedy. But no matter, as witnessing to God's priorities persists.

Herod longed to avoid pain for himself—for example, the criticisms of John the Baptist and embarrassment before his guests. But John and Jesus knew that even great suffering and death were not the end. Jesus carried on from where John left off; and he, like John, would be executed by the powers-that-be.

Second, the reign of God experiments with new kinds of leadership. This threatens the status quo yet allows for the emergence of unanticipated leaders. Part of the confusion of Herod and others related to uncertainty about the roles of John and Jesus. Much of the wonder in the miraculous feeding had to do with the disciples' call into unlikely ministry: Jesus told them: "*You* give them something to eat" (Matt 14:16 CEB; emphasis added).

Finally, God's reign and its new leadership styles bring healing and liberation to all, not just serving the priorities of the few and the elite. Herod aims for his own promotion. Jesus, however, ministered to others even when he appeared to need recuperative and restorative time in "a deserted place." He nevertheless made himself a servant to the well-being of the crowd.

Chapter Six

Competing Visions

The Ongoing Contest between Leadership of this World and God's Leadership

Which Side Are You On?

When I read about the civil rights movement, right and wrong are apparent. I have no trouble knowing whom to cheer and whom to oppose. I like to think that had I lived there I would have been on the right side.

I have been involved in various social issues: writing letters, advocating change, joining protests, even risking arrest. While convicted about causes I embraced, I usually had ambivalence too. I knew thoughtful, well-motivated people, even other believers (relatives, congregants) who saw and believed very differently than I. It was important to take a stand, but I was never comfortable with the clear-cut confidence of the old labor union song "Which Side Are You On?" When we sang that at demonstrations, I always kept my mouth shut.

The Bible is clear, not ambivalent, about the definitive and decisive contest between the kingdoms, powers, rulers of this age and this world versus God's reign or kingdom. This rivalry brooks no compromise. We must choose.

Who Shall Reign Forever and Ever?

Throughout the Bible we observe ongoing struggle between two forms of leadership, God's and the world's. God contends with Pharaoh, Ahab, Caesar—to name only a few of the many leaders who ran afoul of God's prerogatives.

Hazony shows that in Genesis, "from the first moment . . . the Hebrews appear as rebels against the hubris and self-worship of kings and their states."[1] At Babel already an attempt is made to centralize human society: "By virtue of ruling the earth they come to believe that they can rule heaven; by virtue of making themselves a great name they come to believe they can be eternal. They come to think, in other words, that they are themselves God."[2] N. T. Wright contends that the biblical story tells "how Israel's God is taking on the arrogant tyrants of the world, overthrowing their power, and rescuing his people from under its cruel weight."[3] In the Bible, rulers, great and small, almost invariably are self-serving, self-worshipping, self-loving.

This perennial struggle pervades a biblical view of history. And the eschatological hope of Christians is that it will one day be decisively resolved.

> Then the seventh angel blew his trumpet, and there were loud voices in heaven saying,
> "The kingdom of the world has become
> the kingdom of our Lord and his Christ,
> and he will rule forever and always." (Rev 11:15 CEB)

Our God Reigns

Any biblical theology of leadership must be rooted in the Bible's foundational claim that God reigns.

> The Lord has established his throne in heaven,
> and his kingdom rules over all. (Ps 103:19 CEB)

In analyzing how leadership language is employed in the Old Testament, Richard M. Davidson notes that there are eight Hebrew verbs meaning "to lead":

> The vast majority of the references . . . refer to God as the One who leads—almost two hundred occurrences. Repeatedly Scripture mentions that God led Israel out of Egypt and through the wilderness (e.g., Exod. 15:13; Deut. 8:2; Isa. 48:21; Neh. 9:12). The psalmists frequently petition or thank God

1. 46 Yoram Hazony, *The Philosophy of Hebrew Scripture* (New York: Cambridge University Press, 2012), 142.

2. Ibid.

3. N. T. Wright, *How God Became King* (New York: HarperOne, 2012), 129.

> for His leading... The prophets also speak often of God's leading Israel during the time of the Divided Monarchy and His promise to lead His people in the eschatological future (e.g., Isa. 40:11; 42:16; 57:18; Jer. 31:9).[4]

Consider as well how various leadership roles were applied to God:

> The LORD is our *judge*;
> the LORD is our *leader*;
> the LORD is our *king*;
> he will deliver us. (Isa 33:22 CEB; emphasis added)

We confess God's lordship over the universe, creation, history, our lives. Even the mightiest human is subservient to God's power and authority. We all are called to "walk humbly" with God (Mic 6:8 CEB). In 1996, I visited the Desert Monastery of St. Moses the Ethiopian in the Syrian wilderness. To enter the ancient building, one goes through a small door, fewer than four feet high. All of us, in other words, went in on our knees, an appropriate stance for approaching our reigning God.

Worship celebrates these very convictions. God is "enthroned on the praises of Israel" (Ps 22.3b); "Israel's central liturgic act is the symbolic enthronement of Yahweh as king."[5] Worship confirms allegiance to God, renewing our fealty to God's reign. Worship is not primarily about personal inspiration but about *political* realities of celebrating God's rule. My favorite Old Testament professor taught: "Christian worship should be defined as the celebration of the rule of God as experienced in the life of the new community in Christ."[6] In other words, worship is explicitly political. Each worship service should draw us into deeper fealty to God and away from personality cults and earthly loyalties.

4. Richard M. Davidson, "Leadership Language in the Old Testament," in *Servants and Friends: A Biblical Theology of Leadership*, ed. Skip Bell (Berrien Springs, MI: Andrews University Press, 2014), 11.

5. Walter Brueggemann, *Israel's Praise: Doxology against Idolatry and Ideology* (Philadelphia: Fortress, 1988), 30. Oliver O'Donovan cautions: "At no point is the suggestion allowed that the people, by their praises, have *made* Yhwh king" (*The Desire of the Nations: Rediscovering the Roots of Political Theology* [New York: Cambridge University Press, 1996], 48).

6. Millard C. Lind, *Biblical Foundations for Christian Worship* (Scottdale, PA: Herald, 1973), 5.

Sometimes I attend a Coptic Orthodox church. The three-hour Sunday morning liturgy astounds me and—even more astonishing—a good part of every week's service is almost identical. Some scriptures and the short sermon change, but many of the same prayers and hymns recur Sunday after Sunday. On more than one occasion as I worshipped there, listening to the music, smelling incense, hearing prayers in languages I do not entirely understand, something happened within. Captivated by the chanting, overwhelmed by the incense, and impressed by the icons, at some point I surrendered to the worship. *I believe*, I cried out in my heart. I was carried along on the waves of that liturgical celebration.

True worship brings about submission to God who rules.

It is hard to overstate the importance of worship when considering leadership in the Bible. Before Israel had kings, it still fragmented easily into tribes, but worship held it together.[7] Gathering for worship was their primary bond.

From its earliest times, Israelites believed God was their king. Exodus 15 contains an ancient poem (possibly the oldest text in the Bible) that declares: "The Lord will rule forever and always" (Exod 15:18 CEB). God's kingship is rehearsed frequently: Psalms 10:16; 93; 97; 99; 146; Isaiah 52:7. This deeply embedded tradition long meant that Israel had no human king and was the reason that Gideon refused to be crowned (Judg 8).

Israel's worship reinforced the understanding of God as king. Israel gathered to acclaim God as commander-in-chief and to hear God's directives, commands, and laws. The ark was God's *throne*, a political symbol.[8]

This tradition would be tragically betrayed when Pilate brought Jesus before his enemies and said, "Here's your king!" They responded, "We have no king except the emperor" (John 19:14, 15 CEB) rather than the more biblically sound "no king but God."[9] God's place was usurped.

Kingship of God informs the New Testament. The Lord's Prayer says:

> Our Father who is in heaven,
> uphold the holiness of your name.
> Bring in your kingdom
> so that your will is done on earth as it's done in heaven. (Matt 6:9-10 CEB)

---

7. Ibid., 17.

8. Ibid., 21.

9. Wright, *How God Became King*, 146.

This is addressed to a sovereign, *the* Sovereign. We pray that God's reign will triumph, the sphere where God's will and purposes are honored and implemented.

From God's Kingship to Christ's Lordship

New Testament worship built on these understandings. The kingship of God is transmuted into the lordship of Christ. We see this in early church believers:

> They confessed that Jesus is Lord. They proclaimed that He was at the right hand of God, the place of authority in the universe. His authority was also with them since He was with them in the Spirit.[10]

It is easy to lose sight of the political import and ramifications of these professions.

Basic confessions, Acts 2:36 ("God has made this Jesus . . . both Lord and Christ"; CEB) and Romans 14:11 ("As I live, says the Lord, every knee will bow to me, / and every tongue will give praise to God"; CEB), were politically subversive. New Testament confessional creeds use explicitly political language: "Lord" (Phil 2:11 CEB), "Christ" (1 John 5:1 CEB), "God's Son" (1 John 4:15 CEB). We may not realize that these claims rebuked human leaders who held those titles. Applied to Jesus, they had "negative connotations. That is, they were a denial of other messiahs and other lords (i.e. Caesar)."[11] This terminology overtly rejected human rulers and saviors. As Brueggemann reminds us about the Exodus 15 confession of the Lord reigning for ever: "Such doxologies are always polemical; the unstated counter-theme, only whispered, is always 'and not Pharaoh.' "[12] Note the explicit political nature of a famous New Testament hymn:

> Therefore, God highly honored him
>   and gave him a name above all names,
>   so that at the name of Jesus everyone
>   in heaven, on earth, and under the earth might bow
>   and every tongue confess that

---

10. Lind, *Biblical Foundations*, 38.

11. Ibid., 50.

12. Walter Brueggemann, *The Prophetic Imagination*, 2nd ed. (Minneapolis: Augsburg Fortress, 2001), 18.

> Jesus Christ is Lord, to the glory of God the Father." (Phil 2:9-11 CEB)

Many Anglicans, in fulfillment of this promise, actually make a small bow every time the name "Jesus Christ" is mentioned during worship.

The incarnational hymn includes a phrase about Christ who "did not consider being equal with God as something to exploit" (Phil 2:6 CEB). This verse is used to speak of Christ's divinity. But what is easy to miss is the fact that at that time and in that era, equality-with-God was attributed to kings and rulers. For Egyptian and Roman monarchs "the equality in view relates not to ontology—sharing in the divine nature or essence—but to power and status, that is, occupying a godlike position of influence and prestige in the cosmos."[13]

Subversive claims were already suggested during the life of Jesus as we will see in a later chapter. He was accused of political crimes and executed by the powers-that-be (Luke 23:2). All four Gospels report that Pilate asked Jesus a particular political question: "Are you the king of the Jews?" (Mark 15:2; Matt 27:11; Luke 23:3; John 18:33 CEB).

It is essential to understand the intent and implication of using monarchical and kingly language for God and Jesus. Frances Spufford notes: "It may make sense to compare Him to a king, if a king is your best local image of unparalleled majesty, but even if He is like a king, kings are not like Him."[14]

Some leaders claim that God being a ruler—or better, *the Ruler*—means human rulers resemble God. From here come other assertions, for example, the divine right of kings. I am aware of faith communities who judge leaders as "anointed" and thus not to be questioned. (What would be sins for mere mortals—lying or adultery—are tolerated in "anointed" leaders; glaring errors of King David or Jimmy Swaggart do not necessarily discredit their authority.) Here we must be cautious. Spufford notes we need to see how:

> the power of the God of everything differs from all the other manifestations of power.... This power is not exercised from the top of any hierarchy.... It works entirely through presence. Kings and caliphs, emperors and popes, televangelists and household bullies have all wanted to claim

13. Joseph H. Hellerman, *Embracing Shared Ministry: Power and Status in the Early Church and Why It Matters Today* (Grand Rapids: Kregel, 2013), 143.

14. Frances Spufford, *Unapologetic: Why, Despite Everything, Christianity Can Still Make Surprising Emotional Sense* (New York: HarperOne, 2014), 84.

> that their authority is a licensed copy of its universal reach, but their claim must always be incomplete.... In the end, their power and His are unlike. Their power is rivalrous, in the economic sense. It is big because others' power is small. It needs to be extracted from the submission of other apes like themselves. But His power needs nothing, competes with nothing, compels nothing, exists at nothing's expense.[15]

Kingship terminology for God does not justify or excuse power, especially arbitrary abusive power. This language is subversive, reminding us that our highest loyalty is to God and that no human can expect or command our ultimate allegiance. We are called away from placing too much hope in human leadership. Instead we evaluate and judge human leaders to see whether they live up to God's just and merciful priorities.

> By me kings rule,
> and princes *issue righteous decrees*
> By me rulers govern,
> and officials *judge righteously*. (Prov 8:15-16 CEB; emphasis added)

Jesus Is Lord

A central New Testament refrain is the politically charged claim: "Jesus is Lord." Matthew quotes Jesus: "I've received all authority in heaven *and on earth*" (28:18 CEB; emphasis added). Paul believed Jesus was already reigning; you cannot understand Romans or 1 Corinthians or Philippians unless you take that as basic. The book of Revelation celebrates the sovereignty of Jesus from first page to last.

This claim of Jesus as Lord was repugnant to Roman authorities and at the center of deadly controversies for centuries. When aged Polycarp (mid-second century) was on trial, his interlocutor argued: "Come now...where is the harm in just saying 'Caesar is Lord', and offering the incense, and so forth, when it will save your life?"[16]

Art Gish translates this ancient term's connotations into our current context by referring to Jesus as "our President and our Chairman." He argues that Christ's lordship "revealed the nature of truth and reality and God's will for humanity." He contends that lordship entails "the definition

15. Ibid., 83–84.

16. "The Martyrdom of Polycarp," in *Early Christian Writings: The Apostolic Fathers*, trans. Maxwell Staniforth (Toronto: Penguin, 1968), 158.

of reality" and thus it is not unrealistic or idealistic to live by Christ's priorities: "All the compromises made in the name of 'realism' are unrealistic. Jesus Christ is reality."[17] When we profess allegiance to the One who is Lord, that also means committing ourselves to the ethical and practical implications of that commitment.

"Jesus is Lord" confessions relativize all other loyalties: "for *yours* is the kingdom, the power, and the glory" as we say in the Lord's Prayer doxology. The gospel invites the fealty also of others to the Lord Jesus Christ, fulfilling Jesus's mandate: "Therefore, go and make disciples of all nations" (Matt 28:19b CEB). Paul until the very end of Acts, even in Rome the empire's capital, can be found politically "proclaiming the *kingdom of God* and teaching about the Lord Jesus Christ with all boldness and without hindrance" (Acts 28:31; emphasis added).

Sometimes lordship language becomes diminished. A student told me, "First I made Jesus my Savior and later I made him my Lord." This was a statement about personal and individual choice. Acknowledging Christ's lordship is not done as private units. Rather it recognizes what is already and ultimately true. Jesus is Lord, whether we believe it or not; we do not opt to make him Lord. After the 2008 election, some American radio commentators said that Barack Obama was not *their* president; but that is nonsense. Obama was elected president of all in the United States, including those who voted against him. Here in Canada, I have never seen a prime minister who got my vote; yet those elected were nevertheless still prime minister of my country and therefore my prime minister too.

Christians confess that Jesus the Christ sits at God the Father's right hand and thus is *Lord* over all. That is reality, not a call or optional choice for us to make.

Subversive Mysticism

Ecstatic prophetic visions help us see the political nature of God's reality.

Micaiah was tempted to abandon his vocation when faced by two kings: "Now Israel's king and Judah's king Jehoshaphat were sitting on their thrones, dressed in their royal robes" (1 Kgs 22:10 CEB). He declined to be intimidated, in spite of their sartorial finery or the symbols of their office. He told them: "Listen now to the LORD's word: I saw the LORD *enthroned* with all the heavenly forces stationed beside him, at his right and at his left"

17. Arthur G. Gish, *Beyond the Rat Race* (Waterloo, Ontario: Herald, 1973), 165.

(1 Kgs 22:19 CEB; emphasis added). God—no human monarch—controls history.

Isaiah did not worry about devastating political transitions. He knew who truly ruled the world, even when a king perished: "In the year of King Uzziah's death, I saw the Lord *sitting on a high and exalted throne*, the edges of his robe filling the temple" (Isa 6:1 CEB; emphasis added).

Stephen, just before execution, had a political vision: "'Look,' he said, 'I see the heavens opened and the Son of Man standing at the right hand of God!'" (Acts 7:56). These visions proclaimed ultimate political realities.

The mysterious book of Revelation is rooted in worship rhythms, filled with doxologies. In contrast to the plagues, the Beast, and other threats, there is always the *enthroned one* (a political image) who is adored. The "you are worthy" formula in chapters 4 and 5 had been used to extol Caesars, but Revelation usurps and subverts that phrase to glorify God instead, the true ruler of all. Similarly when the multitude cried, "Victory belongs to our God / who sits on the *throne*, / and to the Lamb" (Rev 7:10 CEB; emphasis added), they employ language that Caesars explicitly claimed for themselves.

We are counseled to look to and rely first of all on God. A good thing, too, because the scriptures are predominantly pessimistic about human leadership, especially when it comes to rulers.

Chapter Seven

The Usual Suspects

Biblical Misgivings about Leadership

Put Not Your Trust in Princes

Once in life I was convinced enough by a candidate to put up an election sign. I usually do not declare to the world my particular preference. When I showed my hand this way, I lived in the inner city of Chicago. A resident alien, I could not vote. But I had opinions, strong ones in fact.

After graduating from seminary, I moved with my wife to Chicago within weeks of Harold Washington taking office. He was Chicago's first African American mayor and won by hammering together an unprecedented coalition of African Americans, whites, and Latinos. I got to know many people who supported and campaigned for him, an idealistic lot committed to social change and justice.

I did not endorse everything he did. But I liked what was happening where we lived and gave him a lot of credit. When we first moved to our neighborhood, it showed the ravages of decades of indifference by city departments. Police, fire, and street services were all scanty. Even the public park was neglected. But the longer Washington held office, the more city funds and attention came our way; we saw gradual but steady improvements in our barrio.

So when it was time for another city election, I did not hesitate about allegiance. As a pastor I did not explicitly tell congregants how to vote, but my sermon hints were not exactly subtle. For the first time I put up an election poster, proclaiming my opinion, hoping Washington would win.

And win he did. Once again, the coalition worked. I, like my friends, was euphoric. But the euphoria did not last. Washington was in second term office for little more than half a year when he died of a massive heart attack. Like many, I felt deep grief. With thousands of Chicagoans, I went to city hall to pay honor to the body of a man who had changed us for the better. (I went in the middle of the night when the lines were a little more manageable.)

Within hours of his death, there was a power struggle in city council. More distressingly, the coalition that he tended for years quickly and completely disintegrated. His hard work evaporated. I recalled the psalmist's words:

> Don't trust leaders;
> don't trust any human beings—
> there's no saving help with them!
> Their breath leaves them,
> then they go back to the ground.
> On that very same day, their plans die too. (Ps 146:3-4 CEB)

The Bible's view of "leaders" or "princes" is sobering. Each human ruler—and hence his or her leadership—dies, frequently unpleasantly. In many accounts, evil leaders come to a bad death: Herod eaten by worms (Acts 12) or Jezebel gruesomely assassinated (2 Kgs 9) or King Jehoiahim receiving "a donkey's burial," being dragged "outside the gates of Jerusalem" (Jer 22:19 CEB). Nasty death examples in the book of Judges include Eglon (slaughtered while having a bowel movement), Sisera (assassinated by a woman with a tent peg while he was sleeping), and Abimelech (murdered by a woman throwing a millstone). These stories mock monarchy and its pretensions. They remind us that the Bible regards with suspicion many—if not most—of those in charge and what they accomplish.

Judging the Judges

We earlier saw the Bible's attention to Moses, an unprecedented inimitable leader. His protégé Joshua shared some of his gifts but had no obvious successors. The book of Judges is about the next kind of leaders. (Some translate "judges" as "executive leaders."[1]) While they perhaps sometimes adjudicated disputes, mostly they led Israelites in battles. Buber suggests that the Hebrew word for "judge" meant liberator.[2] These were charismatic

1. Harold Lindsell, *NRSV Harper Study Bible*, ed. Verlyn D. Verbrugge (Grand Rapids: Zondervan, 1991), 329. John Dominic Crossan translates judge as "'leader' or 'prince'" ("Judges," in *The Jerome Biblical Commentary*, ed. Raymond Edward Brown, Joseph A. Fitzmyer, and Roland E. Murphy [Englewood Cliffs, NJ: Prentice-Hall, 1968], 149).

2. Martin Buber, *Kingship of God*, trans. Richard Scheimann, 3rd ed. (New York: Harper and Row, 1967), 66.

leaders, war chieftains, who emerged spontaneously as needed; their "authority...was strictly ad hoc, local, and sporadic."[3] The thrust of the book of Judges is that this spontaneous, charismatic, ad hoc system failed and did so badly. Many judges were *unlikely* leaders and did not seek this office. The judges' abysmal performances were a central factor in why Israelites decided to be like other nations in having a king.

You do not have to be idealistic to have concerns about much of their leadership. Ehud used deception to assassinate. Gideon destroyed idols and conquered enemies against great odds but ended up creating a harmful idol himself. Jephthah won an amazing victory, but a rash promise propelled him to sacrifice his daughter. Samson had a strict religious upbringing but contended with sexual lust and uncontrollable anger; impulse control was not in his skill set. A Levite summoned Israelites to war by cutting his concubine into twelve pieces and sending the bloody remnants to all the tribes. We censor these stories when we tell them to children; they did not have much that was exemplary to offer seminarians and graduate students that I taught either.

Besides bad behavior, their effectiveness is also questionable. Whenever judges died, Israelites did evil again, rejecting God and worshipping idols (Judg 7:11-22). Buber calls the tiresome pattern "a tragic rhythm."[4] This cycle devolved. After Gideon, midway through the book, judges get worse and worse with distressing accounts of Abimelech's slaughter of his seventy brothers, Jephthah's killing of his wife, and Samson's adulterous and murderous shenanigans.

The final verse of Judges reads: "In those days there was no king in Israel; each person did what they thought to be right" (21:25 CEB). The failure of the judges experiment set the stage for another (ultimately unsuccessful) undertaking.

Judges Versus Kings

The book of Judges questions the kingship institution. When grateful Israelites tried to make Gideon and his descendants into a monarchy, he refused: "I'm not the one who will rule over you, and my son won't rule over

3. Joseph Blenkinsopp, *Sage, Priest, Prophet: Religious and Intellectual Leadership in Ancient Israel* (Louisville, KY: Westminster John Knox, 1995), 130.

4. Martin Buber, "Biblical Leadership," in *On the Bible: Eighteen Studies*, ed. Nahum N. Glatzer (Syracuse, NY: Syracuse University Press, 2000), 146. He also notes the book's overwhelmingly "melancholy character" with its tragic pattern of "apostasy-affliction-unification-rest" (Buber, *Kingship of God*, 68).

you either. The LORD rules over you" (Judg 8:23 CEB). Judges 9 contains a quirky parable about trees trying to anoint a king. This story rebuked Gideon's son who tried to crown himself after killing seventy of his brothers. The olive tree, fig tree, and vine all declined the throne. Only the lowly, worthless bramble—a plant that accomplishes and produces nothing—accepted the invitation. John Dominic Crossan says that in this story

> the argument is that the best do not have time to be kings; therefore, it usually falls to the worthless to accept the role of the monarch. The "buckthorn" cannot even furnish shade—the minimum requirement of a tree in a hot country.[5]

Lest we miss this story's sting: "Commentators view this passage as the most abrasive criticism of the institution of kingship in the Bible and the ancient world. Martin Buber, in particular, calls this the 'strongest anti-monarchical poem of world literature.'"[6] This text shows that kingship is not "productive" but "vain," "bewildering and seditious."[7]

Furthermore, battles in Judges were regularly *against* kings. Most nations closely identified gods with monarchs, but Israelites experienced God's intervention in history in *opposition* to kings and the office of kings. Lind calls this the "antagonism of Yahweh toward political rulers."[8] The Bible is full of accounts of God defeating kings. The psalmist reminds us that God "killed mighty kings: Sihon the Amorite king [and] Og the king of Bashan" (Ps 135:10b-11 CEB; see also Ps 136:19-20). Not just a record of two punished monarchs, this conveys the sense that God *rejects monarchy* itself. God makes wars on kingship: "He has pulled the powerful down from their thrones" (Luke 1:52a CEB), as Mary will later sing.

This antagonism was also expressed through mockery:

> Why do the nations rant?
>   Why do the peoples rave uselessly?
> The earth's rulers take their stand;
>   the leaders scheme together

5. Crossan, "Judges," 156.

6. Robert Gnuse, *No Tolerance for Tyrants: The Biblical Assault on Kings and Kingship (*Collegeville, MN: Liturgical, 2011), 76. The citation in the Gnuse quotation is from Buber, *Kingship of God*, 75.

7. Buber, *Kingship of God*, 75.

8. Millard C. Lind, *Yahweh Is a Warrior: The Theology of Warfare in Ancient Israel* (Scottdale, PA: Herald, 1980), 53.

against the LORD and
against his anointed one
"Come!" they say.
"We will tear off their ropes
and throw off their chains!"
The one who rules in heaven laughs;
my Lord makes fun of them. (Ps 2:1-4 CEB)

Other narratives mock kings. Low status (but *named*) midwives defied *unnamed* Pharaoh's order to kill male Hebrew offspring. They fooled him with subterfuge. Another instance of king ridicule is Babylon's Nebuchadnezzar. One day he expressed pride at accomplishments of his "mighty strength and... majestic glory" (Dan 4:30 CEB). He then became like an animal: "He was driven away from other humans and ate grass like cattle. Dew from heaven washed his body until he grew hair like eagles' feathers and claws like a bird" (Dan 4:33 CEB). When restored to sanity, he finally rendered proper worship to God (Dan 4:34-37).

More disdaining examples toward monarchy include the story of King Balak commissioning Balaam to curse the Israelites. This scheme failed for several reasons, including a talking donkey's intervention (Num 22). Pharaoh's hard-hearted reversals in the face of increasingly devastating plagues is a narrative that mocks a king and his office. Or remember Herod, who had mixed feelings about John the Baptist but was finally so overcome by his stepdaughter's dancing that his evil course of action was determined.

Kings by the Eponymous Book

The final verse of Judges reads: "In those days there was no king in Israel; each person did what they thought to be right" (Judg 21:25 CEB). The scene is set for an extended kingship experiment. Ancient kings were regarded as divinely connected, if not divine; but in Samuel we have the "radical political statement that the desire to have a king" meant rejecting God.[9] First Samuel 8:4 suggests that kingship was "a despicable human creation akin to crass idols."[10] Hebrew kingship was a human invention, "made by the people for their own purposes: that's why awe and reverence are absent from First Samuel."[11] In "Second Samuel, there is no hint of the

9. Gnuse, *No Tolerance for Tyrants*, 79.

10. Ibid., 20.

11. Michael Walzer, *In God's Shadow: Politics in the Hebrew Bible* (New Haven, CT: Yale University Press, 2012), 58.

conventional magnifications of monarchy: no mysteries of state, no divine descent, no royal magic, no healing touch."[12]

Hebrew kings were circumscribed compared to peers in other countries. They could neither make nor alter laws but had to obey laws.[13] Deuteronomy warns that kings should not "acquire many horses," "many wives," or "silver and gold," but should stay close to God's law (Deut 17:16-20). The Deuteronomy restriction is a radical innovation ahead of its time. "We have to wait until the thirteenth-century C.E. Magna Charta . . . in England to find a comparable notion that royal power should be limited."[14]

Elsewhere, kings were the most important kind of *leader*. Not surprisingly, given the cultural setting, some biblical accounts speak favorably of kings and kingship, but these are outweighed by negative portrayals. St. Benedict was uneasy with the ambiguity. He recommended that monks *not* read aloud from 1 and 2 Kings after supper, as it is not "good for those of weak understanding to hear these writings at that hour."[15]

The first kings—Saul, David, Solomon—warrant a number of chapters in the Bible. Each reign was ultimately tragic. Saul's succession was torn from his descendants. David, God's beloved, committed adultery and murder and was alienated from spouses and children. (Lipman-Blumen considers David a "toxic leader"![16]) Without questioning the sincerity of his relationship with God, caution needs to be exercised when trying to derive "leadership principles" from David's example.

David's ascent to power was brutal and violent. He therefore was not allowed to build the temple. A scholarly book on him is entitled *David's Secret Demons: Messiah, Murderer, Traitor, King*. God had deep fondness for David—but God oftentimes has a soft spot for rascals (Jacob, the prodigal son, and so on). Rogues are not necessarily leadership role models.

Solomon, although impressively wise, nevertheless sundered loyalty to God by distressing choices. He embraced problematic priorities that Deuteronomy warned kings against (see Deut 17:16-17). Those dangers

12. Ibid., 51.

13. Jonathan Sacks, "God's Politics: The Lessons of the Hebrew Bible," review of *In God's Shadow: Politics in the Hebrew Bible*, by Michael Walzer, *Foreign Affairs*, vol. 91, no. 6 (November/December 2012): 126.

14. Gnuse, *No Tolerance for Tyrants*, 41.

15. St. Benedict, *The Rule of Saint Benedict in English*, ed. Timothy Fry (New York: Vintage Books, 1998), 43.

16. Jean Lipman-Blumen, *The Allure of Toxic Leaders: Why We Follow Destructive Bosses and Corrupt Politicians—and How We Can Survive Them* (New York: Oxford University Press, 2005), 10.

included relying on military strength, alliances and idolatry, and one's own resources—"functional atheism" again. These dependencies eroded reliance on God.

Solomon's ultimate failure was shown after his death; the kingdom was divided into two (because of his oppressive conscription of labor), each ruled by a different king. Judean successor Rehoboam foolishly provoked the populace. Jeroboam seized leadership of Israel and consolidated power by promoting idolatry.

First and Second Kings show consistent critical themes. The citations below are from these two books, and the emphases are added. (Several rulers mentioned in these books are not listed below if there is no overall summary of tenure, although all omitted rulers are also negative examples.)

Kings of Judah	Kings of Israel
(Left alignment)	(Right alignment)

Even after this event Jeroboam *did not turn from his evil way*, but made priests for the high places again from among all the people; any who wanted to be priests he consecrated for the high places. This matter became sin to the house of Jeroboam, so as to cut it off and to destroy it from the face of the earth. (1 Kgs 13:33-34)

[During Rehoboam's reign] Judah did what was *evil in the sight of the Lord*; they provoked him to jealousy with their sins that they committed, more than all that their ancestors had done. For they also built for themselves high places, pillars, and sacred poles on every high hill and under every green tree; there were also male temple prostitutes in the land. They committed all the abominations of the nations that the Lord drove out before the people of Israel. (1 Kgs 14:22-24)

[Abijam] *committed all the sins that his father did before him; his heart was not true to the Lord his God.* (1 Kgs 15:3)

Asa *did what was right in the sight of Lord*, as his father David had done. He put away the male temple prostitutes out of the land, and removed all the idols that his ancestors had made. . . . But the high places were not taken away. Nevertheless the heart of Asa was true to the Lord all his days. (1 Kgs 15:11-12, 14)

[Nadab, the last of Jeroboam's descendants to rule] *did what was evil in the sight of the Lord*, walking in the way of his ancestor and in the sin that he caused Israel to commit. (1 Kgs 15:25-26)

[Baasha] *did what was evil in the sight of the Lord*, walking in the way of Jeroboam and in the sin that he caused Israel to commit. (1 Kgs 15:34)

[Zimri's short reign quickly ends] because of sins that he committed, *doing evil in the sight of the LORD*, walking in the way of Jeroboam, and for the sin that he committed, causing Israel to sin. (1 Kgs 16:19)

Omri *did what was evil in the sight of the LORD; he did more evil than all who were before him.* For he walked in all the way of Jeroboam son of Nebat, and in the sins that he caused Israel to commit, provoking the LORD, the God of Israel, to anger by their idols. (1 Kgs 16:25-26)

Ahab son of Omri *did evil in the sight of the LORD more than all who were before him.* And as if it had been a light thing for him to walk in the sins of Jeroboam son of Nebat, he took as his wife Jezebel daughter of King Ethbaal of the Sidonians, and went and served Baal, and worshiped him. He erected an altar for Baal in the house of Baal, which he built in Samaria. Ahab also made a sacred pole. Ahab did more to provoke the anger of the LORD, the God of Israel, than had all the kings of Israel who were before him. (1 Kgs 16:30-33 [Ahab's reign merits several chapters.])

[Jehoshaphat] walked in all the way of his father Asa; he did not turn aside from it, *doing what was right in the sight of the LORD*; yet the high places were not taken away, and the people still sacrificed and offered incense on the high places. (1 Kgs 22:43)

[Ahaziah] *did what was evil in the sight of the LORD*, and walked in the way of his father and mother, and in the way of Jeroboam son of Nebat, who caused Israel to sin. He served Baal and worshiped him; he provoked the LORD, the God of Israel, to anger, just as his father had done. (1 Kgs 22:52-53)

[Jehoram, also known as "Joram"] did what was *evil in the sight of the LORD*, though not like his father and mother, for he removed the pillar of Baal that his father had made. Nevertheless he clung to the sin of Jeroboam son of Nebat, which he caused Israel to commit; he did not depart from it. (2 Kgs 3:2-3)

[Confusingly enough, Judah had a king named Jehoram, son of Jehosaphat, at this time.] He walked in the way of the kings of Israel, as the house of Ahab had done, for the daughter of Ahab was his wife. *He did what was evil in the sight of the LORD.* (2 Kgs 8:18)

[Ahaziah] also walked in the way of the house of Ahab, *doing what was evil in the sight of the LORD*, as the house of Ahab had done, for he was son-in-law to the house of Ahab. (2 Kgs 8:27)

Jehu *did not turn aside from the sins of Jeroboam* son of Nebat, which he caused Israel to commit—the golden calves that were in Bethel and in Dan. (2 Kgs 10:29)

Jehoash did what was *right in the sight of the LORD all his days*, because the priest Jehoiada instructed him. Nevertheless the high places were not taken away; the people continued to sacrifice and make offerings on the high places. (2 Kgs 12:2-3)

> [Jehoahaz] *did what was evil in the sight of the Lord,* and followed the sins of Jeroboam son of Nebat, which he caused Israel to sin; he did not depart from them. (2 Kgs 13:2)

> [Jehoash] also *did what was evil in the sight of the Lord*, he did not depart from all the sins of Jeroboam son of Nebat, which he caused Israel to sin, but he walked in them. (2 Kgs 13:11)

[Amaziah] *did what was right in the sight of the Lord*, yet not like his ancestor David; in all things he did as his father Joash had done. But the high places were not removed; the people still sacrificed and made offerings on the high places. (2 Kgs 14:3-4)

> [Jeroboam II] *did what was evil in the sight of the Lord*; he did not depart from all the sins of Jeroboam son of Nebat, which he caused Israel to sin. (2 Kgs 14:24)

[Azariah, also called "Uzziah"] *did what was right in the sight of the Lord*, just as his father Amaziah had done. Nevertheless the high places were not taken away; the people still sacrificed and made offerings on the high places. (2 Kgs 15:3-4)

> [Zechariah] *did what was evil in the sight of the Lord*, as his ancestors had done. He did not depart from the sins of Jeroboam son of Nebat, which he caused Israel to sin. (2 Kgs 15:9)

> [Menahem] *did what was evil in the sight of the Lord*; he did not depart all his days from any of the sins of Jeroboam son of Nebat, which he caused Israel to sin. (2 Kgs 15:18)

> [Pekahiah] *did what was evil in the sight of the Lord*; he did not turn away from the sins of Jeroboam son of Nebat, which he caused Israel to sin. (2 Kgs 15:24)

> [Pekah] *did what was evil in the sight of the Lord*; he did not depart from the sins of Jeroboam son of Nebat, which he caused Israel to sin. (2 Kgs 15:28)

[Jotham] *did what was right in the sight of the Lord*, just as his father Uzziah had done. Nevertheless the high places were not removed; the people still sacrificed and made offerings on the high places. (2 Kgs 15:34-35)

[Ahaz] *did not do what was right in the sight of the Lord his God*, as his ancestor David had done, but he walked in the way of the kings of Israel. He even made his son pass through fire, according to the abominable practices of the nations whom the Lord drove out before the people of Israel. He sacrificed and made offerings on the high places, on the hills, and under every green tree. (2 Kgs 16:2b-4)

[Hoshea] *did what was evil in the sight of the Lord,* yet not like the kings of Israel who were before him. (2 Kgs 17:2)

[Hezekiah] *did what was right in the sight of the Lord* just as his ancestor David had done. He removed the high places, broke down the pillars, and cut down the sacred pole. He broke in pieces the bronze serpent that Moses had made, for until those days the people of Israel had made offerings to it; it was called Nehushtan. He trusted in the Lord the God of Israel; so that there was no one like him among all the kings of Judah after him, or among those who were before him. For he held fast to the Lord; he did not depart from following him but kept the commandments that the Lord commanded Moses. The Lord was with him; wherever he went, he prospered. (2 Kgs 18:3-7)

[Manasseh] *did what was evil in the sight of the Lord,* following the abominable practices of the nations that the Lord drove out before the people of Israel. For he rebuilt the high places that his father Hezekiah had destroyed; he erected altars for Baal, made a sacred pole, as King Ahab of Israel had done, worshiped all the host of heaven, and served them. He built altars in the house of the Lord, all of which the Lord had said, "In Jerusalem I will put my name." He built altars for all the host of heaven in the two courts of the house of the Lord. He made his son pass through fire; he practiced soothsaying and augury, and dealt with mediums and with wizards. He did much evil in the sight of the Lord, provoking him to anger. . . . Manasseh misled them to do more evil than the nations had done that the Lord destroyed before the people of Israel. (2 Kgs 21:2-7a, 9b)

[Amon] *did what was evil in the sight of the Lord,* as his father Manasseh had done. He walked in all the way in which his father walked, served the idols that his father served, and worshiped them; he abandoned the Lord, the God of his ancestors, and did not walk in the way of the Lord. (2 Kgs 21:20-22)

[Josiah] *did what was right in the sight of the Lord,* and walked in all the way of his father David; he did not turn aside to the right or to the left. (2 Kgs 22:2)

[Jehoahaz] *did what was evil in the sight of the Lord,* just as his ancestors had done. (2 Kgs 23:32)

[Jehoiakim] *did what was evil in the sight of the Lord,* just as all his ancestors had done. (2 Kgs 23:37)

> [Jehoiachin] *did what was evil in the sight of the LORD*, just as his father had done. (2 Kgs 24:9)
>
> [Zedekiah] *did what was evil in the sight of the LORD*, just as Jehoiakim had done. Indeed, Jerusalem and Judah so angered the LORD that he expelled them from his presence. (2 Kgs 24:19-20)

Every single king of Israel—seventeen named—is described negatively. In most cases, terminology of "evil" is explicitly used. Almost all repeat the sin of Jeroboam, the first ruler of Israel's breakaway kingdom. Several distinguish themselves by not only perpetuating Jeroboam's sin but being even more sinful than predecessors. "Omri did . . . more evil than anyone who preceded him" (1 Kgs 16:25 CEB); Ahab "did evil in the LORD's eyes, more than anyone who preceded him" (1 Kgs 16:30 CEB). There is not one righteous example among Israel's monarchs.

First and Second Chronicles offer a rosier view, looking more positively on the monarchy and its possibilities. However, those books omit subjects: Saul's disastrous rein, David's grievous errors, Solomon's idolatry problems. Little is said of the kings of Israel. It is easier to be optimistic when we overlook this kind of information.

The negative kingly record in 1 and 2 Kings is *slightly* ameliorated by Judean kings. Eleven are described as evil or not doing right. Some committed heinous sins, including sacrificing sons. Eight kings—about two-fifths of the total—are favorably described, but usually the positive record is mixed: six did not remove idolatrous high places, and thus people continued to offer illegitimate sacrifices. Only two well-behaved kings, one quarter of the eight, get unqualified commendation.

No matter how you juggle the numbers, this is a pessimistic portrait. Joining the two lists of kings, twenty-eight are evil and eight (less than a quarter) good; even then only two of those eight (a nineteenth of the total) are beyond reproach.

> What nation normally would produce a national history that takes its royal leaders to task for their sins? This is not the way that annalists or authors wrote in the ancient world, but it is the way that the biblical authors wrote.[17]

Particularly striking is how evil patterns get passed through generations but good patterns not so much. Jeroboam's sin is repeated in most succeeding

17. Gnuse, *No Tolerance for Tyrants*, 68.

kings. The good of the few worthy monarchs does not descend very far into following generations.

All of this is not a surprise. After all, Samuel warned against kingship (1 Sam 8:10-18). Deuteronomy 17 laid out laws for kings and suggested how that office could—and likely would—be misused and exploited.

This is a stunningly pessimistic litany about some of the most famous leaders in scriptures. There is not much to celebrate. Buber soberly summarized: "The history of the kings is the history of the failure of him who has been anointed to realize the promise of his anointing."[18] Monarchy, a divine concession at best, was always ambiguous in its worth.

This hard-nosed biblical assessment about Old Testament monarchs should give us pause. We may object, "Oh, that was *then* and that was *them*, but this is *now* and we are *us*." In other words, previous examples do not apply to us, they are not relevant, and we are above all that. But the biblical delineation of Israelite kings offers discerning insight into the propensities of *all leaders*. Taking scriptures seriously gives no room for easy optimism about the potential of any ruler.

Keeping Kingship in Its Place

A number of factors made Hebrew kingship far less important—and more circumscribed—than monarchy in other contemporary countries.

The first remarkable fact about Hebrew kingship is that it was created by people, not divinely instituted. The Israelites *requested* a king, in part to be "like all the other nations" (and to escape the burden of being ruled by Samuel's corrupt sons; 1 Sam 8:5 CEB). Scriptures point out that people do not necessarily choose well.

> Someone will seize a family member, saying "You have clothing! You be our leader! This mess will be your responsibility!" (Isa 3:6 CEB)

There is no sense of a "divine right of kings." Kingship was not a right but a responsibility bequeathed by people and one requiring (but seldom receiving) careful stewardship.

Another astonishing kingship limitation, as we have already seen, was the fact that the king was not a legislator. Israel was not "like all the other nations," where kings were usually primary lawmakers. God was the source

18. Buber, "Biblical Leadership," in *On the Bible*, 147.

of Hebrew legislation.[19] A basic prerogative of monarchs elsewhere was not assumed in Israelite culture.

This reality meant another restriction on kingship: monarchs, like everyone else, had to submit to the law. Not only that but they were also equal to others under the law. This is why Ahab was depressed at not being able to acquire Naboth's vineyard; he had to be subservient to inheritance legislation.[20]

Moreover, there were specific moral restrictions on the king. Certain laws tried to reign in potentials and possibilities for abuse; "the laws of the nation served to limit the king's inclination toward self-enrichment."[21]

This did not stop kings, of course, from pretensions to power and prestige. This brings us to the final restriction on kingly power: prophetic criticism. When wrong-headed initiatives happened, prophets reminded kings of their proper place, rebuking arrogance and corruption. Walzer notes that Jeremiah 21–22 names and condemns four Judean kings: "the collection of all these antiroyal oracles in one place has a cumulative effect of destroying the sacredness of the institution of kingship." Ezekiel 31 is another text "assaulting. . . common ancient assumptions about the nature of kingship: that kings are divine; wielders of great power; wise; patrons of building projects, trade, and the arts because of their exalted status."[22] When kings overstepped authority, prophets stepped in to criticize and condemn, especially over issues of injustice. Where other nations saw protesting against kings as treason, perhaps meriting death, Israelite culture prioritized this prophetic role.

It is true that some voices in the Bible celebrate kings. Kingship arose in part out of a real need as exemplified by the failures of the judges. There are positive traditions about kingship; see Psalm 89, for example. Even the most pro-kingship passages, however, uphold the idea that Israel's true king is God. Brueggemann argues that the king had a specific purpose: "to arrange and administer power in the face of chaos so that people can be human after the image of God."[23] Even so, he also points out that in the scriptures "the king is at best irrelevant."[24]

---

19. Walzer, *In God's Shadow*, 21–23.

20. Ibid., 23.

21. Marty E. Stevens, *Leadership Roles of the Old Testament: King, Prophet, Priest, Sage* (Eugene, OR: Wipf and Stock, 2012), 26.

22. Gnuse, *No Tolerance for Tyrants*, 28, 36.

23. Walter Brueggemann, *Peace* (St. Louis, MO: Chalice, 2001), 102.

24. Brueggemann, *Truth Speaks to Power*, 101.

Contemporary Implications

In biblical times there was great suspicion of monarchs. Even when God was understood as working through (or in spite of) leaders, leaders themselves were not necessarily to be emulated or trusted. On the whole, the biblical legacy of rulers is tragically disappointing. Think of God's sad conclusion—after rebuking and condemning princes, officials, priests, and prophets—in Ezekiel: "I looked for anyone to repair the wall and stand in the gap for me on behalf of the land, so I wouldn't have to destroy it. But I couldn't find anyone" (Ezek 22:30 CEB).

Here we note something important for contemporary leadership discussions. Most people in most eras did not regard *leadership* positively. This is not only a recent phenomenon; it is also *cultural.* North Americans and Anglo-Saxons have a particular fascination with heroes and exceptional leaders; we romanticize leadership and revere celebrity CEOs, but Europeans tend to be more critical and skeptical.[25] For all our enthusiasm about leadership, some contemporary authors caution us to remember that leadership almost *always* involves compromise, evil choices, villainy.[26] First and Second Kings certainly make that point. Yet only a few contemporary authors soberly remind us that leadership has many dark sides. In fact, leadership research itself is overly focused on positive examples and pays small attention to studying poor leadership.[27]

Positive *leader* terminology is scant in the scriptures. Few office holders are regarded favorably. Official rulers usually look out for interests contrary to God's purposes; their characters are deficient. Good rulers are exceptions.

Christian leadership programs aiming to be biblical must focus more on avoiding leadership deformations, pitfalls, dangers, and temptations than on glorifying positive possibilities of leadership. Joseph Badaracco notes that with many so-called "great people," it is usually the case "that ego, passions, and drives that were somewhat less than angelic often motivated

25. Brad Jackson and Ken Parry, *A Very Short, Fairly Interesting and Reasonably Cheap Book about Studying Leadership* (Thousand Oaks, CA: Sage, 2011), 77, 53.

26. F. G. Bailey, *Humbuggery and Manipulation: The Art of Leadership* (Ithaca, NY: Cornell University Press, 1988), ix, 2.

27. Lars Glasø, Ståle Einarsen, Stig Berge Matthiesen, and Anders Skogstad, "The Dark Side of Leaders: A Representative Study of Interpersonal Problems among Leaders," *Scandinavian Journal of Organizational Psychology* 2, no. 2 (2010): 3. Kathie L. Pelletier, "Leader Toxicity: An Empirical Investigation of Toxic Behavior and Rhetoric," *Leadership* 6, no. 4 (November 2010): 374.

them."[28] Reading the Bible, it is easy to conclude that leadership is *hazardous*. It regularly oppresses the vulnerable and misleads many into idolatry. It is risky as it frequently distorts and dehumanizes those wielding power.

These biblical concerns do not merely suggest that the problem is how people occupied their office. They do not mean things would be better if a good person, a good leader, were in that place. The critique goes deeper. Mere regime changes—substituting good leaders for bad ones—do not improve matters. The leadership enterprise is over and again corrupt and corrupting. We do not need merely good leaders but entirely different conceptions of leadership.

The prevailing scriptural bias is suspicion of leaders. Seldom do we meet anyone exemplary at the top. While we need and long for good leaders, in order to get them, we require deeper understandings of leadership.

28. Joseph L. Badaracco Jr., *Leading Quietly: An Unorthodox Guide to Doing the Right Thing* (Boston: Harvard Business School Publishing, 2002), 40.

Chapter Eight

Counterbalancing Kings

Prophets as Leaders

I Told You So?

During my high school and university years, I spent summers on construction crews building greenhouses. This hot and hard labor always left me with a renewed sense of motivation for pursuing higher education.

One sweltering afternoon, we were working beside a cherry orchard. An employee I'll call Karl got into a heated swearing match with foreman Jim. Karl insisted that if the gables continued to be installed in a particular manner they would fail. The two had worked together for years and Karl was known for exaggeration. I was not surprised when foreman Jim opted to ignore him.

I was surprised, however, when a few hours later the angle iron of a gable suddenly sprang loose from its mooring; an entire corner of the building could collapse. No one was hurt and no parts were permanently damaged, but obviously Karl was right this time. That greenhouse's design could not sustain the weight it was supposed to carry, especially once the snow started falling in several months. We needed to strengthen the structure.

I was even more surprised by Karl's reaction. This middle-aged man enthusiastically bounced up and down, like an overgrown toddler, calling out for everyone to hear: "I knew it! I knew it! I knew it!" He was happy. He may have considered himself a prophet, but he was not one in the biblical sense: "If we are to understand prophetic criticism we must see that its characteristic idiom is anguish and not anger,"[1] let alone glee about being right.

1. Walter Brueggemann, *The Prophetic Imagination*, 2nd ed. (Minneapolis: Augsburg Fortress, 2001), 81.

Prophets

Sometimes we think prophets predict future events, especially catastrophes, and fervently expect their projections to be realized. But faithful biblical prophets are not eager for dire warnings to be fulfilled. They express concerns in the spirit of helping people avert inevitable and disastrous consequences and outcomes. Jeremiah quotes God as saying: "At one moment I may declare concerning a nation or a kingdom, that I will pluck up and break down and destroy it, but if that nation, concerning which I have spoken, turns from its evil, I will change my mind about the disaster that I intended to bring on it" (Jer 18:7-8).

Jonah was unfaithful. He did not want his prophecies to change the attitude (and future) of Ninevites; then he would not be able to gloat triumphantly, "I knew it! I knew it!" When prophets made claims about the future, they hoped to bring about a change in the behavior of listeners and so avert the foretold catastrophe. Prediction was intended to change *present* realities. Unlike gleeful Karl, faithful biblical prophets hoped that grim forecasts would not happen. When bad things occurred, prophets were not cheerful but shared the suffering lot of their fellows. Think of Jeremiah's words:

> Oh, my suffering, my suffering!
> My pain is unbearable;
> my heart is in turmoil;
> it throbs nonstop.
> I can't be silent. (Jer 4:19 CEB)

Not having much official power, prophets adopted outside or "underside" perspectives. They were frequently rejected, not only by the powers-that-be but by the populace as well. Yet they were not merely cranky eccentrics or mentally unstable individuals. No, they had an important role and were *the* major counterbalance to the monarchy's power. In many ways, they were more important than kings. Their prominence shows a remarkable prioritizing of dissent and critique, especially against the rulers and other leaders of the day. A unique aspect of Israelite culture is the unmatched importance of prophets.

Any study of scriptural perspectives on leadership must look closely at their strangely unexpected example.

Prophets as Leaders

Prophets were significant Old Testament leaders. It is hard to overstate their importance. Almost a quarter of the Old Testament is devoted to speeches and poetry in books named after them; these texts are the works of at least fifteen prophets over the course of 250 years.[2] And prophecy—"judgment about the present in the light of the future—judgment arrived at through the authority of God"—was also valued in the New Testament.[3]

As spokespersons for God, they frequently began statements with this phrase: "Thus says the Lord." By speaking the Lord's word, prophets not only reveal God's intentions, but also uncover truths about listeners, especially those with power. A dramatic instance was Nathan's confrontation with King David over the latter's adultery with Bathsheba and the murder of her husband Uriah. Nathan denounced the king thus: "You are that man!" (2 Sam 12:7 CEB).

We sometimes have unfavorable impressions of prophets. An English term, "jeremiad," alluding to one famous Old Testament prophet, has negative connotations. Yet prophets were meant to be heard. When they did not speak, their silence was ominous. "In certain circumstances, Yahweh would punish his people by depriving them of the tough love represented by the prophet's voice. Such was the fate of Ezekiel, when Yahweh made his tongue cleave to the roof of his mouth, apparently for seven and a half years (Ezek. 3.25-6)."[4]

Early on, prophets emerged as a major force. Not coincidentally, they came to prominence around the same time as the monarchy. As we saw, the judges system had failed badly. Two kinds of leaders became an alternative substitution; the role of prophets was to counterbalance powerful kings. This latter point is particularly striking. Surrounding cultures thought of kings as the pinnacle of leadership, responsibility, and power, but the Israelite context continually downplayed their priority, as we saw in the previous chapter.

Not only are prophets central in writings that bear their name, but Elijah and Elisha are the main protagonists in 1 and 2 Kings; "these two characters occupy one-fourth of the whole of the history of royal Israel and

2. Yoram Hazony, *The Philosophy of Hebrew Scripture* (New York: Cambridge University Press, 2012), 41.

3. Hans Walter Wolff, *Confrontations with Prophets* (Philadelphia: Fortress, 1983), 64.

4. Diarmaid MacCulloch, *Silence: A Christian History* (New York: Penguin, 2013), 15.

royal Judah"; so Brueggemann suggests that those books might better be titled as a question "1 and 2 Kings?"[5] Monarchs "are not the definitive players in the true history of this people; the real players are Elijah and Elisha who stand outside and beyond the routines of power, acting variously in defiance or disregard of these occupants of the seats and forms of power."[6] Elisha time and again "trumped" officials.[7] Prophets' authority superseded that of anyone else, including kings. And they, unlike kings, were even allowed to "challenge and change" laws.[8]

On the importance of prophets, consider Jeremiah's call (1:9-10 CEB):

> Then the Lord stretched out his hand,
> touched my mouth, and said to me,
> "I'm putting my words in your mouth.
> This very day I appoint you over nations and empires,
> to dig up and pull down,
> to destroy and demolish,
> to build and plant."

Millard Lind concludes: "This great prophet in Israel, unique to the Near East so far as we know, was regarded by Israel as Yahweh's chief political officer."[9] He observes: "As the ambassador of Yahweh, the prophet rather than the king is presented... as the decisive political leader in Israel."[10]

Prophets had little social standing. They came from every level of society. Women could be prophets (priests and kings were upper-class males).[11] Brueggemann refers to prophets as "uncredentialed" and "without pedigree."[12]

---

5. Walter Brueggemann, *Truth Speaks to Power: The Countercultural Nature of Scripture* (Louisville, KY: Westminster John Knox, 2013), 86, 87.

6. Ibid., 86.

7. Ibid., 97.

8. Michael Walzer, *In God's Shadow: Politics in the Hebrew Bible* (New Haven, CT: Yale University Press, 2012), 23.

9. Millard C. Lind, *Monotheism, Power, Justice: Collected Old Testament Essays*, Test-Reader Series (Elkhart, IN: Institute of Mennonite Studies, 1990), 110.

10. Millard C. Lind, *Yahweh Is a Warrior: The Theology of Warfare in Ancient Israel* (Scottdale, PA: Herald, 1980), 135.

11. Walzer, *In God's Shadow*, 76.

12. Brueggemann, *Truth Speaks to Power*, 90.

Prophetic power was paradoxical. Prophets relied on eloquence and conviction rather than coercion to get people to do their bidding. Yet they were astonishingly influential. For those who think of leadership as "getting things done" or "getting others to do things," it is worth noting that prophets did not embrace the usual manifestations of power. Buber says: "Being a prophet means being powerless."[13]

Courageous prophets risked the wrath of rulers and the opposition of fellow citizens. Some struggled with their call, resisting the impetus to speak, but the fact that they spoke up nevertheless indicates the bravery required. They met with disputation and contention, not only from kings (or other authorities; for example, priests) and crowds but even from other prophets. Both their message and their credentials were frequently challenged from all sides.

Prophets acted in ways that are counterintuitive to contemporary leadership priorities. They did not necessarily "win friends and influence people." They did not speak smoothly or diplomatically; rather they disputed, argued, denounced, condemned. At times they sounded treasonous, a charge in most cultures then that was normally applied to anyone who criticized royalty. Biblical prophets could be threatened with harsh punishment, exile, and even death.

It is vital to remember that prophets and rulers need each other. Both have their place. Neither can play the role of the other and neither can properly function without the other. Hebrew scriptures clearly show that kingly rule requires prophetic criticism. So the issue is discerning their proper relationship: "It is an uneven conversation, but agents of order and vision must listen to each other."[14] Brueggemann indicates that their conversation should always prioritize the powerless. In the Hebrew scriptures, this means kings and prophets working together for the poor (widows, orphans, strangers). In the Gospels this means Pharisees and chief priests being in conversation about the inclusion and redemption of publicans and sinners. This is how shalom is achieved.[15]

Prophetic Credibility

As there are true and false prophets, *discernment* is essential. How does one know whether a prophet is trustworthy? When can we be sure that he

13. Martin Buber, *Israel and the World: Essays in a Time of Crisis* (Syracuse, NY: Syracuse University Press, 1997), 108.

14. Walter Brueggemann, *Peace* (St. Louis, MO: Chalice, 2001), 104.

15. Ibid., 104–5.

or she truly speaks for God? There are scriptural criteria but no guaranteed methods.

An important mark of true prophets is *call.*[16] In Near Eastern cultures elsewhere, call narratives tended to be about kings.[17]

True prophets relied on biblical traditions. They spoke of the *future* by examining what went before: "prophets . . . were more commonly reading the signs of the times as interpreted through lessons from the past (scripture and tradition) that everyone in the community should already have known."[18]

In spite of the high price, prophets felt compelled to speak. Jeremiah cries:

> I thought, I'll forget him;
> I'll no longer speak his name.
> But there's an intense fire in my heart,
> trapped in my bones.
> I'm drained trying to contain it;
> I'm unable to do it. (Jer 20:9 CEB)

Bruce Cockburn, a contemporary prophetic singer, cries out: "a helpless rage seems to set my brain on fire."[19] The prophet had difficult dilemmas. Cornel West, reflecting on the witness of Dorothy Day, puts his finger on a powerful challenge for prophets: "It takes courage to be a nonconformist, to be willing to be a witness to something grander than one's self."[20]

Walzer notes many references to disputes and debates that prophets had with others. Thus a prophet's "true test is this: by his words—rhetoric, eloquence, poetic power, argumentative skill—shall you know him." Prophets relied on eloquence for authority and credibility.[21]

16. Marty E. Stevens, *Leadership Roles of the Old Testament: King, Prophet, Priest, Sage* (Eugene, OR: Wipf and Stock, 2012), 44.

17. Lind, *Yahweh Is a Warrior*, 62, 95.

18. Jamie Gates, "Primer on the Prophets," in *Nurturing the Prophetic Imagination*, ed. Jamie Gates and Mark H. Mann (Eugene, OR: Wipf and Stock, 2012), 2.

19. Bruce Cockburn, "Gavin's Woodpile," *In the Falling Dark* (Toronto: True North Records, 1976).

20. Cornel West, "On the Legacy of Dorothy Day," *Catholic Agitator* 44, no. 1 (February 2014): 1.

21. Walzer, *In God's Shadow*, 74–75, 78, 87.

Being a minority voice was a mark of "prophetic reliability."[22] Many kings had court prophets who spoke favorable words; they were suspect. In 1 Kings 22, Micaiah, who is resented by King Ahab, contradicted four hundred prophets.

Hans Walter Wolff suggests that prophetic words frequently contradicted what people want to hear. This led to another common characteristic of true prophecy. Prophets oftentimes *suffered* repercussions of delivering unpopular messages. Meanwhile, false prophets tailored content for popular approval.[23] False prophets were frequently self-confident with plenty to say. "The true prophet has to wait for the voice of his God and is forced to endure periods of uncertainty." True prophets, intriguingly, regularly show a "lack of self-confidence."[24]

Prophets could be judged by how they live, that is, whether or not they behaved ethically. Jesus later made this clear: "Watch out for false prophets. . . . You will know them by their fruit" (Matt 7:15a, 16a CEB). Jeremiah notes:

> In the prophets of Jerusalem
> I saw something horrible:
> They commit adultery and tell lies.
> They encourage evildoers
> so that no one turns from their wickedness. (Jer 23:14a CEB)

One last means to weigh prophetic legitimacy was the understanding that a prophet did not speak for himself or herself, reporting his or her own priorities or dreams or visions. When the message was difficult, unwelcome, and even overwhelming to the prophets who brought the message, they did not want to say these things but felt compelled, as though they had no choice.[25]

These kinds of criteria do not make discernment infallible or guaranteed but are worth emphasizing. It is instructive to think about this in light of contemporary leadership emphases. Christians would generally agree that leaders should have communication skills, appreciate the past (scripture and tradition), behave ethically, and be called by God. Other prophetic criteria might give us pause. Many leadership definitions nowadays

22. Ibid., 77, 78.

23. Wolff, *Confrontations with Prophets*, 70, 71.

24. Ibid., 70.

25. Ibid., 73.

emphasize the need to recruit and influence followers, but how does this fit the prophetic mark of nonconformist subversion? When leadership teachings stress success, relevance, and effectiveness, what do we make of the reality of prophetic suffering? When popular ideas of gifted leadership include self-confidence, what about true prophets who are tentative and uncertain? Numerous biblical assumptions about faithful prophecy undermine common contemporary leadership perceptions.

Applications

During the 1970s, Archie Bunker and others reprimanded dissenters with a choice: "America, love it or leave it." Frequently protesters said that in fact they *did* love America and that that love compelled them to ask hard questions. (Jonah failed as a prophet because he was unable to love Nineveh, where he preached.) Healthy society makes room for protest and disagreement.

In 1979, I attended a peacemaking conference in Indiana. Several academics spoke about how "Christian" institutions where they taught were still punishing them—denying tenure, promotions, sabbaticals—because in 1972 they had the gall to support George McGovern for president. I was amazed that Christians who supported Richard Nixon could be so self-righteous, since Nixon, once reelected, had to resign in disgrace. I was also dumbfounded that institutions could hold grudges for years and years.

I have since seen firsthand that churches and "Christian" institutions can indeed have long memories and be unforgiving toward dissenters. When that happens, however, we forget the important priority of prophets in God's leadership economy. We *need* people to disagree; sometimes we even need people to be disagreeable. This does not mean complying with every contrary point of view. Instead we listen discerningly and celebrate that the Spirit speaks through all of God's children, and sometimes those voices will shake and disturb us.

Grace in the face of criticism can be hard. I confess that as a young pastor, I resented those who disagreed with me. I was sure that I was on "God's side" and took offence at the effrontery of those who could not recognize this. Gradually I realized both that my perspective was always limited and that opponents can be teachers, perhaps our best teachers.[26] Being human, we are not always so good at tolerating vigorous differences of opinion.

26. That was a major insight in my book *Never Call Them Jerks: Healthy Responses to Difficult Behavior* (New York: Rowman and Littlefield, 1999).

Christian leaders need to realize that criticism, as painful as it may be, comes with the territory. An essential skill is the ability to deal well with inevitable dissent. We need to welcome it even if feeling attacked. We affirm the appropriateness of tough questions. We can adopt a learning stance toward opposing points of view.

We can reframe attitudes that see dissent as inherently negative by viewing it as intrinsically worthwhile. This is not always fun, or easy, but it is a way to learn much about oneself or one's institution and helps one to make needed changes.

What was true during the biblical eras is still true now. Prophets have much to offer. We need them.

Chapter Nine

All Fall Short

Priests and Sages

Seeing Stars?

For years I taught a core leadership development course required for all seminary students, regardless of their majors. One seminary official contended that in this class professors ought to look for one or two "stars," those with obvious potential and charisma to be "true leaders." Then most of the teacher's focus should be on grooming them for success down the road.

This is not advice that I was willing to accept.

For one, this counsel struck me as unjust. This seemed equivalent to offering mandatory group music lessons but only focusing on potential prodigies. Many are called, but few, a very small few, are chosen perhaps?

For another, this advice bought into narrow understandings of leadership as people with attractive upfront gifts of communication, warmth, organization, persuasion. This is not intrinsically Christian. In the Bible, God repeatedly shows a preference for those who are not "stars" and sets aside those who look most predictably like leaders.

Biblical perspectives show that there is not only one form of leadership but many different manifestations (celebrated in Paul's doctrine about multiple gifts). Furthermore God's people continually experiment with how to lead and be led.

Categories of Old Testament Leaders

We considered several different Hebrew leaders to work toward a theology of leadership. We looked at Moses, a leader in a stand-alone category; no one before or after him compares. We studied judges, a leadership experiment. We considered first kings and then prophets, the most prominent and significant types of leaders found in the Old Testament.

Other leaders are mentioned in the Bible. An astonishing passage reminds us of God's treatment of leaders.

> He leads *advisors* away barefoot;
> makes madmen of *judges*;
> unties the belt of *kings*,
> binds a garment around their loins;
> leads *priests* away barefoot;
> overthrows the *well-established*;
> silences the talk of *trusted people*;
> takes away *elders'* discernment;
> pours contempt on *royalty*,
> loosens the belt of the *strong*. (Job 12:17-21 CEB; emphasis added)

Almost all leader-types of the day (except prophets) are here humiliated by God: advisors, judges, kings, priests, the well-established, the trusted, elders, royalty. There are also other leadership lists:

> As a thief is ashamed when caught in his tracks,
> so the people of Israel are ashamed—
> their *kings*, *officials*, *priests*, and *prophets*. (Jer 2:26 CEB; emphasis added)

> Then they said, "Come, let's unite against Jeremiah, for the *priest's* instruction won't fail, nor will the *sage's* counsel, nor the *prophet's* word." (Jer 18:18a CEB; emphasis added)

> Disaster comes upon disaster,
> and rumor follows rumor.
> They seek a vision from the *prophet*.
> Instruction disappears from the *priest*,
> and counsel from the *elders*.
> The *king* will go into mourning,
> the *prince* will clothe himself in despair. (Ezek 7:26-27a CEB; emphasis added)

Traditional leaders are poor sources for hope, wisdom, or strength. Once again, we see a prevailing biblical theme: texts offering discouraging outlooks on leadership.

Note one more thing. Looking at the verses cited above, biblical scholar Marty Stevens concludes that in the Hebrew scriptures there were primarily "four roles: king, prophet, priest, and sage."[1] *Leadership* is never in one form alone. It is to two remaining roles—priests and wise ones—that we briefly turn.

Priests

Priests were common in ancient Near Eastern religions. By connecting to God, they mediated between God and humanity. Unlike the many stories about kings and prophets in the Bible, there are few accounts of priests. There are no complex, nuanced examples of lives to compare with those of Moses and David, for example. Most of what we read is rules, guidelines, laws, or principles.

The priestly office was inherited by males. The Levite tribe was set apart for this role. This was not a mysteriously divine calling; a priest "dispenses salvation by virtue of the office, rather than through personal charismatic endowment."[2] Although the status was inherited, it could be lost or taken away because of abuse (Aaron's sons in Lev 10:1; Eli's sons in 1 Sam 2:17; Samuel's sons in 1 Sam 8:3).

Normally, one could not be a priest without being a Levite. Samuel appears to be an exception; not labeled a priest, he performed priestly duties.[3]

Levites were not apportioned geographical territories like other tribes. They were allotted certain cities and the rest of Israel was expected to support priests, a common Near Eastern practice.[4] Priests were entitled to a portion of sacrifices. Aaron's, Eli's, and Samuel's sons all showed that a hereditary leadership system was subject to abuse and corruption.

The priests' primary role was administering rituals. These included prayer, sacrifices, purification rites, overseeing religious festivals, and discernment by the casting of lots. They were also responsible for teaching the law (Lev 10:11). Sometimes they were the primary leaders. In the Sinai, af-

1. Marty E. Stevens, *Leadership Roles of the Old Testament: King, Prophet, Priest, Sage* (Eugene, OR: Wipf and Stock, 2012), x.

2. Joseph Blenkinsopp, *Sage, Priest, Prophet: Religious and Intellectual Leadership in Ancient Israel* (Louisville, KY: Westminster John Knox, 1995), 79.

3. Stevens, *Leadership Roles of the Old Testament,* 65–66. Samuel represented "apparently contradictory roles... (judge, prophet, priest)" and thus could be considered "the first great religious reformer since Moses." Millard C. Lind, *Yahweh Is a Warrior: The Theology of Warfare in Ancient Israel* (Scottdale, PA: Herald, 1980), 97.

4. Stevens, *Leadership Roles of the Old Testament,* 66.

ter escaping from Egypt, the people of Israel had neither kings nor military leaders "but prophetic and priestly leaders, Moses and Aaron."[5] (Moses was of the tribe of Levi but was never for some reason a priest.)

It is difficult to apply Old Testament priesthood to contemporary leadership. (Many Christian traditions resist calling their clergy "priest.") While frequently pastors are children or grandchildren of pastors, ordination is not usually inherited or inheritable. Furthermore, most clergy no longer have the elaborate ritual demands of the biblical era. (I am, however, astonished by the ritual obligations of a Coptic Orthodox priest friend who will never be permitted to retire.)

Occasional abuses of the priesthood (e.g., sons of Aaron, Eli, and Samuel) imply two cautionary leadership themes. One, it is important to be aware of and resist misuses of office privileges. And, two, the high responsibility of representing God must not be taken lightly.

Yet another Old Testament form of leadership included sages.

Wise Ones

Sages or wise ones (usually but not always men) comprise the most elusive leadership category. This group is not as neatly or tidily definable as kings or priests. This is "the least-institutionalized of the leadership roles under consideration, leaving fewer traces in the biblical records." Those regarded as wise counselors first for family clans and later for royalty are described variously in the Bible: sometimes as *chakam* meaning "the wise," at times as "elders" (*zaqen*), or otherwise as "counselors" (*ya'ats*).[6]

In patriarchal nomadic cultures (Genesis through Ruth), elders helped tribespeople work out disputes and conflicts. Sages of this kind are found in Exodus 3:16 and Deuteronomy 1:13-16. Eventually these people might act as local judges. They may also have been diplomats for their communities, negotiating peace agreements.

These roles gradually evolved into statespeople, counselors, diplomats advising kings. These office holders were part of the elite, interested in protecting institutions and benefitting from special education.[7] There are

5. Lind, *Yahweh Is a Warrior*, 85.

6. Quotations and information in this paragraph are from Stevens, *Leadership Roles of the Old Testament*, 91.

7. William McKane, *Prophets and Wise Men* (Naperville, IL: Alec R. Allenson, 1965), 38, 17.

references to groups of elders giving counsel (Ezek 7:26-27; Lam 4:13-16).[8] King Rehoboam consulted elders after the people ask him to rule more lightly than his father Solomon. He tragically ignored their sage advice and the northern kingdoms rebelled and seceded. On occasion, royal malice co-opted elders. Jezebel used a group of this sort in a conspiracy to have Naboth killed and his vineyard given to Ahab (1 Kgs 21:8-14).

At times, the counsel was devoid of *ethical* content. David (2 Kgs 2:6, 9) spoke of "wisdom" and being "wise" when he recommended that Solomon conduct discreet assassinations. Jonadab (2 Sam 13:3) is "crafty" or "subtle" (KJV). The word can also means "wise," even when Jonadab counsels David's son Amnon to rape his own sister. The Bible is ambivalent about this kind of leadership, sometimes speaking of it positively, at times neutrally, and other times negatively.[9]

Many wisdom ideas infiltrated Jewish thought from elsewhere. Several scripture references allude to sages in other cultures (Jer 50:35; 51:57; Isa 19:11), and the citations are frequently *negative.* Hebrews were suspicious about what passed for wisdom elsewhere.[10] Joseph and Daniel show that royal counselors were not adept at interpreting dreams. Some "wise men" are affiliated with the magic that is rejected by Israelite faith.[11] Isaiah 10:12-16 rebukes the Assyrian king for inappropriately boasting of his own wisdom. William McKane observes:

> It is not, after all, emperors and statesmen who move the world and the resolute humanism of their hard-thinking posture does not win for them a monopoly in the world of politics they suppose it does. It is not they but Yahweh who shapes history; it is he who takes the big decisions and implements them.[12]

Isaiah 31:1-3 also repudiates human wisdom; this time against counsel suggesting an alliance with Egypt.

Jeremiah's sharp prophetic conflicts with statespeople resulted in him being imprisoned and threatened with death (36:26; 37:15, 20-21). When

8. This paragraph is summarized from Stevens, *Leadership Roles of the Old Testament,* 92–99.

9. McKane, *Prophets and Wise Men*, 17.

10. Michael Walzer, *In God's Shadow: Politics in the Hebrew Bible* (New Haven, CT: Yale University Press, 2012), 145.

11. Stevens, *Leadership Roles of the Old Testament,* 100–101.

12. McKane, *Prophets and Wise Men*, 68.

prophets challenged wise ones, they did not just question the so-called wisdom of statespeople but even "the basic presuppositions of the tradition itself." Prophets had deep theological differences with those particular opponents.[13]

Sages did have influence. Wisdom is a significant scriptural stream. Some contemporary leadership books draw heavily on these traditions. Evangelicals have an affinity for Proverbs. The practicality, realism, and searching for success themes in much biblical wisdom literature can resonate with contemporary self-help, how-to-succeed-in-life-and-business, leadership literature. Much of Proverbs explains how to be successful in a king's court and includes learning how to address kings gently, softly, and with patience (rather than the blunt condemnation of prophets).[14]

Much is unknown and unclear about wisdom's role in Israelite leadership, but prophets remained suspicious. Wise counselors were frequently condemned.

> Doom to those who call evil good and good evil,
>   who present darkenss as light and light as darkness,
>   who make bitterness sweet and sweetness bitter.
>
> Doom to those
> who consider themselves wise,
>   who think of themselves as clever. (Isa 5:20-21 CEB)

One issue was that wisdom could come from untrustworthy sources (Jer 8:9; Isa 31:1).[15] Sages frequently reinforced institutions and supported priorities that did not sit well with prophets: "Their . . . good advice is worldly and strategic, aimed at accommodating differences, reaching a compromise, negotiating alliances. . . . The wise are wholly engaged in the world as it is."[16] This kind of wisdom avoided dealing with evil (Prov 4:14-15) "rather than confronting it directly."[17] Such literature focused on prudence, realism, caution. Lind contends that as monarchy became more established, kings less and less consulted God (or listened to prophets) but showed "an increased reliance upon calculation and worldly wisdom"; they drew on "the statecraft

13. This paragraph relies on ibid., 118, 128.

14. Walzer, *In God's Shadow,* 147, 149.

15. Ibid., 150.

16. Ibid., 151.

17. Ibid., 153.

and wisdom of the ancient Near East."[18] This may also reflect a decreasing conviction about God's active—and at times miraculous—involvement in historic events.[19] Even so, not all sages were irreligious or antireligious.[20]

Strong voices contended for prioritizing prophetic counsel over wisdom that is "like other nations." They rejected "ancient Near Eastern concepts of wisdom. Instead...Israel was to rely upon Yahweh's word through the prophet for her decision-making."[21] William McKane, without taking sides, carefully detailed what he calls the "incompatibility between prophet and statesman."[22] Throughout his book he calls this tension a "conflict."

There are not many clear implications from ambiguous portrayals of wisdom for contemporary leadership theology. We are reminded that when it comes to leadership, the Bible has different voices, some of them conflicting with each other.

Nevertheless, one conclusion is wariness about being overly "practical" and "realistic," being cautious of what we now could call "functional atheism." Prophets remind us of the importance not only of behaving ethically but also of relying on God and God's providence.

18. Lind, *Yahweh Is a Warrior*, 120.

19. Ibid., 25, 56.

20. McKane, *Prophets and Wise Men*, 47.

21. Lind, *Yahweh Is a Warrior*, 156.

22. McKane, *Prophets and Wise Men*, 7.

Chapter Ten

Upside-Down Priorities

Scripture's Unexpected Takes on Leadership

Most Unlikely to Be a Leader

Ronald Heifetz, a well-respected Harvard professor and authority on leadership, opens one book with an extended account of Lois. A resident in a small Native American community, she decided to use her experience of becoming sober to help others do the same. But this commitment was demanding. For months and months, she set up a circle of chairs in the community lodge and prayed for others to show up. The chairs stayed empty for a long time. Yet she returned week after week, waiting up to two hours alone. In three years, only a few people appeared. After a decade, however, the meetings were fully attended and the difference was felt throughout her community.

Heifetz regards Lois as a leader even though she held no office and results were slow in coming. For much of the early years, she and another sober community member were misunderstood and dismissed by others. They felt

> out of place..., unwelcome at parties and gatherings where alcohol flowed, so ostracized that even holidays became lonely, solitary events. Indeed, for long stretches of time they spent weekends off the reservation to find people they could talk to. They had put themselves at risk, as well as key relationships with neighbors, friends, and family. Eventually, they succeeded and survived. But for a long time, they could not know. They could have lost everything.[1]

1. Ronald A. Heifetz and Marty Linsky, *Leadership on the Line: Staying Alive through the Dangers of Leading* (Boston, MA: Harvard Business School Press, 2002), 10–11.

So, *when* was Lois a leader? When people showed up? During all those weeks and months prior when she was the only one at a meeting? What if someone did a performance review of her after a month or even a year or three into her efforts, would she have been regarded as a leader? We need to be cautious about measurements. Are we far-sighted enough? Do we pass up good opportunities when we give up too soon?

This contemporary example lines up with the unexpected reversals of biblical leadership. Lois aligns with Martin Buber's vision of prophets:

> The true prophets know the little, bloated idol that goes by the name of "success" through and through. They know that ten successes that are nothing but successes can lead to defeat, while on the contrary ten failures can add up to a victory. . . . When true prophets address the people, they are usually unsuccessful; everything in the people that craves for success opposes them.[2]

Confounded Expectations

The Bible's most intriguing leadership theme is that faithful leadership confounds expectations. While we may identify leadership with prestige and elite standing, the Bible generally commends leadership as a way to pursue justice.

This point of view is communicated by the frequent selection of unattractive and unlikely leaders. Time after time they had no obvious leadership qualities and came from out-of-the-way places—in other words people who would not necessarily stand out as seminary "stars."

Blenkinsopp shows that many judges were disreputable: "The Deuteronomic historian goes out of his way to emphasize the socially marginal origin of most of these 'judges.'" Several may have been of Canaanite descent; "Jephthah was an outlaw and son of a prostitute; Abimelech's mother was one of Jerubaal's concubines."[3] *Unlikely* leaders were "chosen despite visible handicaps such as Jephthah's bastardy, Gideon's youth, or Deborah's sex."[4]

God frequently did not search for the obvious "stars." Surrounding cultures favored oldest males (primogeniture) for parental favor, blessing,

2. Martin Buber, *On the Bible: Eighteen Studies,* ed. Nahum N. Glatzer (Syracuse, NY: Syracuse University Press, 2000), 170.

3. Joseph Blenkinsopp, *Sage, Priest, Prophet: Religious and Intellectual Leadership in Ancient Israel* (Louisville, KY: Westminster John Knox, 1995), 130.

4. Aaron Wildavsky, *Moses as Political Leader* (New York: Shalem, 2005), 253.

and legacy. Yet in the Bible blessings not infrequently went to younger sons: Abel, Isaac, Joseph, Benjamin, the prodigal.

Moses also was an unlikely choice. He was a fringe outsider to both the adoptive Egyptians and Hebrew ancestors. He was a man of wrath, a fugitive from the consequences of a murder that he committed.

Samuel was commissioned to anoint a son of Jesse to be king. None of the impressive obvious candidates were chosen. "But the LORD said to Samuel, 'Have no regard for his appearance or stature. . . . God doesn't look at things like humans do. Humans see only what is visible to the eyes, but the LORD sees into the heart'" (1 Sam 16:7 CEB).

> God uses unexpected persons. . . . Over and again the biblical story tells us that men and women who become crucial to God's purposes would have been overlooked if measured only by the usual human standards. God looked beyond these standards and saw new possibilities.[5]

God deliberately works through unexpected reversals:

> God, who is preached and represented in this world by the One who was crucified and rose from the dead, is the God of paradox: what people consider wise He considers folly, what people regard as madness and a stumbling block is wisdom in His eyes, what people see as weakness He considers strength, what people consider great He sees as small, and what they find small He regards as great.[6]

Scriptures reinforce these themes with the many prospective candidates who were not looking to be leaders. Moses resisted God's assignment. Most judges did not *seek* their positions. Saul hid when nominated to be king. Numerous prophets argued against God's call.

This spirit is still captured in how Amish select ministers. They employ a lot system for this important process. But an Amishman (ministers there are always males) is disqualified if he shows an un-humble sense of being called to ministry. Campaigning for this office is a no-no. In that tradition, ambition is suspect.

5. Lewis A. Parks and Bruce C. Birch, *Ducking Spears, Dancing Madly: A Biblical Model of Church Leadership* (Nashville: Abingdon, 2004), 42.

6. Tomas Halik, *Night of the Confessor: Christian Faith in an Age of Uncertainty* (New York: Doubleday Religion, 2012), 22.

Leadership Never Stands Alone

The office of priest eventually disappeared. It was not a permanent institution, just as kingship proved temporary. These were transitory measures. This raises intriguing questions. One can never talk about, analyze, or evaluate leadership in and of itself. It cannot be examined in isolation. There are always at least two other relevant factors that need consideration.

For one, the context or situation where a leader operates is crucial. Many commend Winston Churchill's style during the Second World War, but his forceful, eloquent, crisis-oriented leadership was not well-received in post-war Britain where he suffered a humiliating electoral defeat.

André Trocmé was a brilliant Reformed pastor who helped lead his village in Vichy France to protect and save Jews during World War II. Yet his gifts so suited for crisis did not always serve him well. After the war, he tried (and failed) to pastor in the village that was no longer in desperate straits.

In both cases, we have an acknowledged and official leader with particular gifts, talents, and capacities (Churchill, Trocmé). In both cases, the leader related to the same followers (people of Britain, villagers of LeChambon) during and after the war. While that combination of leader and follower functioned effectively in war, it was no longer suited when circumstances changed. The altered situation and context made all the difference.

Second, we also take into consideration followers. Good leadership is partly in relationship with those one leads. Jim Jones, Adolf Hitler, Mahatma Gandhi, and Steve Jobs all worked with considerably different constituencies. Styles and approaches that succeed with one group may well fail with another group.

Evolving Roles from Old to New Testament

Our Old Testament survey showed that many roles evolved. Judges, kings, priests, sages, and Moses provided various forms of leadership. Most of those offices faded away. They offered mixes of religious, political, military, judicial, and intellectual counsel. Commonly, one person in a particular role gave several kinds of guidance. Moses, the most remarkable, functioned as tactical strategist (military), intermediary between God and people (religious), dispenser of wisdom (sage), and ruler (political). Likewise, while David was primarily a king, a political leader, he guided the faith of his people (in moving the Ark of the Covenant, for instance, and composing Psalms). Some prophets were priests. Tradition has King Solomon being a sage. So roles are not always clearly demarcated.

Nevertheless, the Old Testament showed movement from virtually no designated roles to eras where roles were increasingly specified and delineated. The Old Testament offered a long retrospective look at a people being formed. As a nation came together, with the emerging importance of various institutions, there was increasing clarity about *who* was responsible for *which* duties.

This will look different in the New Testament, writings from the infant church. The New Testament was written within a hundred years of the life of Jesus Christ. In this emerging movement, roles were more fluid than those established positions at the end of the Old Testament. While various Christians claim the New Testament for their own denominational polities, this is a dubious endeavor. Roles and offices emerge over the coming centuries, but as important and even as valid as they are, they are not clearly and strictly biblically mandated.

Concluding Reflections on Hebrew Scriptures and Leadership

In the next chapter, we turn to the New Testament—especially the history, example, and teachings of Jesus—for further leadership explorations. This is an appropriate place to pause and consider whether the Hebrew scriptures indeed resonated with the earlier claim of three consistently countercultural voices in the Bible about leadership.

First, strains in the Bible constantly question and critique prevailing leadership models of the day. We saw this in several ways. For one, no matter which leadership model was considered—the unparalleled and completely unique Moses, judges, kingship—the Bible is surprisingly forthright about the temptations, delusions, downsides, vulnerabilities, and shadows of each.

More than that, a primary prophetic role is to puncture leadership fallibilities. This office deliberately criticized and at times attacked kings, priests, and sages. Prophets even criticized other prophets.

Second, the Bible shows ongoing experimentation with leadership forms. We could read the Old Testament as a series of leadership tests. Moses arose at a time of unprecedented need. He was prophet, ruler, movement organizer all wrapped up in one, and there has never been his like since. Judges rallied people during crises. Kingship was brought in after the dismal failure of judges. But kings were always counterbalanced by prophets, and, in the long run, kingship also failed.

Third, God prioritizes justice and liberation. God turns power on its head, dethroning the mighty, empowering the vulnerable and excluded.

Moses was an unseemly leadership candidate, and with this desert rebel God overthrew Pharaoh and his slave system. Judges—regularly unlikely and weak themselves—helped Israelites cast off the burdens of oppressive neighbors.

Any form of leadership ultimately fails in God's eyes when it overlooks God's passionate concern for the excluded and downtrodden.

> The two central conflicts of the Bible put it clearly. . . . Pharaoh is the competent manager and desperate retainer of what has been and is. Moses is the terrifying voice of what is promised and surely will come in spite of our best resistances. Jesus versus the Pharisees of his time is the same. The Pharisees and all their allies in Jerusalem and Rome were those who had stabilized their lives and defended their turf powerfully. And Jesus discounted and dismantled their prized situations. He announced that the promises were happening. The kingdom of God is at hand. The coming has come. The promises are being kept. And kings and technicians and pharaohs and Pharisees—all of us who have it stabilized—view newness as a most unwelcome guest. If we can, we shall un-invite this guest.[7]

The only leadership "institution" to survive much beyond the Old Testament is the prophetic tradition; the prophets' primary role was always to undercut the pretensions of the mighty and to give God's voice to the voiceless.

As we turn our attention more deliberately to Jesus and the Gospels and the early New Testament church, we shall see that the Bible's radical critique of leadership goes ever deeper.

---

7. Walter Brueggemann, *Peace* (St. Louis, MO: Chalice, 2001), 125.

Chapter Eleven

A Long Rebuke in the Same Direction

Jesus Christ and the Powers-That-Be

An Argument Worth Losing

I regularly required leadership classes to read the Henri Nouwen classic *In the Name of Jesus*. One mature student objected that Nouwen was not a leader. I explained that Nouwen was a pastor and chaplain, taught seminarians and L'Arche volunteers to offer pastoral care, gave spiritual direction to the famous and not-so-famous, wrote dozens of books translated into many languages, and is considered one of the twentieth century's most important spiritual writers.

My student said, "But he never led a large organization, never rallied followers, never persuaded a group to move in a certain direction."

I took the bait and added that Nouwen was a successful fund-raiser and helped his Daybreak L'Arche community plan, fund, and achieve a retreat center. Only then did the student concede that Nouwen could be regarded as a leader.

I enjoy winning debates, but am sorry for how I made my case. Too much attention paid to leadership, even by Christians, centers around running businesses, nonprofits, and other institutions.

Long concerned that there is not enough quality theological reflection on leadership, I was happy to discover a book entitled *The Bible on Leadership*. But the subtitle startled me: *From Moses to Matthew—Management Lessons for Contemporary Leaders*.[1] Biblical characters—Paul, Isaiah, Peter,

1. Lorin Woolfe, *The Bible on Leadership: From Moses to Matthew—Management Lessons for Contemporary Leaders* (Toronto: American Management Association, 2002).

Luke, Noah, Jesus—are described as "managers." The inside cover promises that this book will teach "core traits—among them honesty, integrity, purpose, courage, and humility"—and link them to contemporary business leaders. Examples include Steve Jobs, Sam Walton, Mary Kay Ash, Ben and Jerry, and Rudolph Giuliani, "who at their best demonstrate some of the same strengths and values as their biblical predecessors." Several of those contemporary examples, of course, can also be remembered for notably not being "at their best." Misdirected emphases are also found in a well-known book called *Jesus, CEO*. The author notes that Jesus's unusual "values in management" were shown in "his approach with his staff."[2] Were the disciples staff, "direct reports"? On the flipside, do we want employees in corporations to relate *as disciples* to CEOs?

Scripturally speaking, there are problems in unduly emphasizing and revering leaders, especially in focusing primarily on those who are on the top of usual and predictable hierarchies.

Leadership Implications of Jesus's Early Life—Titles

All the junctures of Jesus's life—birth, wilderness temptation, ministry beginnings, calling disciples, announcing his mission and impending death, preparing disciples for his coming execution, crucifixion, resurrection, ascension—were deeply revealing about the counterintuitive leadership he embodied.

From the start, language deliberately portrayed him as a leader, one explicitly contrasted with prevailing rulers of his day. The first verse of Matthew's first chapter lists "the genealogy of Jesus the Messiah, the son of David, the son of Abraham," each term pregnant with meaning. "Jesus the Messiah" (repeated again in 1:18) or "Christ" means "'the anointed one,' i.e., the anointed king of the House of David."[3] "Son of David" also emphasizes *royal* ancestry. "Son of Abraham" connects to Israel's primary patriarch. We might not think twice about these claims now, but they were controversial and not only for religious reasons. They were political assertions that flew in the face of Roman imperial claims and priorities.

2. Laurie Beth Jones, *Jesus, CEO: Using Ancient Wisdom for Visionary Leadership* (New York: Hyperion, 1995), xiv.

3. Raymond E. Brown, *The Birth of the Messiah: A Commentary on the Infancy Narratives in the Gospels of Matthew and Luke* (New York: Doubleday, 1999), 59.

Mark's first verse says: "The beginning of the good news of Jesus Christ, the Son of God" (1:1). The "good news" (or "gospel") and even "Son of God" terminology sound familiarly religious. Yet these were *political* terms. "Son of God" was a label claimed by Roman emperors. "Good news" or "gospel" alluded to the current empire's triumphs and military wins. When new emperors took power, this "was cause for 'glad tidings.'"[4]

> There was a human being in the first century who was called "Divine," "Son of God," "God," and "God from God," whose titles were "Lord," "Redeemer," "Liberator," and "Savior of the World." Who was that person? Most people who know the Western tradition would probably answer... Jesus of Nazareth. And most Christians probably think that those titles were originally created and uniquely applied to Christ. But before Jesus ever existed, all those terms belonged to Caesar Augustus. To proclaim them of Jesus the Christ was thereby to deny them of Caesar the Augustus. Christians were... taking the identity of the Roman emperor and giving it to a Jewish peasant. Either that was a peculiar joke and a very low lampoon, or it was what the Romans called *majestas* and we call high treason.[5]

Terms like *gospel* aggressively proclaim Jesus's leadership in defiance of the strongest, most important leader, the emperor, Caesar himself. Mark's Gospel is "a declaration of war upon the political culture of the empire."[6] Mark—like the other Gospels—does not simply showcase Jesus the Christ's particular leadership but starkly contrasts his leadership with other authorities. N. T. Wright says that this is "*the story of the kingdom of God clashing with the kingdom of Caesar.*"[7]

When the angel Gabriel announced that Mary would bear a son, he noted: "He will be great and he will be called the Son of the Most High. The Lord God will give him the throne of David his father. He will rule over Jacob's house forever, and there will be no end to his kingdom" (Luke 1:32-33 CEB). Again, notice the politically loaded leadership language: "great," "throne," "rule," kingdom."

---

4. Ched Myers, *Binding the Strong Man: A Political Reading of Mark's Story of Jesus* (Maryknoll, NY: Orbis, 2008), 123.

5. John Dominic Crossan, *God and Empire: Jesus against Rome, Then and Now* (New York: HarperCollins, 2008), 28.

6. Myers, *Binding the Strong Man*, 124.

7. N. T. Wright, *How God Became King* (New York: HarperOne, 2012), 127.

We associate these familiar texts with churchy ideas or "spiritual realities" (whatever they might be). Yet the Gospels from the beginning use explicit politically tinged language in potentially treasonous ways. Their intention is to contrast Jesus-style leadership with the prevailing leadership paradigms of their day and—we might suspect—future generations as well.

It is loaded to speak of being in "the White House," residing at "10 Downing Street," or living at "24 Sussex Drive." These claims are not just about a location. They are short forms for powerful political leaders: US president, British prime minister, Canadian prime minister. If we call Jesus "commander-in-chief," we usurp the president's title. Early Christian readers knew that "son of God," "son of man," "Messiah," "son of David," "Christ" are not polite spiritual titles; they have bite, even subversive implications. They implicitly suggest that if God is king or Christ is lord then no one else is king or lord. This carries on a theme already seen in the Old Testament.

Leadership Implications of Jesus's Early Life—Making Way for Jesus

Just as titles for Jesus make leadership claims that contest the presumptions of contemporary rulers, his beginnings function similarly.

For example, the prediction of John's birth begins, "During the rule of King Herod of Judea there was a priest named Zechariah" (Luke 1:5 CEB). Luke is not just reporting merely *when* the events happen. Rather, he shows that God's most important work does not necessarily occur through the high and mighty, the strong and the powerful. God acts, rather, through unlikely and unknown, out-of-the-way fringe folks, in this case an old priest and his aging, barren wife.

Luke 2:1-2 reads: "A decree went out from *Emperor* Augustus...while Quirinius was *governor* of Syria" (emphasis added). Two rulers are mentioned before we learn about God's actions. Later we read: "In the fifteenth year of the rule of the *emperor* Tiberius—when Pontius Pilate was *governor* over Judea and Herod was *ruler* over Galilee, his brother Philip was *ruler* over Ituraea and Trachonitis, and Lysanias was *ruler* over Abilene, during the *high priesthood* of Annas and Caiaphas—God's word came to John son of Zechariah in the wilderness" (Luke 3:1-2 CEB; emphasis added). Luke names leading luminaries: emperor, governor, important religious officials. These are the normal newsmakers, of course, the ones in charge. (Intriguingly many offices named in early Luke—king, governor, high priesthood—will be implicated in Jesus's arrest, trial, and execution.) In actuality marginal folks—Mary, Joseph, John the Baptist—will be God's unexpected channels, the *real* sphere of God's transformation, the center of God's actions, where *good news* is found and embodied. Note, too, that God's word came "*in the wilderness*," showing again that familiar biblical contrast between centers of power and the wilderness.

There is a lovely twist on these kinds of leadership lists in "The Martyrdom of Polycarp" (second century). After narrating events around Polycarp's sacrificial death, the author notes: "The official responsible for his arrest was Herod; the High Priest was Philip of Tralles; and the proconsul was Statius Quadratus—but the ruling monarch was Jesus Christ, who reigns for ever and ever. To him be ascribed all glory, honour, majesty, and an eternal throne from generation to generation. Amen."[8] The author—structuring the account with biblical allusions—names religious and political luminaries but makes clear where true authority lies.

Early in Luke we learn that a young unmarried virgin, out-of-the-way from capitols and power centers, "found favor with God" (1:30) and will be mother of the Messiah. The angel prophesied: "He will *rule* over Jacob's house forever, and there will be no end to his *kingdom*" (1:33 CEB; emphasis added). Once more, note the explicit political language.

Mary later acknowledged the unlikeliness of being chosen: "he has looked with favor on the *low status* of his servant" (1:48a CEB; emphasis added). Her response is inspiring: "I am the Lord's servant. Let it be with me just as you have said" (1:38 CEB). Daniel Wolpert argues that her "radical openness" makes her a "model of leadership."[9] While leadership may be regarded as the ability to cause things to happen or to persuade others to do things, Wolpert suggests that Mary's faithful *leadership* made room to let God act. Mary was not achieving so much as actively assenting to God.

Later the young virgin sang the Magnificat canticle. This praise hymn makes clear the expectation that God works dramatic leadership reversals.

> My soul magnifies the Lord,
>   and my spirit rejoices in God my Savior,
> for he has looked with favor on the lowliness of his servant.
>   Surely, from now on all generations will call me blessed;
> for the Mighty One has done great things for me,
>   and holy is his name.

---

8. "The Martyrdom of Polycarp," in *Early Christian Writings: The Apostolic Fathers*, trans. Maxwell Staniforth (Toronto: Penguin, 1968), 132.

9. Daniel Wolpert, *Leading a Life with God: The Practice of Spiritual Leadership* (Nashville: Upper Room Books, 2006), 51.

His mercy is for those who fear him
from generation to generation.
He has shown strength with his arm;
he has scattered the proud in the thoughts of their hearts.
He has brought down the powerful from their thrones,
and lifted up the lowly;
he has filled the hungry with good things,
and sent the rich away empty.
He has helped his servant Israel,
in remembrance of his mercy,
according to the promise he made to our ancestors,
to Abraham and to his descendants for ever. (Luke 1:46-55)

God is described with overt leadership terminology, "Lord" and "Savior." God's political agenda defeats and overturns powers-that-be. Not only will there be a dramatic reversal of fortunes for those in power, but also the oppressed—"the lowly" (v. 52; echoing Mary's earlier description of herself, "the low status of his servant"), "the hungry"—will be liberated and rescued from suffering.

The radical implications of this prayerful song at times can mean great risks for those who take or recite it prayerfully. Nouwen observed back in the early 1980s: "These words . . . have taken on so much power and strength that, in a country like El Salvador, they are considered subversive and can lead to torture or death."[10]

An Unlikely King Is Born—Jesus's Nativity

The circumstances of Jesus's birth include his parents-to-be traveling to Bethlehem for a census. This is a heavily loaded detail. The census was a reminder of the Roman Empire's oppressive power on colonialized peoples. In our day, many resent taxes—even when revenue benefits us by supporting schools, emergency services, road repairs. But Jews of Jesus's time suffered under an exploitive foreign occupying government; taxes went abroad to enrich others elsewhere. Furthermore, biblically minded people know that, theologically speaking, a census is bad news: "The census stands in Israel for the ability of the royal apparatus to regiment people against freedom and justice. Thus

10. Henri Nouwen, *¡Gracias! A Latin American Journal* (Maryknoll, NY: Orbis, 1993), 68.

it evokes curse (2 Samuel 24)."[11] Here are other not-so-subtle digs directed at those oppressors who think that they control the world and reality.

Luke shows Jesus's *poverty*. He was born in a manger, an animal's trough, "because there was no place for them in the inn" (Luke 2:7b). Later, his parents gave the poor person's offering of pigeons during the temple presentation of Jesus. The first human witnesses were shepherds, people in Jesus's day who "were often considered as dishonest, outside the Law."[12] They were hardly credible witnesses and did not add prestige to the occasion.

Our culture enjoys stories that begin with poverty, rags-to-riches motifs, not to mention prosperity gospel promises of liberation from poverty by miraculous provision. But Jesus never moved from "rags-or-swaddling-bands-to-riches." Rather he would be crowned with thorns and given a purple cloak as mockery. He did not in life achieve notable power and affluence. He was downwardly mobile.

The angels announced "good news," a phrase alluding to "an imperial proclamation"; this was "Luke's gentle counterpropaganda that Jesus, not Augustus, was the Savior and source of peace whose birthday marked a new beginning of time."[13] The angels' canticle included the phrase "on earth peace among those whom he favors" (Luke 2:14b CEB). Again, this directly rebuked and countered Caesar Augustus who claimed to be responsible for world peace; "he was remembered as the founder of the Empire who had pacified the world" and was called "savior" and even "savior of the whole world."[14]

Matthew's details about Jesus's birth also pose a distinct contrast to leadership models. Herod was a fearful, anxious *king*, threatened when he heard from the "wise men from the East" of "the child who has been born *king* of the Jews" (Matt 2:1-2; emphasis added). These wise ones, Gentiles from afar ("we three *kings*," we often sing), unlikely examples of faithfulness, desired to "honor" (Matt 2:2, 11 CEB) the child. Who was the worthy leader: "the newborn king of the Jews" (Matt 2:1 CEB) or an anxious, deceptive, murdering tyrant? Like a demented Pharaoh, Herod had all Bethlehem's children, two years of age and under, slaughtered. His action forced Joseph and his family to flee as exiled political refugees to Egypt.

11. Walter Brueggemann, *The Prophetic Imagination*, 2nd ed. (Minneapolis: Augsburg Fortress, 2001), 144n2.

12. Brown, *The Birth of the Messiah*, 420.

13. Ibid., 424.

14. Ibid., 415.

Baptism and Leadership

Jesus was baptized by outsider John the Baptist in the wilderness, a frequent location for oppositional alternatives to rulers. For all the lofty language about Jesus, he *submitted* to baptism. John was aware of this irony; in one version he wanted to be baptized by Jesus rather than baptize Jesus (Matt 4:14). Elsewhere he said of Jesus, "I'm not worthy to untie his sandal straps" (John 1:27 CEB).

The baptism shows that Jesus was endowed by the Spirit (Matt 3:16) and rehearses titles for him: "This is my Son, the Beloved" (Matt 3:17). As we already saw, "Son of God" terminology is politically loaded vocabulary commonly used for Caesar. This text also alludes to the promised messianic leader in Isaiah:[15]

> But here is my servant, the one I uphold,
> my chosen, who brings me delight.
> I've put my spirit upon him;
> he will bring justice to the nations.
> He won't cry out or shout aloud
> or make his voice heard in public.
> He won't break a bruised reed;
> he won't extinguish a faint wick,
> but he will surely bring justice. (Isa 42;1-3)

Mark includes a curious detail: Jesus "saw the heavens torn apart" (1:10). This apocalyptic language suggests the end of one era and the launching of another by God. Later, Mark uses the same imagery after Jesus dies and "the curtain of the temple was torn in two, from top to bottom" (15:38), again reminding us that one system is being dramatically superseded by another. (Following the ripping of the curtain, a Roman centurion—probably the man in charge of Jesus's beatings and execution—declared Jesus "God's Son," again that political title.)

Jesus's baptism functioned as commissioning into ministry on behalf of the reign of God, an unprecedented rulership that will compete with and against contemporary leaders and rulers.

Temptations of Jesus

Jesus went to the *wilderness* (that loaded location) and was thrice tempted. Parker Palmer calls these "Temptations of Action."[16] This scenario immedi-

15. Myers, *Binding the Strong Man*, 129.

16. Parker J. Palmer, *The Active Life: Wisdom for Work, Creativity, and Caring* (San Francisco: HarperSanFrancisco, 1990), ch. 6.

ately followed his baptism and had everything to do with the kind of ministry and leadership he would exercise. Bill Wylie Kellermann says that these are allurements about personal identity and power: "The Confuser's scheme is for Jesus to forget who he is by getting lost in how he'll work, so that the One who is the beginning and end will be swallowed up in the means."[17]

Matthew and Luke order the diversions differently but report the same enticements. In two of three of the temptations, the devil taunted, "If you are the Son of God" (Matt 4:3, 6; Luke 4:3, 9), using a term that we now understand to be political, one claimed by various Caesars. These were temptations about *kingship*; "all the options laid before Jesus by the tempter are ways of being king."[18] Clarence Jordan is right, this was not merely theological but political; Jesus was being tested on his political qualifications: "It has... to do with his right to rule. If you are going to rule—to be the leader of this movement..."[19]

These lures concern how Jesus lives out ministry and leadership. Clarence Jordan sees them as temptations about ruling others: gaining influence by materialism (bread), ecclesiasticism (pinnacle—"Be the head of a great church movement!"), or "political power based upon militarism" (worshipping the devil).[20] W. Paul Jones speaks of possession, power, and prestige.[21]

Henri Nouwen masterfully summarizes these as temptations for success and relevance (bread), popularity and spectacle (throwing oneself from a pinnacle), and power and control.[22] One does not have to look far in "church world" to see methods and priorities employed in the service of *effective* ministry, having *influence*, gaining *power*—key terms common in leadership literature.

Jesus encountered the same kinds of allures in John. After a miraculous feeding, "Jesus understood that they were about to come and force him to be their king, so he took refuge again, alone on a mountain" (John 6:15 CEB). Success and relevance were not his priority. He disregarded

17. Bill Wylie Kellermann, *Seasons of Faith and Conscience: Kairos, Confession, Liturgy* (Eugene, OR: Wipf and Stock, 2008), 159.

18. John Howard Yoder, *The Politics of Jesus*, 2nd ed. (Grand Rapids: Eerdmans, 1994), 25.

19. Clarence Jordan, *The Substance of Faith and Other Cotton Patch Sermons*, ed. Dallas Lee (Eugene, OR: Cascade, 2005), 60.

20. Ibid., 60–62.

21. W. Paul Jones, *A Season in the Desert: Making Time Holy* (Brewster, MA: Paraclete, 2000), 7.

22. Henri J. M. Nouwen, *In the Name of Jesus: Reflections on Christian Leadership* (New York: Crossroad, 1989).

his brothers' advice: "Leave Galilee. Go to Judea so that your disciples can see the amazing works that you do. Those who want to be known publicly don't do things secretly. Since you can do these things, show yourself to the world" (John 7:3-4 CEB). Popularity and spectacle were not among his aims. Jesus also refused to bow before Pilate's threats: "Do you not know that I have power to release you, and power to crucify you?" (John 19:10). Power and control were not Jesus's goal.

It is helpful to see how people have interpreted these three temptations:

materialism	ecclesiasticism	militarism (Jordan)
possessions	prestige	power (Jones)
success/relevance	popularity/ spectacle	power/control (Nouwen)

All of these are addressed and refuted by the Lord's Prayer. There we confidently address God as "Father," not allowing "if-you-are" doubts about God-relatedness to be undermined. There we entrust mundane material needs ("daily bread") to God. We refuse to distract God by bogusly begging for miracles, committing ourselves rather to God's reign and will. We decline to worship anything or anyone less than God, for God's name is to be hallowed.

Strikingly, leadership temptations are oftentimes spoken of in threes:

Marcus Borg	achievement	affluence	appearance[23]
Gary Hoag et al.	lust of the flesh	lust of the eyes	pride of life
	control	idolatry	pride[24]
Wes Granberg-Michaelson	money	sex	power[25]

23. Marcus Borg, "Dialogue #1: Marcus Borg," interview by Kristina Lizardy-Hajbi, United Church of Christ website, October 2011, www.ucc.org/education_dialogue-1.

24. Gary G. Hoag, R. Scott Rodin, and Wesley K. Willmer, *The Choice: The Christ-Centered Pursuit of Kingdom Outcomes* (Winchester, VA: ECFA Press, 2014), 16. They are referring to 1 John 2:15-17.

25. Wesley Granberg-Michaelson, *Leadership from Inside Out: Spirituality and Organizational Change* (New York: Crossroad, 2004), 13. He notes that these are counterbalanced by traditional monastic vows.

Daniel Goleman	narcissist	Machiavellian	psychopath
	"dreams of glory"	ends justify means	"other as object"[26]
Fyodor Dostoyevsky's "Grand Inquisitor"	miracle	mystery	authority[27]
Ronald Heifetz	power/ control	affirmation/ importance	intimacy/ delight[28]
Rev. Dr. Martin Luther King Jr.	safety/ cowardice	expediency/ politics	vanity/ popularity[29]

Jesus's example reminds us that some goals—as noble as they sound—are not worth prioritizing and that contemporary leaders, even successful ones, are not always our best models. Eugene Peterson amusingly reflects on Jesus's choices:

> Why didn't Jesus learn from Herod? Why didn't Jesus take Herod as his mentor in getting on in the world?...All Jesus had to do was adopt and

26. Daniel Goleman, *Social Intelligence: The New Science of Human Relationships* (New York: Bantam, 2006), 118–29.

27. In the "Grand Inquisitor" parable: Fyodor Dostoyevsky, *The Brothers Karamazov*, vol. 1, trans. David Magarshack (Toronto: Penguin, 1958), 299. After detailing the inadequacies of the Savior's accomplishments, the Inquisitor adds: "We have corrected your great work and have based it on *miracle, mystery, and authority*," a phrase he later repeats (pp. 301, 305; emphasis added).

28. Ronald A. Heifetz and Marty Linsky, *Leadership on the Line: Staying Alive through the Dangers of Leading* (Boston, MA: Harvard Business School Press, 2002), ch. 8. They are concerned about leaders who do not manage those normal hungers and thus go awry.

29. This is summarized from one of Martin Luther King's last sermons at Ebenezer Baptist Church. Parts of the sermon are excerpted in Chris Hedges, *The Death of the Liberal Class* (Toronto: Knopf, 2010), 188.

> then adapt Herod's political style, his skills, his tested principles, and put them to work under the rule of God.[30]

Jesus's refusals rejected what Parker Palmer called "functional atheism," a "belief that ultimate responsibility for everything rests with us."[31] Dangers of buying into this mode, according to Palmer, include potential burnout, depression, or despair. Leadership literature regularly reflects a motivational, can-do tone about all that one might accomplish just by following certain principles. Success and relevance, popularity and spectacle, and power and control seem winsome and attractive. Nevertheless they can divert us from what is most worthwhile.

Kingdom, Disciples, and Congregants

Once launched in ministry, Jesus's earnest preaching is summarized in Matthew: "Change your hearts and lives! Here comes the kingdom of heaven!" (4:17 CEB).

> Faith in the coming of the Kingdom... implied an act of political recognition directed to Jesus himself.... To recognize God's rule was to see him as the figure who satisfied the hopes and expectations which had been vested in the reappearance of traditional monarchical leadership. In that sense the coming of the Kingdom was proved by the acknowledgment of Jesus as king.[32]

"Kingdom" is explicit political language—even if it sounds like church vocabulary now. It shows who is in charge and who ought to be ruling. This terminology is related to the repeated prophetic criticisms of how the world is run.

In the first sermon in Luke, Jesus claimed to fulfill an Isaiah prophecy:

> The Spirit of the Lord is upon me,
> because the Lord has anointed me.
> He has sent me to preach good news to the poor,
> to proclaim release to the prisoners

30. Eugene H. Peterson, *The Jesus Way: A Conversation on the Ways That Jesus Is the Way* (Grand Rapids: Eerdmans, 2007), 203.

31. Parker J. Palmer, *Let Your Life Speak: Listening for the Voice of Vocation* (San Francisco: Jossey-Bass, 2000), 88.

32. Oliver O'Donovan, *The Desire of the Nations: Rediscovering the Roots of Political Theology* (New York: Cambridge University Press, 1996), 117.

> and recovery of sight to the blind,
> to liberate the oppressed,
> and to proclaim the year of the Lord's favor. (Luke 4:18-19 CEB)

This resoundingly political sermon almost earned Jesus an early execution.

Jesus conducted his kingdom campaign through teaching.

> Jesus' teaching-ministry... is a disclosure of the reign of God, through which the authority of God asserts itself. Jesus' authority consists in this capacity to bring us directly into contact with God's authority.[33]

By unexpected teachings, worldview exploding parables, dramatic actions toward outcasts, and healing of the rejected, Jesus manifested the arrival of God's reign.

Jesus began calling individuals. Inviting people to *follow* also suggests leadership terminology; some people define leadership simply as *having followers*. The people Jesus called reveal his reign's inverse priorities. The first four, two sets of brothers (Simon Peter and Andrew, James and John) fished for a living. They were working class, probably illiterate. Later, "leaders, elders, and legal experts" recognized that the "followers of Jesus" were "uneducated and inexperienced" (Acts 4:5, 13 CEB). At that time, society could be divided into "urban ruling elites," about 1 or 2 percent (rulers, aristocrats, government and religious officials); "service class" retainers, 5 to 8 percent (lower officials, soldiers, some priests, scribes, merchants, servants to the elites); and rural peasants, 90 percent (farm workers, fishers, "laborers, and artisans, as well as radically marginalized people such as beggars, outcasts, and other 'expendables'").[34] (This is intriguing given one of Occupy's most famous slogans, "We are the 99 percent.") Jesus's disciples were mostly rural peasant class. He was regularly in conflict with the ruling urban elite.

Jesus found purpose for fishers even though they did not have worldly status or maybe *because* they did not have it. He affirmed their background, using their work as a ministry metaphor: "I'll show you how to fish for people" (Matt 4:19 CEB). He frequently used common labor—farming, housekeeping, domestic service—as images for God's reign, showing the dignity of mundane ways to make a living.

Jesus's disciples were motley, some even disreputable (e.g., Matthew the tax collector in Matt 9:9). The Old Testament tradition of designating

33. Ibid., 89.

34. Marcus J. Borg, *Conflict, Holiness, and Politics in the Teachings of Jesus*, rev. ed. (New York: Continuum, 1998), 11.

unlikely leaders here continues. Yet Christians now think strategically about recruiting others. Some believe that drawing celebrities—politicians, movie stars, entertainers, athletes—makes our faith more attractive. I confess that decades ago I was thrilled when a favorite singer-songwriter, Bob Dylan, was "born again." (In the long run the conversion did not hold, but a few good songs came out of that particular "phase.") Wanting the famous and the powerful on our side has more to do with our proclivities (success, relevance, popularity, spectacle temptations). Even disciples fell for such allurements; they tried to exclude children, but Jesus responded: "Allow the children to come to me... Don't forbid them, because the kingdom of heaven belongs to people like these children" (Matt 19:14 CEB). The shabby followers Jesus chose shows that God's criteria are not ours.

God's peculiar standards were also demonstrated by the odd company Jesus kept. Marginal people recognized Jesus's significance or received his ministry. He attracted ridicule, rejection, repulsion, and even outrage for willingness to associate with outcasts and rejects. He healed and touched lepers (Matt 8:1-4). Religious leaders disparagingly asked disciples: "Why does your teacher eat with tax collectors and sinners?" (Matt 9:11 CEB). An early compassionate act toward a disabled person turned key leaders against Jesus so that they "got together... to plan how to destroy him" (Mark 3:6 CEB). Jesus was disdained by a Pharisee when a sinful woman anointed him (Luke 7:36-50). Even Jesus's disciples were startled about his earnest heart-to-heart with a woman who was not only a Samaritan but had a disreputable moral history, thinking to themselves, "Why are you talking with her?" (John 4:27 CEB).

Jesus not only affiliated with the poor, rejected, or marginalized; he also resembled them. His itinerant ministry lifestyle isolated him from his birth family, leaving him essentially homeless: "Foxes have dens, and the birds of the air have nests, but the Human One has no place to lay his head" (Matt 8:21 CEB). This was no accident but, according to Paul, a central aspect of incarnation: "You know the grace of our Lord Jesus Christ. Although he was rich, he became poor for our sakes, so that you could become rich through his poverty" (2 Cor 8:9 CEB).[35]

The spirit of that example can be seen in Rev. Dr. Martin Luther King Jr. Rev. Billy Kyles, a close friend of King's, discussed King's accomplishments and potential: "Here was a man who earned a Ph.D. degree, a Nobel Peace Prize, had oratorical skills off the charts, and of all things he could have been, university president, senator, leader of megachurches around the country";

35. Brueggemann, *The Prophetic Imagination*, 112.

yet he died in a campaign helping "garbage workers. My God! What a way to give meaning to your life. And what a message to send to your country."[36]

Jesus had less time for those with affluence or influence, but they were not completely overlooked. There were positive interactions behind the scenes. Jesus benefitted from the support of women possibly from well-off families (Luke 8:3-4); strikingly, one had a connection to *Herod's* household. Notably, these cited supporters are *women* even though women did not have explicit power or prestige. A wealthy "good and righteous" man (Luke 23:50 CEB), Joseph of Arimathea, is named as a "disciple of Jesus" (Matt 27:57 CEB); his tomb was used for burying Jesus.

Yet wealthy, powerful people had to go out of their way to get Jesus's attention. He did not cultivate an influential network or leverage connections. He did not intentionally seek to address or minister to key powerful persons. Sadducees and Pharisees had to track him down for their questions. A centurion came to Jesus when he wanted his servant healed (Matt 8:5-13). Jairus, a synagogue leader, pursued Jesus about his fatally ill daughter (Mark 5:22-43). Herod was eager to speak to Jesus but unable to manage this except by Pilate's assistance after Jesus's arrest (Luke 23:8-12). The wealthy young *ruler* had a question but upon hearing the answer, "went away saddened" (Matt 19:22). Phil Needham remarks that Jesus "shows little or no deference for people in high positions, secular or religious; in fact, what he says about them usually brings them down a few notches."[37]

The Mutual Hostility of Jesus and the Powers-That-Be

In order to articulate a theology of leadership, we must consider Jesus's attitude toward leaders. Sarah Coakley writes: "What Jesus has to say about authorities and power, and what he demonstrates in his own acts of witness and in his passion, are absolutely crucial."[38]

Jesus's agenda was *political*, about how people relate to one another, how people lead and are led, how people function in communities and society:

---

36. Billy Kyles, interview by Bruce Feiler, in *America's Prophet: Moses and the American Story* (New York: William Morrow, 2009), 273–74.

37. Phil Needham, *When God Becomes Small* (Nashville: Abingdon, 2014), 5.

38. Sarah Coakley, "Sarah Coakley: Living Prayer and Leadership," interview by Jason Byassee, *Faith & Leadership*, August 17, 2009, www.faithandleadership.com/qa/sarah-coakley-living-prayer-and-leadership.

> Jesus cannot simply be assigned to the category of "religious preacher"; his message was... political.... To speak of the kingdom of God in a land ruled by Jewish client kings or Roman governors had clear political repercussions. So too did the selection of twelve men as representatives of the restored twelve tribes of Israel.... It should come as no surprise... that Jesus annoyed... political leaders of the day.[39]

The examples are *Legion*. Jesus was "intentionally provocative" toward leaders.[40] In the good Samaritan parable, scoundrels were a priest and a Levite. In another parable, the elder brother of the prodigal son was a thinly disguised rebuke of religious leaders. Jesus's distrust of leaders was shown in his saying: "But if a blind person leads another blind person, they will both fall into a ditch" (Matt 15:14 CEB; cf. Luke 6:39). Luke's Beatitudes included startling woes:

> But woe to you who are rich,
> . . . .
> Woe to you who are full now,
> . . . .
> Woe to you who are laughing now,
> . . . .
> Woe to you when all speak well of you, for that is what their ancestors did to the false prophets. (Luke 6:24-26)

The rich, content, merry, and well-esteemed are the privileged people in the know and in charge. Meanwhile, blessings are addressed to "nonpersons consigned to nonhistory."[41]

> Blessed are you who are poor,
> . . . .
> Blessed are you who are hungry now,
> . . . .
> Blessed are you who weep now,
> . . . .

39. Helen K. Bond, "Political Authorities: The Herods, Caiaphas, and Pontius Pilate," in *Jesus Among Friends and Enemies: A Historical and Literary Introduction to Jesus in the Gospels*, ed. Chris Keith and Larry W. Hurtado (Grand Rapids: Baker Academic, 2011), 246.

40. Anthony Le Donne, "Jewish Leaders," in *Jesus among Friends and Enemies*, 210.

41. Brueggemann, *The Prophetic Imagination*, 109.

> Blessed are you when people hate you, and when they exclude you, revile you, and defame you on account of the Son of Man. (Luke 6:20-22)

Placing blessings and woes beside each other gives a vision of two strikingly different kingdoms where vastly contrasting leadership visions prevail.

In a polemical tirade, Jesus lambasted Pharisees and scribes (Matt 23). He insisted on proper deference to the teaching ministry of those who "sit on Moses' seat" but immediately qualified that counsel by noting that those leaders/teachers "do not practice what they teach" (23:2-3). He warned against being named rabbi, father, or instructor; only God fulfills those designations. As the Old Testament cautioned against giving ultimate recognition to human kings, Jesus denounced designating humans for God's place. Matthew 23 sternly criticized scribes and Pharisees, using repeated "woes" and accusing them of hypocrisy, foolishness, and blindness: "You snakes! You children of snakes! How will you be able to escape the judgment of hell?" (Matt 23:33 CEB). Matthew 23 is Jesus's longest, sustained teaching on leadership; most of it is negative invective.

The New Testament elsewhere does teach a certain deference to leaders: "For the sake of the Lord submit to every human institution. Do this whether it means submitting to the emperor as supreme, or to governors" and even, "honor the emperor" (1 Pet 2:13-14a, 17b CEB). Yet this is not about high expectations of how leaders would behave. We pray for those with authority in that we hope (but by no means assume) that they will not unjustly persecute believers. God's created people need good rulers; "the world works best when ruled by wise stewards, human beings who are humble before God and hence effective in bringing fruitful order to his world."[42] These texts, however, do not establish a divine right of kings or justify all that rulers do.

> Saying that the creator God wants his world to be ordered under the rule of human beings is not saying that whatever human rulers do must be right. . . . All it means . . . is that human rulers are answerable to God for what they do with the power he has lent them.[43]

Texts like 1 Peter advise treating leaders with caution as leaders are dangerous.

Again and again, Jesus engaged in heated debates with Herodians, Sadducees, and Pharisees. They kept trying to entrap him, and he responded

42. Wright, *How God Became King*, 169.

43. Ibid.

with sarcasm, subterfuge, or outright anger. Not only the religious powers attracted his negative attention but also the political powers-that-be. Mention familiar names of rulers then—Herod (more than one, first the father and then the son), Pilate—and we think of cowardice, violence, connivance. Not one is exemplary. No political rulers mentioned in the Gospels or indeed in the entire New Testament are unambiguously good. Given the universality of New Testament criticism toward rulers, a strong case can be made that it is not only critiquing leaders who are named but shows that *all* people of power must be scrutinized with suspicion. Leadership as the world knows and practices is found wanting.

Jesus was deeply critical of both the religious *and* political leadership models of his day. Later, at the last supper, he sarcastically wrote off political leadership: "The kings of the Gentiles rule over their subjects, and those in authority over them are called 'friends of the people'" (Luke 22:25 CEB).[44]

Sometimes when we ponder leadership, we note that different kinds are appropriate for varying contexts. Fair enough. Jim Collins wrote a useful book called *Good to Great*, an extensive study of businesses. Later, in a small monograph, *Good to Great and the Social Sectors: Why Business Thinking is Not the Answer*, he indicated that successful business leadership is not necessarily appropriate in social service enterprises.

Some Christians speak of a "two kingdom" theology, suggesting that guidelines for Christians in personal lives (e.g., the Sermon on the Mount's high demands) do not necessarily apply to governments. A striking aspect about Jesus's leadership critiques—including the "other kingdoms" of Gentile rulers—was that he judged them by the standards of "Jesus' teaching on service and humility" and "the basis of the social patterns desired by God."[45] I am glad Jim Collins freed churches from complying with "best practices" of successful corporations, but Christian theology would suggest that even successful corporations should be judged by the high standards of God's reign!

It is no great wonder that authorities and rulers opposed Jesus. Not merely disagreeing with him, they sought his destruction. Consider this: "The chief priests, the legal experts, and the foremost leaders among the people were seeking to kill him" (Luke 19:47 CEB). Herod also wanted to

44. Richard J. Cassidy notes the sarcasm here in *Jesus, Politics, and Society: A Study of Luke's Gospel* (Eugene, OR: Wipf and Stock, 2015), 39.

45. Ibid., 60.

eliminate Jesus; a threat that prompted Jesus to refer to him scornfully as "that fox" (Luke 13:31-32 CEB).

This sort of wrath did not abate after his death. Animosity from religious and political leaders was not limited toward Jesus. Deep hostility continued against his followers. Jesus matter-of-factly warned about persecution *from leaders*: "When they bring you before the synagogues, the rulers, and the authorities..." (Luke 12:11). *When*, not *if.* Jesus observed: "They will take you into custody and harass you because of your faith; they will hand you over to synagogues and prisons, and you will be brought before kings and governors because of my name" (Luke 21:12 CEB).

Meanwhile, people recognized something different about Jesus: "The crowds were amazed at his teaching because he was teaching them like someone with authority and not like their legal experts" (Matt 7:28-29 CEB). He contradicts contemporary leadership.

On Palm Sunday, we recall people welcoming Jesus with a political chorus: "*Hosanna! Blessings on the one who comes in the name of the Lord!* Blessings on the coming kingdom of our ancestor David! Hosanna in the highest!" (Mark 11:9-10 CEB). This action is connected to Old Testament political prophecies: "Say to Daughter Zion, 'Look, your king is coming to you, humble and riding on a donkey, and on a colt the donkey's offspring' " (Matt 21:5 CEB). While there are regal elements, the emphasis is *humility*. The prospective ruler rides a donkey not a military stallion. In fact Matthew's words (alluding to Zech 9:9) explicitly include the word "humble."

The triumphal entry was soon followed by a highly charged challenge to the authorities, clearing the temple. Directly after this, "the chief priests and legal experts... tried to find a way to destroy him" (Mark 11:18 CEB). Shortly thereafter, "the chief priests, legal experts, and elders came to him. They asked, 'What kind of *authority* do you have for doing these things? Who gave you this *authority* to do them?" (Mark 11:27-28 CEB; emphasis added). Authority, of course, is a central leadership issue.

Trial and Crucifixion

The powers-that-be succeeded in having Jesus arrested, tried by both religious and secular leaders, and finally crucified.

All major religious and political power players were involved. Matthew tells us that "the chief priests and the elders of the people gathered in the courtyard of Caiphas the high priest. They were plotting to arrest Jesus by cunning tricks and to kill him" (Matt 26:3-4 CEB). Mark's similar version writes of "chief priests and the legal experts" (Mark 14:1 CEB). John pins the conspiracy on "the chief priests and the Pharisees" (John 11:45-54). Luke includes "officers of the temple guard" (Luke 22:52 CEB). John names Pharisees at the arrest (John 18:3). After an inquisition before Caiaphas, the high priest (Matt 26:57-68), "chief priests and the elders of the people" (Matt 27:1 CEB; and scribes, according to Mark) delivered him to Roman governor Pontius Pilate. Pilate sent Jesus to Herod because of jurisdictional issues (Luke 23:6-12). "In his darkest remark,... the evangelist tells us that collaboration over the case of Jesus sealed a political friendship between these two rulers (23:12). What bound them together was their mutual consciousness of impotence."[46]

A key phrase, "king of the Jews," appears over and again, making clear that the arrest, trial, conviction, and execution were *political.* This phrase was on the sign attached to the cross to explain why Jesus was executed. In the four Gospels, "king of the Jews" shows up fifteen times. Matthew and Mark each additionally use the phrase "king of Israel."

Roman soldiers abused Jesus (stripping, beating, spitting on, insulting) and executed him (Matt 27:27-31); this was all supervised by a Roman centurion (Matt 27:54). While he was on the cross, "the chief priests were making fun of him among themselves, together with the legal experts" (Mark 15:31 CEB).

What was it about Jesus that allied this diverse group of scribes, elders, chief priests, Roman officers, Roman governor, and puppet king? The point is not just that they were bad leaders or on the wrong side of a cosmic conflict. *All* contemporary leaders were mistaken and finally impotent and powerless.

These passages are a sustained, deliberate, constant, and determined attack on all who people then understood to be leaders. Jesus alluded to inverted views of power. After rebuking Peter's swordplay, Jesus said: "Or do you think that I'm not able to ask my Father and he will send me more than twelve battle groups of angels right away?" (Matt 26:53 CEB). When Pilate boastfully tried to intimidate, Jesus responded: "You would have no authority over me if it had not been given to you from above" (John 19:11 CEB). Hauerwas writes of Jesus's refusal to engage in discussion with Pilate: "The silence of Jesus before Pilate can now be understood for what it was—namely, that Jesus refuses to accept the terms of how the world understands power and authority."[47] (Dostoyevsky's "Grand Inquisitor" also has the Sav-

46. O'Donovan, *The Desire of the Nations*, 140.

47. Stanley Hauerwas, *Cross-Shattered Christ: Meditations on the Seven Last*

ior chillingly silent before his accusing persecutor.) It was not actually Jesus on trial in the Gospels but Pilate and all leaders.[48] In the end, Paul describes the effect of Jesus's suffering and execution: "When he disarmed the *rulers* and *authorities,* he exposed them to public disgrace by leading them in a triumphal parade" (Col 2:15; emphasis added).

The gruesome execution of Jesus became a coronation. "The result—the climax of the gospel, and for John the climax of Israel's entire story—is the paradoxical 'enthronement' of Jesus on the cross, the final moment of the fulfillment of the great scriptural story."[49] Authorities mocked Jesus's alleged kingship: with a robe and crown of thorns, granting him a reed scepter, kneeling and hailing the king, paying him homage (as the prior Herod once claimed he intended to do), and affixing a sign to his cross that read "king of the Jews." Brueggemann writes: "The fully energized Lord of the church is . . . the slain lamb who stood outside the royal domain and was punished for it."[50]

Ironically these events showed him to be regal. Others conspired against him and trumped up charges and employed intimidation and torture, but he remained true to his vocation, even as he suffered deeply. In the midst of pain, he ministered redemptive healing to a fellow victim who had a political request: "Jesus, remember me when you come into your kingdom" (Luke 23:42 CEB). Even a centurion was stunned by what he witnessed, exclaiming, "Truly this man was God's Son" (Matt 27:54). This political title and "exclamation is rendered even more dramatic given the likelihood that he had been in charge of Jesus' crucifixion."[51]

> Calling Jesus "God's son" echoes, of course, the voice at Jesus's baptism (1:11). But when a Roman centurion says those words, we assume he didn't know what had happened on that day. For him, the phrase "God's Son" would normally have meant one person and one person only: Tiberius Caesar, son of the "divine" Augustus. That's what the coins all said—including the coin they showed Jesus a few days before.[52]

Words (Grand Rapids: Brazos, 2011), 51.

48. Brueggemann, *The Prophetic Imagination*, 96.
49. Wright, *How God Became King*, 79.
50. Brueggemann, *The Prophetic Imagination*, 113.
51. Cassidy, *Jesus, Politics, and Society*, 72.
52. Wright, *How God Became King*, 94–95.

Jesus is "the real king and the model for how kings and people with power are to conduct themselves."[53] Expectations, convictions, and assumptions are completely overturned. Christopher P. Momany writes, "The atonement is an indictment of all that the world assumes about power."[54] The crucifixion narratives alter our view of reality and critique standard ways of thinking about leadership.

Resurrection and Ascension

The resurrection itself was a political act. The seal on the stone meant that it was illegal for the body to be moved, and thus Jesus's resurrection is actually civil disobedience![55]

The resurrection vindicated God's leadership: "the resurrection . . . declares that the cross was a victory, not a defeat. It therefore announces that God has indeed become king on earth as in heaven."[56] The resurrection demonstrated that worldly power and effectiveness do not have the last word. God's power is decisive, even in the face of apparent defeat:

> That genuinely historical event has important political dimensions, as is recognized especially in Matthew. On the one hand, it is as seen as a threat to the regime (Matt 28:11-15), whereas, on the other hand, the risen Jesus announces his new royal authority. He is now the king who displaces the king.[57]

Jesus not only rose again but ascended; another "vindication of Jesus."[58] The Apostles' Creed asserts that he "is seated at the right hand of the Father." Oliver O'Donovan observes: "The Son of Man is presented before the Ancient of Days and receives the Kingdom. Precisely because it attracts this political imagery to itself, the Ascension is of great importance to political theology."[59] And, we might add, to any Christian theology of leadership.

53. Walter Brueggemann, *Peace* (St. Louis, MO: Chalice, 2001), 97.

54. Christopher P. Momany, "Affirmation of Being," *Christian Century* 131, no. 3 (February 2014): 25.

55. Kellermann, *Seasons of Faith and Conscience*, 186.

56. Wright, *How God Became King*, 246.

57. Brueggemann, *The Prophetic Imagination*, 113.

58. Wright, *How God Became King*, 177.

59. O'Donovan, *The Desire of the Nations*, 144.

Conclusions

Each and every stage of Jesus's life and ministry as reported in the Gospels has huge implications for leadership theology. When William Stringfellow used to write or preach about church feasts or seasons—Epiphany, Holy Week, Easter—he liked to comment in his dryly mischievous way that each particular feast or season was the most political of all![60] There was truth in what he asserted, because *all* of Jesus's life and ministry were indeed highly political.

Some have attempted to fit Jesus into unlikely molds. Famously, "in 1925 advertising honcho Bruce Barton published *The Man Nobody Knows*, depicting Jesus as the ultimate entrepreneur. . . . *The Man Nobody Knows* was the number four best-selling book of 1925 and the number one best-selling book of the following year."[61] More recent attempts include *Jesus, CEO.* Such well-meant efforts are misguided because they fundamentally distort what the scriptures show about Jesus and his leadership.

Jesus briefly achieved some popularity that quickly dissipated well before he was killed. When he died, he had almost no followers. He did not win much in the way of friends or influence many people. The Bible is all about unexpected and unlikely reversals and inversions. The first are last; the cursed are blessed; one wins by losing and lives by dying. These are not ways to build guaranteed steps or create "irrefutable laws" of leadership success.

60. I spent a week in late October 1980 with Stringfellow in London, Ontario, listening to his sermons and lectures in a variety of Christian settings.

61. Feiler, *America's Prophet*, 212.

Chapter Twelve

Look Before You Lead

Counterintuitive Implications of the Leadership Teaching of Lord Jesus Christ

Faithfully Dying

A remarkable Christian witness was captured in the Academy Award–winning French film *Of Gods and Men* (2010). This account is based on events at a French Trappist monastery in Algeria during the 1990s; the background of the story is worth rehearsing.

Christian de Chergé grew up in Algeria where his father was a military officer protecting French colonial interests.[1] Not a particularly religious child, de Chergé was impressed by the devotion of Muslims. Years later, he was in Algeria as a soldier himself. In one violent encounter with local militants, an Algerian Muslim police officer, Mohammed, saved Chergé from being killed. That rescue resulted in Mohammed's assassination the next day. De Chergé converted to Christian faith, won to a vision of God's love by the sacrifice of another human.

Later ordained a priest in France, he returned to Algeria to be a monk in a Trappist monastery, eventually becoming its prior. He and the monks lived contemplatively near Muslims in the small village of Tibhirine. Tibhirinites recognized Trappist monasticism as being similar to Muslim values. (Muslims not infrequently are otherwise shocked by how little Christians pray.) De Chergé studied Islam, particularly the Qur'an.

In the 1990s, an Islamic rebel ultimatum demanded that all foreigners leave Algeria. During these turbulent years, 60,000 to 100,000 people died violently. The Trappists wrestled hard with whether to stay in the country

1. The story of de Chergé and his community is told compellingly in John W. Kiser, *The Monks of Tibhirine: Faith, Love, and Terror in Algeria* (New York: St. Martin's, 2002). Information in this section is from that book.

or leave. They knew the risk of remaining but decided that if they lost their lives to terrorism then they would make this sacrifice willingly. They opted for maintaining a prayerful witness of love and hospitality. Their monastery remained a refuge for Christians and Muslims to work, pray, and talk together.

Repeatedly, as violence against expatriates increased, well-meaning friends and reputation-conscious government officials urged the monks to depart. The Trappists stayed, declining military protection. Finally, in 1996, Islamic militants raided the monastery and kidnapped seven brothers. Only their heads were found, a little less than two months later. Some see this shocking event as a turning point in Algerian politics, one that helped gradually lead to the reduction of violence.

De Chergé left behind a letter to be opened in the event of his death. He wrote: "If the day comes... that I am a victim of the terrorism that seems to be engulfing all foreigners living in Algeria, I would like my community, my Church, and my family to remember that I have dedicated my life to God and Algeria."[2] He pleads with readers that his death not be used to caricature Islam or perpetuate violence. Islam was his "very first church"; as a child he marveled at the religious devotion of Muslims and as an adult his life was saved by the sacrifice of a Muslim police officer.[3] The letter closes with a prayer for his murderer: "And to you... my friend of the last moment,... I wish this thank-you, this 'A-Dieu,' whose image is in you also, that we may meet in heaven, like happy thieves, if it pleases God, our common Father. Amen! Insha Allah!"[4]

These contemporaries of ours exemplified crucial aspects of leadership that Jesus promoted and taught.

In the previous chapter of this book we reflected on what we can learn about leadership from Jesus's life. Besides being informed by the events and circumstances of his ministry and life, we can also benefit from his teachings on the implications of faithful leadership within God's kingdom. Jesus taught by contrasting his understandings with negative contemporary examples. We see this, for example, when he spoke of John:

> When John's disciples had gone, Jesus spoke to the crowds about John: "What did you go out to the wilderness to see? A stalk blowing in the wind? What did you go out to see? A man dressed up in refined clothes?

2. Ibid., 244.
3. Ibid., 245.
4. Ibid., 246.

> Look, those who wear refined clothes are in royal palaces." (Matt 11:7-8 CEB)

This chapter focuses particularly on four constructive themes arising from the teaching of Jesus—following, serving, suffering, and witnessing.

Disciples of Our One and Only Leader

The current faddishness of *leadership* is difficult to justify by a straightforward reading of the Gospels. Jesus had different priorities than teaching us to *lead.* "Follow," however, comes up explicitly over thirty times in the Gospels. Whether or not all of us or anyone are called to leadership is not at stake; we all are called to be followers. Discipleship is first and foremost about *following. Disciple* indicates one who follows Jesus, "a relationship that involves both commitment and cost."[5]

"Follow" is the phrase Jesus used to call people; some complied and others did not. He summarized the essence of faithfulness as being about following:

> "Those who don't pick up their crosses and follow me aren't worthy of me." (Matt 10:38 CEB)

> "All who want to come after me must say no to themselves, take up their cross, and follow me." (Matt 16:24 CEB)

> "I am the light of the world. Whoever follows me won't walk in darkness but will have the light of life." (John 8:12 CEB)

> "Whoever serves me must follow me. Wherever I am, there my servant will also be. My Father will honor whoever serves me" (John 12:26 CEB)

To be a disciple, to follow, means to learn from one's master. This relationship is not a commuter school where consumers take elective courses. It is rather an all-encompassing environment intended to change one entirely. It is not enough to go temporarily in the same direction as Jesus. Rather, to follow Jesus is a whole-hearted, life-altering commitment.

James and his brother John (like Peter and his brother Andrew ahead of them) made a radical sacrificial move to follow Jesus. They *immediately*

5. Terence Donaldson, "Guiding Readers—Making Disciples: Discipleship in Matthew's Narrative Strategy," in *Patterns of Discipleship in the New Testament,* ed. Richard N. Longenecker (Grand Rapids: Eerdmans, 1996), 44.

left behind their boat (income). Their story paralleled Peter and Andrew's but with an added detail: they also relinquished their father (family loyalty). Neither action was lightly done in that culture. Yet they showed no hesitation. Their example reminds us of when Elijah threw his mantle over Elisha while the latter was plowing; Elisha slaughtered his oxen, burned their yokes, cooked and gave away the meat. This was his first step in following Elijah, and there was no returning to his former work. James and John emulate that decisive move.

James, John, and Elisha contrasted with some later would-be followers: "Lord, first let me go and bury my father" or "let me first say farewell to those at my home" (Luke 9:59, 61). True disciples boldly embark on a course affecting the rest of their lives. They spend all their time with Jesus because they have much to learn. Jesus demanded and commanded from would-be followers an all-consuming following that nevertheless had its own rewards:

> Peter said to him, "Look, we've left everything and followed you."
>
> Jesus said, 'I assure you that anyone who has left house, brothers, sisters, mother, father, children, or farms because of me and because of the good news will receive one hundred times as much now in this life—houses, brothers, sisters, mothers, children, and farms (with harassment)—and in the coming age, eternal life."(Mark 10:28-30 CEB)

Current leadership fascinations sometimes suggest that leadership is, in and of itself, a primary goal. But for Christians, the first priority is *followership*. Some people define leadership very simply as "having followers." Yet in the Christian perspective, since *we* are followers, it can faithfully and truthfully be said that only Jesus is the leader. To paraphrase Jesus: call no one your leader on earth, for you have one leader, the Messiah himself, and you are all followers. That journey begins with an act of faithfulness, following Jesus, the place that all Christian leadership starts: following, imitating, and modeling ourselves after him.

This following is voluntary, uncoerced. Jesus does not manipulate us into obedience, threaten punishments, force our hand, torture, or punish us until we obey. He does not withhold wages or promotions; neither carrot nor stick operates here. He gives his example and invites imitation. We pattern ourselves and our lives after his paradigmatic model. Outside the Gospels and Acts, *imitation* language is employed in the New Testament to describe what is required. Ultimately, discipleship is about how we become like Jesus and, in fact, resemble God.[6]

Challenges of following Jesus and imitating God are not only how we grow in and with Jesus. They show how we are to lead as well. John Stott says: "The Christian leads by example, not force, and is to be a model who invites a following, not a boss who compels one."[7]

Priority of Service

Jesus never explicitly said that we are to be leaders but commanded us all—specifically in contrast to the leaders and rulers of this age—to be *servants*.[8] This servanthood instruction may be his *most important* term when speaking of leadership; "leadership means service, understood as taking up the role of a servant."[9]

Servanthood language has infiltrated leadership literature. *Servant leadership* was popularized by Quaker-influenced Robert Greenleaf. We might assume he got his notion from Jesus, but he attributed it to Hermann Hesse's Buddhist-inspired book, *Journey to the East*.[10]

Service, in the Gospels, has to do with being vulnerable and at the disposal of a higher cause. We hear a lot about "public *service*" but that phrase is not always clear. I am alarmed by how many politicians leave office to become wealthy consultants. In these cases, the meaning of "service" is demeaned. When Jesus commissioned disciples, his instructions included the following: "You received without having to pay. Therefore, give without demanding payment. Workers deserve to be fed, so don't gather gold or silver or copper coins for your money belts to take on your trips. Don't take a backpack for the road or two shirts or sandals or a walking stick" (Matt 10:9-10 CEB). The disciples go on a demanding excursion with little in

6. See L. Ann Jervis, "Becoming like God through Christ: Discipleship in Romans," in Longenecker, *Patterns of Discipleship in the New Testament*, 144.

7. John R. W. Stott, *The Message of 1 Timothy and Titus: Guard the Truth* (Downers Grove, IL: InterVarsity, 1996), 120.

8. Siang-Yang Tan, "The Primacy of Servanthood," in *The Three Tasks of Leadership: Worldly Wisdom for Pastoral Leaders*, ed. Eric O. Jacobsen (Grand Rapids: Eerdmans, 2009), 78. In John, Jesus once sets aside the term "servant," calling disciples "friends" instead.

9. Alan G. Padgett, *As Christ Submits to the Church: A Biblical Understanding of Leadership and Mutual Submission* (Grand Rapids: Baker Academic, 2011), 52.

10. Robert K. Greenleaf, "Introduction," in *On Becoming a Servant Leader*, ed. Don M. Frick and Larry C. Spears (San Francisco: Jossey-Bass, 1996), 5.

the way of provisions or official authority. They are vulnerably reliant on circumstances and strangers.

Service and servant language loom large in the Gospels. Consider Mary's response to Gabriel: "Here am I, the servant of the Lord; let it be with me according to your word" (Luke 1:38). Jesus contrasted contemporary rulers when he speaks of servanthood as priority.

> But Jesus called them over and said, "You know that those who rule the Gentiles show off their authority over them and their high-ranking officials order them around. But that's not the way it will be with you. Whoever wants to be great among you will be your servant. Whoever wants to be first among you will be your slave—just as the Human One didn't come to be served but rather to serve and to give his life to liberate many people." (Matt 20:25-28 CEB)

The emphasis is clear.

> But the one who is greatest among you will be your servant. (Matt 23:11 CEB)

> Whoever wants to be first must be least of all and the servant of all. (Mark 9:35 CEB)

Jesus also used servanthood metaphorically for teaching: "The kind of work used by Jesus for analogies and insights into the kingdom of God is servant's work."[11] He showed that roles demeaned in the eyes of the world nevertheless have great worth.

Jesus was not inviting us to be mindless automatons. Rather, service is the heart of what Jesus himself chose and was about, as Paul reminds us:

> Adopt the attitude that was in Christ Jesus:
> Though he was in the form of God,
> he did not consider being equal with God as something to exploit.
> But he emptied himself
> by taking the form of a slave
> and by becoming like human beings.
> When he found himself in the form of a human,
> he humbled himself by becoming obedient to the point of death,
> even death on a cross. (Phil 2:5-8 CEB)

---

11. Lucy Bregman, *The Ecology of Spirituality: Meanings, Virtues, and Practices in a Post-Religious Age* (Waco, TX: Baylor University Press, 2014), 214.

We are called to follow Jesus in this stance, to imitate him; this is how God works. This in itself is a startling critique of how leaders normally act. Philippians 2 is

> a thoroughly political image concerned with the willing surrender of power; it is the very thing kings cannot do and yet remain kings. Thus the entire royal self-understanding is refuted. The empty one who willingly surrendered power for obedience is the ultimately powerful one who can permit humanness where no other has authority to do so.[12]

Jesus repeatedly lived out reversals that do not make sense by worldly calculations of effectiveness. The first shall be last; the last shall be first. The least are the greatest. Or the phrase that Paul attributed to Jesus: "It is more blessed to give than to receive" (Acts 20:35 CEB). Christians are not in the business of promoting ourselves, putting our interests first. We are not to follow the example of Pharisees, who "loved human praise more than God's glory" (John 12:43 CEB).

These are startling admonitions in the context of leadership literature. We may regard leaders as people who assert themselves, put themselves forward, make their cases persuasively, build an online presence. Many of my seminary students concluded that they are not leaders and not fit to be leaders. Some pulled back because of temperament; "typical leadership" actions and attitudes do not come naturally for introverts, for example. But there are also theological reasons for caution. What looks like a temperamental disadvantage in the wider world's understanding of leadership may actually be an advantage when trying to lead faithfully according to Jesus Christ's model.

Christian service goes in two directions at once: both serving God and serving neighbors, worship and work. Thus we fulfill the two great commandments. This is especially important to remember for anyone in charge of institutions. Just as humans are called to serve God and others, our institutions are called to be directed to the same ends, praising God and caring for God's creatures and creation.

These unified priorities, worship and work, offer an important caution. Institutions—even "Christian" ones—can become preoccupied with survival as a goal and end. William Stringfellow and Jacques Ellul, among others, address this issue. Stringfellow believed institutional self-preservation could undermine ministry. Institutions are prone to forget that they exist

12. Walter Brueggemann, *The Prophetic Imagination*, 2nd ed. (Minneapolis: Augsburg Fortress, 2001), 98.

for the service of others. Any aspiring "Christian" endeavor must realize that survival is not a primary priority. Jesus called us to be willing to lose our lives, power, successes, reputations. Stringfellow's harshest criticisms were directed at so-called "Christian" institutions. He scathingly described churches "so entrapped in preserving and proliferating a cumbersome, costly, self-serving, officious, indulgent, soft ecclesiastical apparatus that it becomes easy to think that they don't have to care about the world any more since they are so much consumed in caring for themselves." In this way, he said, churches "most resemble the worldly principalities and powers."[13]

Ellul warned against becoming too reliant on—or too devoted toward—institutions: "Once a movement becomes an institution, it is lost."[14] He was particularly concerned when the church prioritized "developing and strengthening itself institutionally."[15] He was convinced that inevitable administrative implications of institutionalization contradicted gospel imperatives of worshipping God and serving God's priorities in the world.[16]

In many languages, the same word, *service*, is used for both worship of God and attending to others' needs. Praising and worshipping God is not separate from caring for and loving fellow humans and God's creation; together they are our primary purpose.

Servants Suffer

While leadership literature prefers to focus on success, Jesus soberly cautions: faithful Christians, servant followers of Jesus, *suffer*.

Church websites are prone to announce and describe their staff members' *passions*: activities, objects, hobbies, or priorities that fill them with energy and motivation. These passions range from bungee jumping to Starbucks coffee to antique cars to wondering about faith, tackling "impossible" challenges, and discipling believers. Having passions apparently makes organizations more attractive. In Christian terms, however, *passion* refers to suffering and affliction, what Jesus endured in his final days. Think of Mel Gibson's film *The Passion of Christ* (2004) or of medieval passion plays.

13. William Stringfellow, *A Private and Public Faith* (Eugene, OR: Wipf and Stock, 1999), 74–75.

14. Jacques Ellul, *Perspectives on Our Age: Jacques Ellul Speaks on His Life and Work*, ed. Willem H. Vanderburg, 2nd ed. (Toronto: House of Anansi, 2004), 20.

15. Jacques Ellul, *The Humiliation of the Word* (Grand Rapids: Eerdmans, 1985), 190.

16. Jacques Ellul, *The Subversion of Christianity* (Grand Rapids: Eerdmans, 1986), 21.

Realistic assessment of likely *suffering* can frighten people away from service. Numerous people called by God in the scriptures knew there would be a cost: "This is going to hurt. I'm going to suffer." Jesus encountered reluctant prospective followers. In the Old Testament, eventual prophets were frequently ambivalent about their calling. Moses tried to get out of what God wanted; Jonah too. Jeremiah complained at length about his calling:

> Lord, you enticed me, and I was taken in.
> You were too strong for me, and you prevailed.
> Now I'm laughed at all the time;
> everyone mocks me. (Jer 20:7 CEB)

The Hebrew here is rougher and rawer than the polite CEB; Jeremiah complained of being seduced if not actually *raped*! Probably not the kind of passion we want to proclaim in social media.

Paul connected faithful suffering with what Jesus experienced. Central to 2 Corinthians, the theme of adversity comes up in most chapters:

> "The sufferings of Christ overflow to us" (1:5); "we always carry around the dying of Jesus" (4:10); "we groan, longing to be clothed with our heavenly dwelling" (5:2); "as servants of God we commend ourselves through great endurance in troubles, hardships, and distresses" (6:4); "when we came into Macedonia . . . we were harassed at every turn" (7:5); "I have known hunger and thirst . . . I have been cold and naked" (11:27); "I delight in weakness, insults, hardships, persecutions, and difficulties" (12:10); and "we are weak in him" (13:4).[17]

In the early church, numerous people we now regard as commendable saints resisted ordination. They did not count themselves worthy enough or up for the challenges. Prospective ministers fled to the desert and hid in caves rather than accept church leadership. This was not because they did not believe in ordination. Nor was it because they liked spelunking or wilderness hiking ("passions" one could put on a webpage). They knew how hard it would be to accept this office. Frequently a church crowd would locate the Jonah-like candidate and drag him (always a him then) back to town, sometimes in chains, and *forcibly* ordain him! Christopher Beeley claims all "major early pastoral theologians sought to avoid priestly office

17. Linda L. Belleville, "'Imitate Me, Just as I Imitate Christ': Discipleship in the Corinthian Correspondence," in Longenecker, *Patterns of Discipleship in the New Testament*, 133.

in one way or another, on account of its challenges and burdens."[18] Ordination dodgers include Augustine, Gregory Nazianzen, John Chrysostom, Ambrose, and Gregory the Great.

Mark 10:35-45 is one of only a few explicit Gospel passages about leadership. It begins with James and John making a request about their leadership: "Allow one of us to sit on your right and the other on your left when you enter your glory" (CEB). They misconstrued the nature of "glory." Jesus explains that they will drink the same cup and receive the same baptism, that is, *suffer* like him. Finally, Jesus shows how worldly rulers are self-serving, concluding that his own leadership is about being a servant and slave and giving "his life to liberate many people" (Mark 10:45 CEB).

Suffering and service time and again go together. (When joined, we speak of *sacrifice.*) Isaiah's suffering servant songs are frequently applied to Jesus. Jesus foretold his own affliction and death. His passion predictions were met with denial and even rejection by his closest followers.

This kind of resistance is portrayed dramatically in Matthew 16. Peter was at first commended for correctly naming Jesus's identity: "Happy are you, Simon son of Jonah, because no human has shown this to you. Rather my Father who is in heaven has shown you" (Matt 16:17 CEB). More lavish praise quickly follows. But when Jesus predicted his suffering, Peter, perhaps emboldened by the recent affirmation, "took hold of Jesus and, scolding him, began to correct him: 'God forbid, Lord! This won't happen to you.' " Jesus turned on Peter: "Get behind me, Satan. You are a stone that could make me stumble, for you are not thinking God's thoughts but human thoughts." (Matt 16:22-23 CEB).

Passion predictions implicated worldly leaders. In Matthew 16 Jesus foretold that "he had to go to Jerusalem and suffer many things from elders, chief priests, and legal experts" (16:21 CEB). He would suffer because of the *leaders of his day*, just as cousin John was executed by a king. The promise of persecutions serves as a "radical criticism" and "ultimate criticism" of the "royal consciousness" and the usual "dominant theories of power"; they "are the decisive dismissal of every self-serving form of power."[19]

Many Christians integrate the reality of Jesus's suffering into their theology. Yet we are also invited to *imitate* Jesus in his passion; not only did he suffer for and with us, but we will suffer also. Faithfulness results in our

18. Christopher A. Beeley, *Leading God's People: Wisdom from the Early Church for Today* (Grand Rapids: Eerdmans, 2012), 25.

19. Brueggemann, *The Prophetic Imagination*, 95.

own costly service, too, whether we choose it or not. Our suffering, our cross, is not just any kind of sorrow and mourning—bad bosses, illness, unpleasant in-laws, family problems. No, it is about cruciform *consequences* of faithfulness. Furthermore, adversity—like Jesus's tribulation—will be at the hands of leaders. The disciples are explicitly warned: "Watch out for people—because they will hand you over to councils and they will beat you in their synagogues. They will haul you in front of governors and even kings because of me" (Matt 10:17-18 CEB).

This suffering directly results from faithfully proclaiming Jesus, and our affliction resembles his in that way. Much of 1 Peter is a rehearsal of the link between Christ's passion and ours. Consider, for example, 1 Peter 2:21-23:

> You were called to this kind of endurance, because Christ suffered on your behalf. He left you an example so that you might follow in his footsteps. He committed no sin, nor did he ever speak in ways meant to deceive. When he was insulted, he did not reply with insults. When he suffered, he did not threaten revenge. Instead, he entrusted himself to the one who judges justly. (CEB)

On the basis of such passages, a minority of Christians (e.g., peace church traditions that include Mennonites and Quakers) discerned a gospel mandate to peacemaking, nonresistance, and nonviolence—never returning violence for violence, never using deadly force, not even in the most righteous causes. In the New Testament one does not find examples of a believer faithfully employing violence in self-defense but many instances of believers being unjustly victimized.

The ancient church was matter-of-fact about the centrality of suffering. It honored the memory—and testimonies—of martyrs. It prioritized the witness of confessors, those who paid a high cost for the faith.

This call to embrace suffering might be the gospel's most difficult aspect. The important phrase "follow me" includes a readiness to embrace the pain inflicted upon Jesus: "Those who don't pick up their crosses and follow me aren't worthy of me. Those who find their lives will lose them, and those who lose their lives because of me will find them" (Matt 10:38-39 CEB). In so doing, we join God's kingdom work: "Instead, rejoice as you share Christ's suffering. You share his suffering now so that you may also have overwhelming joy when his glory is revealed" (1 Pet 4:13 CEB).

Be My Witnesses

A fourth aspect of the leadership that Jesus commended can be summed up in the word *witness*. Our role is not to draw attention to or promote ourselves. Rather, we point to Jesus, orienting others to the reign of God. Jesus told the apostles: "You will be my witnesses in Jerusalem, in all Judea and Samaria, and to the ends of the earth" (Acts 1:8b). In fact "witness" terms are used almost two dozen times in the book of Acts alone.[20]

This stance is exemplified in John the Baptist. When questioned about his identity and purpose, he denied being the Messiah, Elijah, or even "the prophet." He summed up his function by citing Isaiah:

> "*I am a voice crying out in the wilderness,*
> *Make the Lord's path straight,*
> just as the prophet Isaiah said." (John 1:23 CEB)

John came "to testify concerning the light" (1:7 CEB) and "John testified about him" (1:15 CEB). The Greek word for "testimony" is *martyria* and can also mean "witness," obviously related to the term *martyr*.

Much of Jesus's training and equipping of disciples was to prepare them to be able to give witness to the reign of God.

These central marks of a Christian—following, serving, suffering, and witnessing—also must be at the heart of our understanding of Christian leadership.

---

20. C. Kavin Rowe, *World Upside Down: Reading Acts in the Graeco-Roman Age* (New York: Oxford University Press, 2010), 120.

Chapter Thirteen

They Laid Hands on Them

Early Emergence of Christian Leadership

Multiplying Titles

The longer I live, the more titles I acquire. Some people call me "pastor," "teacher," "reverend," "professor," or "doctor." Since becoming an Anglican priest, now not only my children refer to me as "father." Such titles always give me pause. After all, Jesus sternly warned against calling people "rabbi," "father," "instructor." Am I a stumbling block to others' faithfulness when they address me in such ways?

I have gradually come to an uneasy peace with all of this. I tell both students and parishioners that how they address me is up to them. Some call me by titles, others do not. (Sometimes it depends on culture; in Toronto many people are from countries where deference is prioritized.) No matter, as far as I am concerned.

I am reluctant to employ my titles. In commercial transactions I never tell people that I am "Reverend Boers" or "Father Boers." Nor do I invite students to call me "Professor" or "Doctor." (I admit, though, to being pleased when they address me as "Pastor.") Titles, as I see them, should be put at the service and for the good of others. I might cite them when I contact a hospital about someone. Similarly, when advocating for a person at a disadvantage, especially when dealing with bureaucracy, I cheerfully use titles. It is like the first time I wore a clerical shirt: I was visiting a local jail and figured that garb might help me with police officers in heavily Catholic Chicago.

Titles are about *power* and power leaves many ambivalent. I am amused by how many important people have official e-mail addresses that informally employ their first name: FirstName@MajorInstitution.org. This suggests an accessible intimacy that is perhaps attractive but deeply untrue. For the last forty-plus years in North America, we've experienced a growing fascination with informality and deceptive egalitarianism. People with power need to recognize and deal responsibly with the potential and actual authority they hold. That we have it is clear, whether we like that fact or not.

In one seminary where I taught, many prospective pastors were irresolute about authority. Their denomination permitted people to be ministers without ordination; numerous graduates put off ordination, some never accepting it. A number of them sincerely asserted that this was for good sound theological reasons (e.g., everyone is called to ministry and no one should be singled out). "In recent decades, . . . some have suggested that in order to promote the ministry of all the baptized and to strengthen the people of God, ordained leaders need to get out of the way, or relinquish their duties—the idea being that strong laity require weak or absent clergy."[1] Sometimes this is defended as an implication of "the priesthood of all believers." Believers' priesthood (the doctrine that none of us need a mediator other than Jesus Christ) does not necessarily mean that there are no specific gifts, roles, offices, or responsibilities within church life.[2] Like Christopher Beeley, I reject the idea "that the success and well-being of both leaders and people inevitably conflict with one another—that the church is, in short, a zero-sum game, where one person's good or voice or authority can only exist at the expense of another's."[3]

Ironically, those who are never ordained can do more harm and easily avoid accountability. I once heard a pastor (who resisted ordination) change the trinitarian formula of baptism. Upon inquiry I learned that he had done this on his own initiative, not having consulted with other church leaders or authorities, either in that congregation or the denomination. This minister, then, single-handedly altered the classic formula and put himself out of step with what the church has long held to be important.

---

1. Christopher A. Beeley, *Leading God's People: Wisdom from the Early Church for Today* (Grand Rapids: Eerdmans, 2012), 11.

2. I agree with Beeley that a significant

> confusion is the belief that pastoral authority is about bossing people around and seeking one's own honor and prestige. . . . Pastoral authority is never meant to inflate the egos of leaders at the expense of those they lead. . . . Such treatment is very far from the power of Jesus Christ, and in fact it betrays an underlying *lack* of strength, and an absence of real authority. (Ibid., 12)

3. Ibid., 18.

Power is a fact, a reality, whether recognized or not. When we do not acknowledge it, power grows less accountable and more hazardous. The point of ordination is not that the candidate's personality is so holy that he or she deserves unique status. Rather, the minister now puts his or her gifts and capacities at the church's service. It is problematic for a pastor to alter baptism's time-tested formula, thinking that he or she has the individual authority to do this; that pastor puts church traditions at his or her own service. An ordained minister is continually reminded—by virtue of ordination—that he or she is just not that special.

MaryKate Morse delineates four kinds of social power: expert, character, role, culture.[4] Titles refer to one or more of these. *Expert* has to do with knowledge, education, experience—perhaps achieving an MDiv or other seminary degree. *Character* deals with how others perceive one's attributes. *Role* is about one's place in an organization (e.g., treasurer, CEO, rector). *Culture* covers what's valued in a group, congregation, organization, denomination, or nation; students from certain places accord me deference and respect simply because I am a teacher. It does not work to ignore such forms of power; they cannot be easily discarded. Korean students may bow to me whether I am comfortable with that or not. Traditional Anglicans call me "Father," no matter what I think of the practice. So the question is: *How* do we deal with our power and be good stewards of it?

It does not suffice to ignore titles and pretend one does not have certain kinds of power, playing at being "just one of the gang." That is the opposite error of clinging to power for the sake of "influence." Our power always must be at the service of God's reign, especially on behalf of the marginalized, the voiceless, the vulnerable.

This is how I read some unusual Bible stories about privilege. The Esther narrative is not a fairy tale story where a commoner, a Jew no less, is elevated to be a queen. Esther is willing to risk all—title and life—for her people. The risk pays off, but she would not have thought her life a failure if she were executed. She said matter-of-factly, "if I am to die, then die I will" (Esth 4:16 CEB). Survival is not a biblical priority. She is convinced by Mordecai that her privilege and access to the king needed to serve others: "Maybe it was for a moment like this that you came to be part of the royal family" (Esth 4:14b CEB).

The Old Testament has other stories of Jews in unlikely positions of influence in a foreign place: Joseph (first with Potiphar and then with Pharaoh), Moses (rescued by Pharaoh's daughter), Daniel and the other young

4. MaryKate Morse, *Making Room for Leadership: Power, Space and Influence* (Downers Grove, IL: InterVarsity, 2008), 43–47.

men, and Nehemiah. In each case, they served God's purposes and priorities. Shadrach, Meshach, and Abednego refused to bend the knee and were not worried about whether God would save them:

> We don't need to answer your question. If our God—the one we serve—is able to rescue us from the furnace of flaming fire and from your power, Your Majesty, then let him rescue us. But if he doesn't, know this for certain, Your Majesty: we will never serve your gods or worship the gold statue you've set up. (Dan 3:16b-18 CEB)

There was no whiff of "leveraging" advantages and position. For Christians, privilege is only a priority for promoting the faith and advocating for and protecting the vulnerable. It is not to be pursued for itself, certainly not for our own benefit or advantage.

The *kenōsis* (self-emptying) hymn of Philippians 2 offers perspective. There we learn that Christ did not regard "being equal with God" (a designation generally applied then to kings) "as something to exploit" (CEB). Hellerman points out that this can be translated: "did not consider this position of equality with God as something to be used for his own advantage."[5] Positions of power and priority are not necessarily problematic. Certainly not for Christ. Many believers were also thrust into responsibility. But the New Testament constantly cautions against using such advantages for our own benefit. They ought always be at the service and for the good of others.

Acts and Early Church Leadership

Looking at Jesus and leadership is one challenge; another is to consider early church leadership, especially among the first apostolic communities. Many New Testament texts (primarily epistles) were written *before* the Gospels and Acts. So early various forms of church leadership were already in play—and possibly being commented upon—when the Gospels were composed.

For several years, my wife and I attended a congregation that centered on an intentional community; a few dozen families pooled and shared incomes. They lived in a poor neighborhood in large households and had few private possessions. Lorna and I were never able to make such a commitment; the sacrifice felt too great. Yet we were impressed by the dedication of a congregation that based itself on literally imitating the first church:

5. Joseph H. Hellerman, *Embracing Shared Ministry: Power and Status in the Early Church and Why It Matters Today* (Grand Rapids: Kregel, 2013), 144.

"All the believers were united and shared everything. They would sell pieces of property and possessions and distribute the proceeds to everyone who needed them" (Acts 2:44-45 CEB). Like many such communities founded in the 1970s, this one eventually lost its communal focus. Yet such idealism still animates a number of impressive church models today, including monasticism, the Bruderhof, and Reba Place.

Throughout church history, renewal movements longed to return to the pristine early church. Yet carefully reading Acts and the Epistles disabuses us of the idea that those early communities were full of harmony and exemplary behavior. There were conflicts aplenty and startling sinning too. People struggled with what it meant to be faithful. Leadership and authority were unclear. Early Christians fumbled and stumbled, just like we do now. The early church was influenced by a wider culture that stressed hierarchy, one that was heavily class conscious.

For example, a perennial problem was that Christians could be tempted to play favorites with patrons or other powerful people. Sometimes this was based on appearances. The book of James notes the hazard of partiality to richly dressed people versus those who are shabbily attired. Clothing was "a public status symbol," as New Testament scholar Joseph Hellerman reminds us. The Philippians 2 emphases on Jesus setting aside the "form of God" and "taking the form of a slave" have to do with "outward appearance." Thus Paul made a radical claim about Jesus sacrificing his visible rank and standing; this is not just theological but ethical. Similarly to James, Paul warned against favoring important people and advocated becoming like Jesus in giving honor where the world sees dishonor: "Adopt the attitude that was in Christ Jesus" (Phil 2:5 CEB).[6] After all, as James wrote: "Hasn't God chosen those who are poor by worldly standards to be rich in terms of faith? Hasn't God chosen the poor as heirs of the kingdom he has promised to those who love him?" (Jas 2:5 CEB).

It is difficult to extract a definitive New Testament church leadership model. I have been closely acquainted with various systems: autonomous congregational networks, hierarchical episcopacies, collegial Presbyterian arrangements. Every manifestation claims biblical authority and precedent. Some claim to be the *only accurate* rendering of New Testament intentions. Historians of the early church joke about this; one commented that efforts to found denominational structures on the New Testament era over and over result in seeing "the investigator's own denominational face at the bottom of a deep

6. Ibid., 39.

well."[7] No clear models can be derived from the lists of roles and possible offices: apostles, prophets, overseers/bishops, teachers, elders, deacons, widows, virgins, exhorters, miracle workers, healers.

Our understanding of many of these roles is vague. In Acts 1, for example, it is decided that they need another apostle (to replace Judas, who betrayed Jesus and committed suicide). Matthias was chosen by lot. While the Amish still use lots to choose ministers (as many Mennonite congregations also did until well into the twentieth century), this is not a form of discernment that commends itself to many of us today. And Matthias, we note, is never heard from again in the scriptures. We are not sure what his role was or why it was necessary to appoint him or someone like him.

A few chapters later, unequal treatment leads to a need for practical service. The apostles asserted: "It isn't right for us to set aside proclamation of God's word in order to serve tables" (Acts 6:2 CEB). They said that they needed to "devote ourselves to prayer and the service of proclaiming the word" (6:4 CEB) and chose (no mention of a lot) seven people "of good standing, full of the Spirit and of wisdom" (6:3). We connect this practical ministry position with the term *deacon*.[8] "Deacon" itself is not explicitly mentioned here as it is elsewhere in the New Testament, but the Greek word for "wait on" or "serve" is *diakonia*. The first name in the list of these servants is Stephen, "a man endowed by the Holy Spirit with exceptional faith" (6:5 CEB). The next thing we know about him is that he, "who stood out among the believers for the way God's grace was at work in his life and for his exceptional endowment with divine power, was doing great wonders and signs among the people" (6:8 CEB). So he was not confined to practical table service. He was arrested, preached mightily, and became the first in the church to be killed for the faith, our protomartyr. Intriguingly, six more table-servers are named. Only one, Philip,

7. Frances Young, "Ministerial Forms and Functions in the Church Communities of the Greek Fathers," in *Community Formation in the Early Church and in the Church Today*, ed. Richard N. Longenecker (Peabody, MA: Hendrickson, 2002), 157. Or this: "In the history of the study of church order one constantly finds explicit or implicit statements of the writer's own fundamental convictions and of the direct ecclesial interest motivating the work" (Alistair C. Stewart, *The Original Bishops: Office and Order in the First Christian Communities* [Grand Rapids: Baker Academic, 2014], 12).

8. In some traditions, deacons are laypeople appointed from a congregation to care for financial and practical needs in the congregation. In episcopal traditions (those with bishops), deacons are the first of three orders of ministry. (Next are priests, then bishops.)

shows up another time; the others are never heard from again. For most, their significance goes no further than that original appointment.

These leadership selection narratives did not provide precedent-setting models. They demonstrated the inevitable necessity of official forms of leadership. Some of my more radical church friends believe that setting apart someone—or some people—to be in charge is a compromise. Acts, however, is more matter-of-fact. Such appointments began before Pentecost, happened in the early flushes of ecstatic church life when the Spirit came upon the believers, and continued as more and more churches emerged. Leaders were set apart by laying on of hands (Acts 6:6; 13:3). (In a delightful overlap of language, the KJV uses "laid hands on them" also when designating *arrests*! See 4:3; 5:18; 21:7.)

At this time of creativity, flux, and entrepreneurial experimentation, there were no fixed models. No matter what church organizing system we now embrace, "the only head of any congregation, of any diocese, of the universal church, is Christ; of him and of his mysteries are we stewards and servants."[9] Wanting church leadership arrangements to be biblical is commendable; however, the New Testament offers no definitive blueprint.

Sketching the Sketchiness of New Testament and Political Leadership

A further observation is in order. While much of the Old Testament involved explicitly political leaders and while a number of political leaders are referenced in the Gospels (almost always negatively), little is said about political leaders in the New Testament outside of the Gospels and Acts.

Most of what is written about political leaders is how to get along with them given their potential for persecution and great damage. Romans 13 is the New Testament's lengthiest, most positive statement about political rulers, encouraging subjection to "the authority of the government": "So pay everyone what you owe them. Pay the taxes you owe, pay the duties you are charged, give respect to those you should respect, and honor those you should honor" (Rom 13:1, 7 CEB). Some authors note that Romans 13 is best read and held in tension with Revelation 13, a startling text that shows how terrifying governments ("the Beast") can be.[10] Ever since Stalin's

9. Stewart, *The Original Bishop*, 356.

10. See, e.g., William Stringfellow, *Conscience and Obedience: The Politics of Romans 13 and Revelation 13 in Light of the Second Coming* (Eugene, OR: Wipf and Stock, 2004).

terrors, Nazism's holocaust, Mao's mass starvations, the Khmer Rouge's annihilations—to name just a few twentieth-century *leader-mandated* slaughters—we can no longer be naive about the truly evil possibilities of the state and those in charge. "It is a disturbing paradox of modern history that, parallel to the advance of so-called Enlightenment and autonomy in the modern world, there has emerged wave after wave of irrational authoritarianism and repression."[11]

While the New Testament has advice for relating to political leaders, there is no explicit counsel for the rulers themselves. There is Old Testament material about how kings should behave: for example, Deuteronomy 17 and prophetic confrontations. But we do not find corresponding material in the New Testament.

Why not?

The simplest answer is that at this point no political rulers were believers.

Other interpretations are possible. For example, New Testament writers may have found it inconceivable that Christians would ever hold political office and thus did not address the possibility. There was an early presumption that should a governing official become a believer, he or she must give up the position. In the church's earliest centuries, government officials who wanted to be baptized first had to relinquish their offices. The third-century *Apostolic Tradition* document, for example, makes clear that certain professions (including sorcerers, prostitutes, and magistrates) were not eligible for baptism without a change in occupation.

Some Christian traditions argue that the New Testament shows that there is something deeply awry in the idea of Christians possessing coercive political power. Many Anabaptists, for example, not only are suspicious of the possibility of faithfully holding government office but also abstain from voting. As counterintuitive as all of this might seem, there are serious Christian thinkers (not just Anabaptists) who argue that it is impossible for a Christian to be at one and the same time a faithful disciple of Jesus Christ and a responsible president of the United States, for example.[12] This is not a

11. Paul D. L. Avis, *Authority, Leadership and Conflict in the Church* (London: Mowbray, 1992), 42.

12. Clarence Jordan considered being president completely incompatible with being a Christian. See my article, "The Prophet or the President?," *The Other Side* 24, no. 1 (January/February 1988): 32–36.

See also United Methodist Bill Wylie Kellermann, *Seasons of Faith and Conscience* (Eugene, OR: Wipf and Stock, 2008), 101–2; and Episcopalian William Stringfellow, *An Ethic for Christians and Other Aliens in a Strange Land* (Waco, TX:

question of arguing about whether or not Jimmy Carter or George W. Bush were sincere in their claims of being born again; it is rather the simple assertion that there are inherent irreconcilable contradictions between honoring the Sermon on the Mount and being the commander-in-chief of the most powerful military in all of history.

Those are debates for others elsewhere; we simply note that since the New Testament offers only sketchy counsel at best for political rulers and leadership, we cannot be too cocksure that the Bible has an unconditional positive regard of the potentials of public office.

Paul's Challenging Context for Leadership

When considering New Testament leadership, aside from looking at Jesus and the Gospels, Paul emerges as a primary focus. His conversion, subsequent ministry, arrest, and jail time get considerable attention in Acts. Besides, more New Testament books are ascribed to him than to anyone else (even including only those that scholars are *sure* that he wrote). He was key in brokering an agreement that helped the church through a major crisis (Acts 15). His preaching, as in Athens, was creative and innovative. He was instrumental in establishing new churches beyond Palestine. He more than anyone helped make clear that Gentiles were to be included in the church and were also beneficiaries of the redeeming reconciling work of Jesus the Christ.

In spite of striking accomplishments, Paul is not always admired by Christians. His attitude toward women has been much scrutinized and debated. Some lament that Paul is too authoritarian, a stance incompatible with contemporary egalitarianism. Others contend that during Paul's time, the church in its increasing institutionalization already began to fall away from the glorious early days when it was characterized by love, charismatic signs, and wonders.

Criticisms of Paul can be anachronistic. Failing to understand his context, we try to apply twenty-first-century understandings of democracy,

---

Word, 1973), 88–89. They argue—using Pauline Ephesian powers and principalities terminology—that the entrenched dynamics, priorities, and momentum of powerful institutions (political parties, the Pentagon, and so on) cannot be overcome, no matter an elected official's good intentions, good will, or political resolve. Kellermann writes of "the fundamental impotence, even incapacitation, of the president. To sit in that office is to live at the vortex of incredibly powerful forces, material and spiritual" (*Seasons of Faith and Conscience*, 101). I marvel that while one of President Barack Obama's first promises was to close Guantanamo, he never achieved that straightforward commitment, in spite of all his supposed presidential power.

equality, group process, and psychology to what he did or said. Not surprisingly, he is found wanting and does not always appear in a favorable light. We might not agree with him about women, but at the very least we need to understand how women were treated in the cultures where he was working before we can evaluate his stances.

Thus when we consider how Paul exercised and spoke of leadership, it is appropriate to investigate how leadership was understood in the wider context. Andrew Clarke shows a number of factors deeply impacting Christian perspectives: voluntary associations, families and households, Jewish synagogues, and Greco-Roman city assemblies.[13] The latter, by the way, were called *ecclesia*, the same word that the New Testament uses for "church," thus showing the influence of a contemporary political arrangement on the church's self-perception.

There is neither time nor space to explore all of Clarke's findings and insights, but a short summary is helpful to our considerations[14]:

- Greco-Roman assemblies (*ecclesia*) were civic assemblies but usually run by wealthy people and controlled by elites, leaders preoccupied with their own status and reputation.
- Roman colonies and cities were ruled by officials elected because "of their status and wealth."
- Voluntary associations did not necessarily include only elites, yet they tended toward hierarchy, honor, and status.
- Roman families gave great authority to the *paterfamilias* who headed the household. There were marked differences between how slaves and free people were treated.
- Jewish synagogues adopted wider cultural values by according great honor and respect to leaders: people who were wealthy and could afford to be generous.

Clarke concludes that these diverse settings had remarkable commonality in their stratified hierarchy: status and honor went to a privileged few. Different standards applied depending on rank. He also notes that in most

13. Andrew D. Clarke, *Serve the Community of the Church: Christians as Leaders and Ministers* (Grand Rapids: Eerdmans, 2000), 145.

14. The points below are quoted or summarized from ibid., 145–46.

settings, political, social, religious, and ritual responsibilities were intermingled and not distinguishable.[15]

One might expect that the ways that these structures were organized, their ethos and assumptions, influenced how the church regarded status, hierarchy, inclusion, and exclusion. But Clarke shows that the New Testament discouraged churches from the plague of social division.

Paul's churches were to be countercultural examples that raised provocative questions. Pauline texts demonstrated how important it is for Christians to model different kinds of leadership, authority, and ministry than those offered by other organizations, ones that relied on and reinforced status, prestige, and privilege.

The Church at Corinth

First and Second Corinthians are among the most explicit New Testament texts addressing Christian leadership. Paul rejected dividing the congregation into party loyalties (1 Cor 1:12). He would have nothing to do with personality cults. He mocked self-important teachers as "super-apostles" (2 Cor 12:11 CEB). How, then, should Christians today regard parachurch ministries or denominations named after founders or reformers? And how would Paul respond to the current fascination with "branding"?

Paul demolished usual leadership credentials: "wisdom of the wise, . . . the intelligence of the intelligent" (1 Cor 1:19 CEB), debating skills (v. 20), being "powerful" or "from the upper class" (v. 26 CEB), and having "lofty words or wisdom" (1 Cor 2:1). Paul and his coworkers rejected obvious benefits of achievement. Throughout the Corinthian correspondence, Paul paradoxically boasted of his own foolishness, weakness, and vulnerability. "We have become the scum of the earth, the waste that runs off everything, up to the present time" (1 Cor 4:13 CEB). It is hard to imagine how to translate such sentiments into the kinds of leadership literature published and promoted these days. Paul's rebuke of many aspiring Christian leaders also has implications for outside leaders too: "None of the present-day rulers have understood" (1 Cor 2:8 CEB).

The Corinthian church struggled with "a competitive spirit of social upward mobility."[16] Significant problems arose because of divisions—and differing treatments—of rich and poor.[17] There was social diversity, as the

15. Ibid., 148.

16. Ibid., 174.

17. Gerd Theissen, *The Social Setting of Pauline Christianity: Essays on Corinth,*

church included both those who mostly were not and a few who were "wise," "powerful," or "upper class" (1 Cor 1:26 CEB). Those with high status according to external standards could also have extraordinary influence within the church. This was demonstrated in several ways. For those familiar with the Corinthian church's issues, it is eye-opening to read Clarke's analysis of how many concerns dealt with overcoming and reversing cultural standards of status, success, and power.

For one, Paul's letter forbids boasting. Bragging was common in that culture, as a way to build status.[18] (It also figures in much contemporary leadership literature, especially where creative entrepreneurs or prominent individuals detail accomplishments and innovations.) In the face of such writings, we might recall Paul's caution: "So let no one boast about human leaders" (1 Cor 3:21).

Another contentious matter was so-called wisdom and rhetorical proficiency.[19] Some preferred church leaders who measured up to the surrounding culture's standards of speaking well and demonstrating sagacity. Paul refused this acculturation; he was not interested in siren temptations of "relevance." He repeatedly came back to themes of contrasting the world's wisdom with God's wisdom: "The foolishness of God is wiser than human wisdom, and the weakness of God is stronger than human strength" (1 Cor 1:25 CEB).

Paul also denounced and forbade believers from suing each other in secular courts (6:1-11). Lawsuits were a common way for the wealthy to persecute and afflict people of lesser status.[20] (We see this also in Jas 2:6 (CEB): "Don't the wealthy make life difficult for you? Aren't they the ones who drag you into court?") This invidious behavior was practiced by powerful Christians against poorer members of their own community.

Similarly, specified immoral practices (5:1-5; 6:12-20; 7:1-2) were instances where people "used licentious behaviour as a means of drawing attention to their comparatively elevated social status."[21] Paul urged confronting such behavior. He knew that it was difficult to rebuke powerful

---

ed. and trans. John H. Schütz (Philadelphia: Fortress, 1982).

18. Clarke, *Serve the Community of the Church*, 178. Boasting is also addressed in 2 Cor (ibid., 186–87).

19. Ibid., 179–80. The matter of worldly appearances being employed against Paul also comes up in 2 Cor (ibid., 187–88).

20. Ibid., 181.

21. Ibid., 182.

people within the congregation, the likely reason why they had not been challenged.

Furthermore, eating idol-sacrificed food also had to do with status. Those who were well off participated in pagan feasts to connect with other affluent people and to advance their own rank.[22]

Even male head coverings were a matter of status. In Roman public events, only the most senior man covered his head; everyone else was bareheaded. Believers showed high outside cultural status by covering their heads in church services. "In Paul's view . . . it is inappropriate for men to have their heads covered, because the chief official in their community and at their community functions is Christ."[23]

High and low status divisions were most scandalously evident at the Lord's Supper. Some were able to be at the meal early and eat lavishly. Poorer members did not have the leisure to attend early, and by their arrival there might be no food left.[24] Eating together had implications for hierarchy, exclusion, and inclusion: "Meals establish and reinforce relational boundaries in all cultures."[25] It is not surprising, then, that much of Jesus's ministry and teaching was conducted around tables and meals and that he disparaged those who "love to sit in places of honor at banquets" (Matt 23:6 CEB). Status games do not belong in church.

Without understanding the culture, we might not see that these issues—boasting, rhetoric, lawsuits, immorality, idol food, Communion, and meals—reinforced social divisions. Yet all too frequently in the Corinthian church, we now understand, status was demonstrated and played out.

Anyone somewhat acquainted with Paul's letters to Corinth is familiar with those issues. But what is not obvious is that so many of these matters had to do with status, role, authority, honor, and politics. When I remember arguments I have heard over the years about head coverings, who is permitted at Communion, and lawsuits between Christians, I am astonished by how we missed Paul's actual point: he was passionately concerned that the Christian community not be torn asunder by misguided divisions or worldly status standards. He would have had a thing or two to say about believing that "leadership stars" should be privileged over other seminarians.

Prestige and privilege can be invisible to those who hold them. When Lorna and I moved to an inner-city Chicago neighborhood, we had a dif-

22. Ibid., 183.

23. Ibid., 184.

24. Ibid., 184–85.

25. Hellerman, *Embracing Shared Ministry*, 42.

ficult time finding housing. One day, I noticed a second-floor apartment that looked empty but had no "For Rent" sign. The (absentee) landlord lived in a distant suburb and was hard to track down. I finally found his phone number, but he insisted on meeting in person. When we finally met, the young landlord quickly confirmed that the apartment was available and let us rent it for a ridiculously small amount of money. After we lived there for some time, I realized that he rented to us because we—like him—were white. There was no "For Rent" sign because the place was not available to the general public. Only acceptable candidates need apply, a process that was face-to-face or by recommendation. Although we did not do this deliberately, we benefitted from a racist and discriminatory practice.

It is dishearteningly easy for groups to slide into divisions of status and rank, even well-meaning organizations. In one of my churches, we decided to have a talent auction. People offered services for sale: cooking a gourmet dinner in your home, washing and detailing your car, a day on a local dairy farm, and so on. The purpose was commendable: raising money for missions. The result not so much. What happened—and we should have seen this coming—was that people with extra money to spend purchased most services; they had lots of fun. In my first church, an inner-city congregation, a rummage sale was a major annual fund-raiser. We stocked this event with donations from affluent partner congregations in the suburbs. This seemed a good way to distribute useful items affordably to the neighborhood (e.g., baby supplies such as cribs). I am embarrassed to remember how we church folk regularly benefitted the most; we secured the best items for ourselves before the sale. How quickly and easily dynamics of status, privilege, and access distort church life and mission.

While Corinth is the most detailed example of a church community wrestling with divisions based on power, status, honor, and prestige, Clarke demonstrates that this was also at stake in other Pauline congregations.

- Romans 12:1-7's admonition not to "think of yourself more highly than you ought to think" (CEB) rebukes Roman honor emphases. Additionally, "Paul's exhortations concerning the weak and the strong in the community [Rom 15:1-7] urge the latter firstly to imitate not the principles of Graeco-Roman society, but Christ who did not seek to please himself, and secondly to accept those, presumably of lower status, in the community."[26]

26. Clarke, *Serve the Community of the Church,* 191.

- The book of Philemon is difficult to interpret, but one priority is clear: how master-slave relationships need to be substantially changed in the Christian community.[27] Especially astonishing is the fact that Paul did not demand and command this.[28] There was no coercion or hierarchical power play here, only invitation.

Paul constructed, both by argument and practice, new theological understandings of leadership and authority. Paul was not authoritarian, manipulative, or controlling. In the most bitter debates, "Paul's agenda was not to impose on the Corinthian community a conformity to his own values; rather . . . it was to establish a tolerance by the strong towards the weak, and to let the categories of love rather than knowledge dictate ethics; his concern was not to see Pauline conformity but rather Christian liberty conditioned by love."[29]

Paul gave up his rights, for example for compensation (1 Cor 9), and invited other "high-status" Christians to surrender rights too. He declined to be drawn into competition with Apollos, asserting that God works through both Paul and Apollos. He refused to draw on normal credentials of wealth, power, or wisdom. His countercultural leadership and authority views were particularly apparent in how he saw himself in terms of fatherhood, modeling, and being an apostle.

- **Father:** Paul willingly included many people, not only himself, as being worthy of fathering credit.[30] His own preference as a father figure was to deal lovingly and gently with people.
- **Model:** Paul spoke of himself as a model but not as the sole model; he modeled himself after Christ.[31] He employed countercultural metaphors for ministry including "agricultural, artisan and household imagery in 1 Corinthians 3–4 (specifically the lowly task of gardener, builder and servant) [that] may well have been regarded as offensive to those in the Christian community who sought to base their own authority on such widely-

27. Ibid., 202–7.
28. Ibid., 206.
29. Ibid., 214–15.
30. Ibid., 218–23.
31. Ibid., 223–28.

held criteria as secular honour and status."[32] Paul did not work for his own benefit, not accepting support or glorification—unlike many opponents and unlike the surrounding cultures: "the culture of... [Greco-Roman] leadership was dependent on self-promotion and the elaborate pursuit of public popularity."[33] This last quotation is stunning to consider when we reflect on how many forces today, including social media and "branding" emphases, focus on self-promotion.

- **Apostle:** Paul frequently claimed this title, one we might view as authoritarian. His credentials were in contrast to false apostles, "Paul's authority...lies not in his abilities (or lack of them) but in his commissioning by the Lord."[34] He was not building empires or power bases. Different than ostensible apostles who cited strengths and status, he emphasized weakness, foolishness, suffering, and the cross.

Paul ministered in a cultural context with "an exceptionally developed pattern of social hierarchy where high status was clearly recognized and publicly honored."[35] Intriguingly, he seldom used explicit leadership language or titles, preferring to emphasize service, ministry, and being coworkers:

> For Paul, the nature of the Christian [*diakonia* or service] demands a significantly different model of organization from that which prevailed.... It is then all the more anomalous that considerable focus is given in many modern contexts to church 'leaders' and church 'leadership.'[36]

Such conclusions fit what we have seen throughout our biblical-theological reflections, namely that leadership and power are organized and practiced differently within the upside-down reign of God.

Philippian Counterculture

Much could be written about the book of Philippians as a leadership treatise, especially the Philippians 2 hymn.

32. Ibid., 217.
33. Ibid., 228.
34. Ibid., 231.
35. Ibid., 249.
36. Ibid.

An issue for Philippians was that some high-status believers lost privileges in the wider world because of Christian involvements. Sometimes consequences were financial. Paul tried to encourage them in the midst of such setbacks. This makes the hymn in Philippians 2 more powerful; Jesus himself did not cling to "the form of God." Rather, he "emptied himself by taking the form of a slave" and "humbled himself" (CEB).[37] Therefore, believers losing privileges were imitating Jesus.

Philippians 2 is not primarily about Christ's deity but is *ecclesiological* in intent. It commends arranging churches to prioritize humility not hierarchy and power.[38] In this context is the astonishing claim that Jesus took "the form of a slave" (2:7 CEB). We no longer grasp what slavery meant then. Rather than focusing on a lack of freedom, the issue was "the social shame of servile status"; Paul used shocking language to convey the enormity of Jesus's sacrifice.[39] Jesus practiced a downward mobility that was incomprehensible to Roman society or culture.

This might also be hard for us to comprehend. Outside Regis College, a Jesuit school affiliated with the University of Toronto, there is a sculpture of Christ as a sleeping person huddled on a bench. It is lifelike and some mistake it for an actual homeless person. The sculpture reminds us of the connection between Christ's incarnation and the suffering of those on our streets today. Such vivid imagery also helps us understand Paul's language about Christ's slavery.

Another phrase in this hymn speaks of Christ's shame, "to the point of death—even death on a cross" (2:8). We tend to focus on the physical pain of an execution. In Good Friday sermons beyond numbering, I have heard excruciating details about how crucifixion worked and the torment it caused lungs and limbs. The New Testament, however, makes clear that crucifixion was about Jesus being "socially degraded"; it had to do with "social stigma."[40] Jesus "endured the cross, disregarding its *shame*" (Heb 12:2; emphasis added). Early Christians, and their critics and opponents, "were highly sensitive to the anomaly associated with the worship of a crucified deity. One might even say that the very expression 'crucified God' was socially oxymoronic."[41]

---

37. Ibid., 192–97.
38. Hellerman, *Embracing Shared Ministry*, 139–40.
39. Ibid., 148–49.
40. Ibid., 155.
41. Ibid.

Philippians 2:6-11 can be misread. A New Testament scholar comments:

> American evangelicals have generally failed to appreciate Paul's subversive, anti-imperial rhetoric in passages like Philippians 2:6-11. Our familiar emphasis on Jesus as a personal savior, along with the separation of church and state in America, have led us to privatize and spiritualize much of what was public and political in Paul's letters.[42]

Philippians is another crucial New Testament text for understanding how power and authority are to be put at the sacrificial service of others, even to the point of suffering.

Leadership in the Early Centuries of the Church

As the church spread and congregations were planted in diverse places, various organizational structures were put into place. There is much that can be helpfully noted about how ancient Christians thought and theologized about leadership.

First, early church theologians stressed over and again that God is our leader. "Jesus is Lord" was an essential confession. Ancient theological teachers emphasized that God is ruler in all spheres, our only teacher and shepherd: "Christ is not only the devotional focus of the church's life and the goal toward which pastors are guiding their flocks; he is always the source, the standard, and the primary agent of that ministry."[43]

Second, early theologians were first and foremost *pastors*. The most famous theologians, even acclaimed bishops with huge administrative burdens, without exception had responsibility for local parishes. While many different forms of leadership are called for by Christians within the church and beyond, our primary example of human leadership has always been pastors; "all types of church leadership are rooted in pastoral ministry."[44]

42. Ibid., 167.

43. Beeley, *Leading God's People*, 23.

44. Ibid., 7. Regarding "the great theologians of the early church," Beeley observes, "all . . . were practicing pastors, whether bishops overseeing congregations or leaders of monastic communities" (p. ix).

Third, early on significant church leaders were deeply rooted in and connected to monasticism. Many were formed in monasteries, not always intending to be pastors or bishops. Some, once they were in active ministry in the wider world, returned regularly to monasteries for retreat and reorientation. Monastic traditions affected how they taught others. This means, by the way, that they were shaped in and by the desert, or—in terminology that keeps coming up for us—*the wilderness*.[45] Furthermore, desert traditions have continued to inspire and reform ever since. Jesuit scholar Irénée Hausherr wrote: "Each time that there is a spiritual renewal in the Church, the desert fathers are present."[46]

Fourth, for ancient church leaders, Christian ministry and leadership had two priorities: first, glorifying and giving praise to God, and, second, edifying the church and aiding human thriving.[47] In other words, fulfilling Christ's great commandment of loving God and loving others.

Fifth, church leaders needed social abilities. First Timothy 3:1 says: "This saying is reliable: if anyone has a goal to be a supervisor [bishop] in the church, they want a good thing" (CEB). Then it delineates how this church leader or overseer "must be without fault" (3:2 CEB), including in how one relates to spouse or children, household and money: "The quality listed first and last is that a bishop must have a good reputation both within the church and in the wider community. This is not because ministry is a popularity contest; it is because leadership is a preeminently social occupation, and in order to function well leaders must be truly respected by others."[48]

Sixth, in the first centuries the two most authoritative spiritual leaders were confessors, who were persecuted "for the faith but not to the point of death," and martyrs, "people who lost their lives because of the faith." Confessors were especially eligible for church offices.[49]

---

45. These points were made by David Rylaarsdam, "Leadership and Christian Formation in the Early Church" (seminar, Calvin Theological Seminary, Grand Rapids, MI, July 7–11, 2014).

46. Irénée Hausherr, "Pour comprende l'orient chrétien: La primauté du spirituel," *Orientalia Christiana Periodica* 33 (1967): 359, as translated and quoted in David G. R. Keller, *Oasis of Wisdom: The Worlds of the Desert Fathers and Mothers* (Collegeville, MN: Liturgical, 2005), xv.

47. Rylaarsdam, "Leadership and Christian Formation in the Early Church."

48. Beeley, *Leading God's People*, 34–35.

49. David Rylaarsdam, "Leadership" (handout at "Leadership and Christian Formation in the Early Church" seminar), 2.

Seventh, early on there was a huge variety of church roles, including exhortation, healing, exorcism, reading, hosting meals, and so on. People so chosen might have low social status outside the congregation. Early church priorities recognized that the Spirit has a certain wide wildness: including many forms of ministry that may settle on people regarded as being of little worth in respectable society. This does not argue against emerging structures and institutional traditions; they have their validity. Given the rapid growth of early Christianity, it was appropriate that careful organization was required.[50] Church structures and traditions serve best when they find ways of continuing to be channels of the Spirit's unexpected works of grace.

Pauline Conclusions

We have only begun to scratch the surface, but Paul's emphases reveal deep concerns that we not misconstrue Christian leadership. He abhorred dividing Christians on the basis of status; he rejected the leadership standards and claims of his day.

The two preeminent New Testament figures are, first and most obviously, Jesus and Paul. Paul, like Jesus, reinforced cautionary perspectives on leadership.

First, Paul questioned and criticized what some regarded as exemplary leadership models, not only celebrating weakness and foolishness but prioritizing Christ's self-emptying example. He did not regard leadership language of his day as appealing or compelling and declined to employ that vocabulary.

Second, Paul did not have only one leadership model in mind.

Third, Paul showed concern that power not be concentrated or centered on particular leaders. He held authority lightly. His emphasis on spiritual gifts meant Christians were encouraged to see the Spirit's manifestation in a range of capacities. (We shall have more to say about such understandings later when we reflect on "spheres of leadership.") This was also seen in his use of "coworker," repeatedly in the New Testament: Romans 16:3, 9, 21; 1 Thessalonians 3:2; 2 Corinthians 8:23; Philippians 2:25; 4:3; Colossians 4:11; Philemon 1, 24.[51] He deliberately emphasized partnership and mutuality; his understanding of leadership undermined hierarchy, power, and getting credit for oneself.

50. This point was made by Rylaarsdam, "Leadership and Christian Formation in the Early Church."

51. Hellerman, *Embracing Shared Ministry*, 195.

New Testament Conclusions

Our New Testament leadership exploration also points to the three prevailing themes that we saw in the Old Testament.

First, here too there is a wariness of most leaders, both religious and secular. Jesus criticized the leaders of his day and was persecuted by the same. Paul ran afoul of the authorities and powers of his time. While some New Testament writers counseled praying for leaders, in the hopes that they would provide peace, such prayer indicates fears about how awry leadership can go.

Second, here too we see experimental leadership among disciples. Unexpected (even disreputable) people were among those called and following Jesus. Leadership innovation was evident in the early church. There was no one set structure among the first Christian congregations. *Deacon* and *elder* terms were fluid, under construction. Most strikingly, new gifts and capacities were called out among more and more people. Leadership, rather than narrowing its focus, expanded its embrace.

And, finally, New Testament leadership emphases always stress the priorities of serving God and humanity with justice, loving kindness, and mercy. Jesus's harshest criticisms were reserved for leaders on this score. His ministry invited people into God's compassionate embrace. And Paul fought hard for churches under his care to honor justice and compassion; he resisted social division among Christians.

Part Three

Constructive Suggestions toward a Contemporary Theology of Leadership

Please give your servant a discerning mind
in order to govern your people
and to distinguish good from evil,
because no one is able to govern
this important people of yours
without your help.

(1 Kgs 3:9 CEB)

Chapter Fourteen

Orienting and Turning toward God and God's Reign

Defining Christian Leadership and Ministry

Disillusion in the Book Aisle

I was already having a bad day. I do not remember why. But I recall how I decided to address my doldrums: I visited a local bookstore, one of my self-soothing tactics. This time my strategy was about to make me feel even worse.

I went to the used bookstore's theological section and was surprised to see something I had written. I pulled it off the shelf for a closer look and was even more intrigued that I had personalized and signed this to someone.

This was no random autograph from a book event. I had especially chosen and given this book to a beloved congregant who requested baptism a few years earlier. A troubled fellow, I spent a lot of time with him and felt like we grew close in the process. For his baptism, I thought of my book as a personal gift.

Not only that, I carefully selected and inscribed a Bible verse for him. I admired how he had worked hard to overcome adversities, including losing a parent at a young age. So I chose a verse about courage. Not just any verse, it was the very one that an influential minister had given me when I was baptized.

This was a long time ago. In retrospect I can see all kinds of dynamics I did not notice then. I had misread our relationship. I had become unduly attached to the fellow, a case of counter-transference. Some observers might raise relevant questions about my inappropriate "boundaries." Fair enough.

Nevertheless I was shocked to see that book on the shelf, on sale for a couple bucks. The gift I had chosen so carefully was sold to a used bookstore for a few quarters. That was all it was worth to my young friend, the price of a bottle of soda.

I do not know what happened to that long ago parishioner. Today, I am grateful for that discarded book. Yes, the incident shook me at the time. Yet it also reminded me vividly and unforgettably that leadership and ministry are always at the service and even mercy of others. And, that being so, they are not ultimately measured by narrow understandings of success; this hard leadership lesson has deep Christian resonance.

A Metaphor for Christian Leadership

Christian leadership, as I understand it, is always closely related to *ministry*. All Christian leadership should concern itself primarily with whether or not it directs attention to God and God's kingdom.[1]

Turning attention to God is one way of speaking about worship. This turning of course happens not only once a week on Sunday or only in church or only at the hands of pastors or other officially designated leaders. True worship means people direct themselves toward God in all of their lives and activities. Prayer has been called, by Stanley Hauerwas and William Willimon, "bending our lives toward God" or "bending our wants toward what God wants."[2] That is what Christian leaders urge people to do, very much in the spirit of Romans 12:1-2: "So, brothers and sisters, because of God's mercies, I encourage you to present your bodies as a living sacrifice that is holy and pleasing to God. This is your appropriate priestly service. Don't be conformed to the patterns of this world, but be transformed by the renewing of your minds so that you can figure out what God's will is—what is good and pleasing and mature" (CEB).

Terminology of directing people or groups to God is theologically rich. *Turning* is an important term in the Bible. In the Old Testament, people can be distracted from God by turning aside or away (*natah, sur*). Similarly the Old Testament equivalent of repentance (*shub*) means either turning away

1. The following section is derived from my essay, "The Pastor as Spiritual Orienteer: A Pastoral Theology Approach," in *The Heart of the Matter: Pastoral Ministry in Anabaptist Perspective*, ed. Erick Sawatzky (Telford, PA: Cascadia, 2004), 162–75.

2. William H. Willimon and Stanley Hauerwas, *Lord, Teach Us: The Lord's Prayer and the Christian Life* (Nashville: Abingdon, 1996), 18, 19.

from evil and sin or turning toward God. The New Testament *epistrephō* has a similar sense (Acts 11:21; 14:15). There are other relevant biblical themes. Walter Brueggemann, reflecting on Psalms, writes on the Christian life as one of moving from orientation (well-being, settledness, contentment) to disorientation (anguish, crisis, loss of control, meaninglessness) to the joyful and unexpected surprise of reorientation or new orientation.[3]

Turning attention to God is not a one-time event but a lifelong task and discipline, where we need the help of others. On Sunday in worship, we turn to God by giving praise, hearing scriptures read and expounded upon, talking with God about essential things, being bonded with fellow believers, remembering we are not alone, presenting offerings to God, and celebrating the sacraments.

On Sundays, we test our directions against the direction of God's reign. We see the need to readjust. Then God's reality and priorities inform and orient us throughout the week, in mundane life and in difficult crises. We need ongoing orientation and reorientation.

I see Christian leadership metaphorically as spiritual *orienting* or *orientation. Orient* itself was originally a noun that meant "east." It became a verb in the context of Christian *worship*, meaning to arrange or align a church sanctuary to face east. It is a worship word. Another term, *orienteering*, is a sport of finding one's way through difficult territory or wilderness relying only on a map and compass. It is participatory. Someone (not always the most skilled or adept person) is designated to hold and consult the map or compass. Yet it is a team effort; the strong and the weak rely on each other and work collaboratively together.

Leaders are spiritual orienteers; they are also on the journey and also need constant orientation and reorientation. They, too, require the compass and map of scriptures, accountability, community, formation, and worship. A major part of this work is prayer, not just for ministries or people they encounter but so that they are formed to be fruitful and so that they have something to offer others. Nouwen said: "To contemplate is to *see*, and to minister is to *make visible*; the contemplative life is a life with a vision, and the life of caring for others is a life revealing the vision to others."[4] A leader, as orienter or orienteer, helps others perceive God's kingdom priorities.

3. Walter Brueggemann, *The Message of the Psalms* (Minneapolis: Augsburg, 1984).

4. Henri J. M. Nouwen, *Clowning in Rome: Reflections on Solitude, Celibacy, Prayer, and Contemplation* (New York: Doubleday, 2000), 84.

Proposing a Definition for Christian Leadership

Earlier we noted that not only is it difficult to arrive at a definition of leadership, it is particularly challenging for Christians to do so. Certain terms do appear over and again when people try to come up with a definition: someone others follow, making a difference, having influence, using power, helping others solve or overcome challenges. But are any of these sufficient?

At the very least, *good* leadership assumes that people accept responsibility and take initiative to improve the lot and lives of others around them. The opposite of a leader is a bystander or a bypasser (like the religious leaders in the parable of the good Samaritan). Leadership, then, could mean being the first to pull the fire alarm when one spots smoke, making sure that the guest at church feels welcome, or chairing a committee or an organization, in each case initiative and responsibility are key.

As someone interested not just in *good* leadership but particularly in *Christian* leadership, I define it this way:

Inspiring, challenging, or empowering people or groups to join God's mission of redemption and healing.

Some leaders *inspire*; their demeanor, words, or ideas encourage people to join in God's work. Some leaders provoke and *challenge*, sometimes prophetically. And some leaders *empower*, constructively and practically helping people and groups to do new things. A very few do all three.

There are a number of things to highlight about this definition's implications:

- All Christians ought in some way to be about this kind of leadership: inspiring, challenging, or empowering others to join in the mission of God's reign. This is not an elitist definition, not a revised or modified form of clericalism.
- Leadership is not solitary or done alone; it involves others; it entails relationships, collegiality.
- In this collaborative relationship everyone grows, benefits, is enriched in the process, both the leader and the led.

- It is not unilateral, not necessarily from the top down, but invites the agency and participation of all. Inspiring, challenging, and empowering can also come from behind or underneath or off to the side.
- It is not for one's own benefit or self-promotion but is at the service of others and of God's priorities, purposes, vision, values, mission.
- It is not coercive and cannot be forced; rather it is invitational and thus always vulnerable to rejection. My congregant had every right to sell cheaply a book that I regarded as a special gift.
- It invites us into the work of God, the *missio Dei*, that is already underway. Ruth Haley Barton writes: "at the heart of spiritual leadership is the capacity to notice the activity of God so we can join . . . in it."[5]
- The how, the means—and the character—of leadership are crucial. If our means contradict priorities that we promote, then we subvert and corrupt the gospel.
- This leadership is a process that gradually unfolds and involves growth and new insights. Leadership can take a long time and might not be recognized until well after the fact. Quaker John Woolman did not appear to achieve much in his lifetime, but by several decades after he was gone, most American Quakers were convinced and convicted abolitionists.

You Are Salt and Light

If I had to choose just one Bible text to encapsulate a Christian theology of leadership, I would not go first to Proverbs or 1 and 2 Kings or Nehemiah or the book of Revelation. I would turn to the Sermon on the Mount (admittedly among my favorite Bible passages), specifically Matthew 5:13-16, where Jesus said:

> You are the salt of the earth. But if salt loses its saltiness, how will it become salty again? It's good for nothing except to be thrown away and trampled under people's feet. You are the light of the world. A city on top of a hill can't be hidden. Neither do people light a lamp and put it under

5. Ruth Haley Barton, *Strengthening the Soul of Your Leadership: Seeking God in the Crucible of Ministry* (Downers Grove, IL: InterVarsity, 2008), 68.

> a basket. Instead, they put it on top of a lampstand, and it shines on all who are in the house. In the same way, let your light shine before people, so they can see the good things you do and praise your Father who is in heaven. (CEB)

Jesus emphatically asserted that we *are* salt and light. This was not a command or a recommendation. Jesus was not giving us options of ability or agency or attempts or even imperatives. He matter-of-factly stated this reality. I like Jacques Ellul's point: "Things cannot be otherwise; the Christian has no choice."[6] Since Jesus was not asserting here that we *could* or *should* be salt and light, it is proper to conclude that all Christians are called to some form of leadership, that is, being a redemptive, healing influence on behalf of God's reign. The purpose of this ministry is that others will, as Jesus said, "praise your Father who is in heaven" (CEB). In other words, we point and orient others to God and God's priorities.

Note something else: John Stott marvels at the range of the influence: "salt *of the earth*" and "light *of the world*." In an explicitly Jewish gospel, it is significant that all of creation—not just "chosen people"—are embraced in this statement.[7] No one has to aim for, plan toward, or strategize about how Christians will have far and wide-ranging influence. Influence is an inevitable consequence of faithfully living our calling. We are not called to "brand" ourselves as salt or as light or to proclaim great things about who we are or what we accomplished. No, Jesus commended us to be who we are and therefore to practice "good works"; these are the means of drawing others into God's reign.

Salt and light are humble domestic metaphors. No explosions or fireworks here. Yet we know the huge difference that a properly seasoned dish or properly preserved food (another use for salt) can make; the difference between bland and tasty meals or the difference between safe and repulsively decaying (even ill-making) fare. Or the contribution that proper lighting makes, to the atmosphere and mood, to the ability to perform tasks, to the perception of the expressions on others' faces, and on and on. Salt and light, even as small as a chemical crystal or a guttering candle, can affect and shape entire meals or large rooms. Humble means can have huge effects; but that does not downplay their essential humility. In fact, salt and light are intrinsically opposed to self-promotion or self-adulation. Helmut Thielicke

6. Jacques Ellul, *The Presence of the Kingdom*, 2nd ed. (Colorado Springs, CO: Helmers and Howard, 1989), 5.

7. John R. W. Stott, *Christian Counter-Culture: The Message of the Sermon on the Mount* (Downers Grove, IL: InterVarsity, 1978), 58.

pointed out that they "have one thing in common: they give and expend themselves."[8] Salt and light are at the sacrificial service of other priorities.

In this text are two dramatic reversals of what we generally mean when we talk about leadership.

For one, this entire passage aims toward the purpose expressed in the final words, "so they can . . . praise your Father who is in heaven" (CEB). When I was ordained to the Anglican priesthood, Eugene Peterson preached. He mentioned my name only once, almost in passing early on, and then waxed as eloquently as I have ever heard him on Jesus's short prayer, "Father, glorify your name" (John 12:28 CEB). It was a cautionary reminder to me that ordination was not about me, not a celebration of my ministry, but a call to dedicate life ever more faithfully toward God's glory. I have been trying to make that phrase the watchword of my life: "Father, glorify your name." This is an important constraint for all of us who are interested in leadership, see ourselves as leaders, or are pressed by others to be leaders. What we do is not about us, not about our advancement, not about our promotion or our self-promotion, but always for God's glory and priorities.

One other aspect of this passage needs noting. Immediately preceding these words, Jesus "blesses" those who will be reviled, persecuted, or spoken of falsely. At least one Bible commentator clusters the "salt and light" passage with earlier verses 11-12, the "blessed are you when people revile you" passage (Matt 5:11).[9] Notice that is *when*, not *if*; persecution is certain and inevitable. This catches our attention because "salt of the earth" and "light of the world" could be seen as rather grandiose in their influence. Yet here is an anticipated rejection by the wider world. By putting salt and light terminology in the context of predicted persecution, Jesus reminds us that when we look like failures, are rejected and misunderstood, are falsely accused and persecuted, even and especially then, we represent God's reign. It is another stunning expectation reversal. What looks like failure to ourselves or others might be the most important aspect of our leadership. Paradoxically, we may be most influential when our influence is not evident at all. Jesus's words are not just an imperative challenge; they console and encourage when efforts may feel fruitless and misdirected. They warn against following one of two common temptations when we suffer opposition, either we

8. Helmut Thielicke, *Life Can Begin Again: Sermons on the Sermon on the Mount* (Cambridge, England: Lutterworth, 1966), 33.

9. F. W. Beare, *The Gospel according to Matthew* (Peabody, MA: Hendrickson Publishers, 1982), 135.

"might withdraw from the world" or get involved but "lose [our] distinctiveness and become just like everyone else."[10]

Being salt or light does not necessarily mean being famous or powerful, at the front or on the top, a higher-up or a hierarch. Salt and light properties of Christians will be less noteworthy, at least in the world's eyes. In God's reign, the human king is not primary nor necessarily the eldest son. Here, rather, domestic servants, fools for Christ, disreputable tax collectors and prostitutes, exiles and strangers, are just as likely—if not more likely—to reveal God and God's priorities.

Being salt or light is not only about what one does. There is something intrinsic to salt that makes it salt, otherwise it would not be salt, and the same is true of light. Kingdom saltiness and reign-like light have everything to do with who we *are*, our being, our core. Our character cannot contradict our purpose and achievements.

With these convictions in mind, it would be helpful to consider various spheres where God's people can be "ambassadors for Christ" (2 Cor 5:20).

10. Alan Kreider, *Social Holiness: A Way of Living for God's Nation* (Eugene, OR: Wipf and Stock, 2008), 241.

Chapter Fifteen

Spheres of Salt and Light

Leadership Happens Everywhere

More Than One Way to Be Called

Older adults in the last church I served still remembered calling leaders by lot. Sometimes this worked well, sometimes not so much. One pillar of the church, Marcus, would from time to time shake his head and smile ruefully about occasional disasters of people with no gift for preaching being forced to speak from the pulpit.

Daniel, for example, was a fervent and committed believer. Because of his devotion, people assumed that he had a "call." Eventually that was confirmed through the unpredictable mechanism of the lot. But from day one, this calling did not take. While some questioned the Holy Spirit's guidance—not to mention the wisdom of still relying on the lot—no one doubted the fact that Daniel was no preacher. His congregation knew it. His family knew it. And he knew it. Being forced into this leadership was agony for everyone involved. Eventually, Daniel was released from that ministry.

He went on to a joyful career for his remaining decades. He became a maintenance man for a local Christian school. He had great impact on that institution and on its faculty, staff, and students. He was well appreciated and admired. And he was very, very happy in his work.

Too many times we overlook these kinds of stories.

Once at a retreat, I met middle-aged Keith. He had a lot of education but decided not to pursue the profession for which he was academically qualified. Rather, he enjoyed giving care to older people in a local nursing home. "I love my work," he told me. "I make a difference." He took his responsibility seriously: "I have the power to make someone's day go well or horribly. So I try to be a good steward on God's behalf to help a person's day be good."

Spheres of Leadership

Our biblical survey disabused us of the notion that the most important people in God's kingdom are the obvious leaders at the top of the heap or in control of organizations or institutions. Up front and highly visible people have their place, no question. But they are part of a wider network that serves God's purposes. Thus I propose that we consider spheres of leadership influence and impact.

By talking about *spheres* of leadership, I suggest something resembling Paul's use of *body* imagery to describe the church and its gifts and functions. There are different but significant domains where Christians are salt and light. It is dangerous to value, prize, or esteem one sphere over others. Again, Paul makes a similar point: "If the whole body were an eye, what would happen to the hearing? And if the whole body were an ear, what would happen to the sense of smell?" (1 Cor 12:17 CEB). We must neither exclude nor dismiss the importance of each person in the body of Christ, even those deemed "less honorable."

I used to windsurf, an activity that took place at the intersection of several forces and features. In terms of forces, there could be no windsurfing without wind, obviously, or without the gravity that held my board down on the water, not to mention buoyancy, which kept it on top of the water, and waves that always made the journey more intriguing. The sport is named after "wind," but airy draughts, as essential as they are, are not the *only* important force or even the *most* important. Without gravity and flotation, there is no windsurfing. The board was constructed to catch and contend with competing influences: a sail for the wind, a large board to stay on the water, and a keel to help the device move in a straight line. Furthermore, different requirements were made of me: balance on the board so that I did not tip into the brink, muscles to hold the sail, sufficient weight (seldom a problem for me) to keep the board on the water, and brains to calculate the best ways to take advantage of the wind. If any of those—balance, weight, intellect, or strength—were missing, again there would be no sport.

Pondering windsurfing, people commonly think only of the wind or the sail (the sport is also called "sailboarding") but may not realize that the whole enterprise could be sunk (perhaps literally so) without a host of other factors. Pondering leadership, we too often consider only the most obvious candidate—a person with character, temperament, or charisma or one who holds office or is persuasive and heads up groups and gets things done. But the reign of God requires far more.

So let us explore seven spheres where Christians exercise influence on behalf of God's reign. This list is not all-inclusive nor are the spheres considered in order of importance. Yet this exercise gives a sense of the sweep of possible ways to be salt and light. While the various spheres are not always neatly separable, it is helpful to consider different aspects of exercising influence on behalf of God's priorities.

I propose seven spheres:

- community faithfulness sphere
- support roles and "doers" sphere
- guides and coming alongside sphere
- creators, innovators, and entrepreneurs sphere
- dissent, prophetic witnesses, and martyrs sphere
- movement organizers sphere
- managers and rulers sphere

Community Faithfulness Sphere

This sphere simply includes "wherever you have been planted." We are called to be salt and light in whatever community, family, congregation, neighborhood, school, workplace, or interest group that we are located. Furthermore, we are residents, if not citizens, of particular nations and inhabitants of God's good creation and there, too, are called to be salt and light.

Community faithfulness means that we are all invited to be leaders to stand for God's priorities, extend God's hospitality and grace, and promote the well-being of God's creatures and creation. Each and every one of us is implicated.

We are invited to exercise leadership on God's behalf toward all. In Genesis 1, humans are assigned to "have dominion . . . over every living thing" (Gen 1:28). *Dominion* is a leadership word having to do with *domain* of authority or responsibility. This verse is sometimes misused to suggest *domination* or exploitation. It is better understood as caring stewardship. Receiving this privilege from God, we are accountable to God about what we do with it.

We could tap and rely on many scripture passages when we consider these challenges. We might ponder Paul's exhortation to be God's ambassadors of reconciliation (2 Cor 5). We could consider the good Samaritan parable or Jesus's parable of sheep and goats (Matt 25). We could explore stewardship of creation.

If I were to choose a biblical theme, it would be the following: "Promote the welfare of the city where I have sent you into exile. Pray to the LORD for it, because your future depends on its welfare" (Jer 29:7 CEB). Strikingly, people *in exile* are called to act redemptively in the very place of their dislocation and oppression; they are invited to care for their oppressors, their enemies who are also their neighbors.

Christian tradition shows many sources for learning about community faithfulness: emphases on creation care; the Benedictine commitment to stability; New Monasticism's and Move-In's prioritization of neighborhoods; workplace and marketplace faithfulness; Brother Lawrence's "practicing the presence of God" in the kitchen; and Jean-Pierre de Caussade's emphasis on staying faithful to God in day-to-day obligations—to name only a few of the countless examples.

Support Roles and "Doers" Sphere

There are people who, either because of inclination or duty, are responsible for practical day-to-day caregiving (of children, parents, people with special needs), maintenance, administrative assistance, custodial duties, or hospitality. This crucial role too frequently does not get much credit or gratitude.

When I was a pastor, one tragedy our congregation faced was the death of a little boy. Many congregants did not necessarily know what to say, but they could *do*. They provided meals for the family. Whipped up a banquet for after the funeral. Quilted a pall for the casket. And two strong farmers hand-dug the grave—in sub-zero December—to save on grave-digging costs. These were all practical examples of giving support. They were all instances of leadership.

Biblically, I think of the widow caring for Elisha, Ruth keeping faith with her mother-in-law, doorkeepers in the sanctuary (Ps 84:10), Joseph's faithfulness to Mary and the baby who was not his biological son, Peter's mother-in-law serving after being healed, Joanna and Susanna giving support to Jesus's ministry (Luke 8:3), and the sacred act of footwashing.

If I chose one biblical theme character, it would be Martha. While she became "distracted by her many tasks" (Luke 10:40), I believe her problem was mostly in being preoccupied with what Mary was or was not doing. That preoccupation distracted Martha from her commendable hospitality.

In the Christian tradition, we look to various exemplars: Mother Teresa's Missionaries of Charity; the L'Arche movement; Little Brothers and Little Sisters of Jesus; diaconal orders (Catholic, Anglican, Methodist, Lutheran); worker-priests.

Guides and Coming Alongside Sphere

There are leaders who contribute to the growth, healing, and learning of others by coming alongside. I include pastors, social workers, spiritual directors, therapists, coaches, mentors, teachers, patrons, sages, nurses, doctors, and wise people. Their main function is to facilitate and encourage the agenda of people that they serve.

Biblically, I think of Jethro giving needed counsel to his son-in-law Moses, Elizabeth encouraging her pregnant relative Mary, Philip with the Ethiopian eunuch, Ananias with Saul after his conversion, Samuel's ministry, and much wisdom literature.

For me, a preeminent biblical mentor is Barnabas, the so-called "son of encouragement" who advocated both for Paul and later for John Mark. As well as helping plant churches, he and Paul were part of achieving a major reconciliation for the Jerusalem church in Acts 15.

In Christian streams, we remember Carmelite and Jesuit spiritual direction; the Sisters of Saint Joseph, who emphasize nursing and education; George Herbert's *The Country Parson*; Gregory the Great's pastoral instructions; Eugene Peterson's approach to spiritual theology; Henri Nouwen's ministry and teachings; and various mission movements.

Creators, Innovators, and Entrepreneurs Sphere

Every generation is blessed with—and challenged by—out-of-the-box thinkers and innovators. Creative leaders in our midst—including artists, writers, poets, business entrepreneurs, inventors, and architects—imaginatively invent new objects, artifacts, realities, enterprises, and organizations.

Biblically and theologically, I think of psalmists, song creators and singers (Miriam, Hannah, Mary, Zechariah, Simeon), and artisans of the temple and tabernacle. I love the fact that many psalms have little prefatory notes that read "to the *leader*" (see, e.g., Ps 4; emphasis added).

As a primary figure, I would suggest Bezalel, who was a tabernacle artisan. God says of him: "I have filled him with the divine spirit, with skill, ability, and knowledge for every kind of work" (Exod 31:3 CEB).

Christian tradition draws on a long line of sculptors, painters, hymn writers, composers, musicians, poets, iconographers. There are many examples, of course, including Gerard Manley Hopkins, J. S. Bach, Rembrandt van Rijn, *Image* magazine, and Andy Crouch's *Culture Making*.

Dissent, Prophetic Witnesses, and Martyrs Sphere

There is little doubt that, biblically speaking, dissent and prophetic witness are a crucial form of leadership.[1] Even so, not everyone would agree that this is a leadership category because such people may or may not influence and they do not necessarily mobilize others. These are generally people of conscience. Christians think especially of prophets, witnesses to the truth, and, of course, martyrs. This sphere also embraces prayerful contemplatives and visionaries. We must not underestimate their leadership contribution.

We are all familiar with prophetic types, people who seem unruly and subversive, embracing stances at times that are not appreciated by others. Rejected by his fellow villagers, Jesus warned: "I assure you that no prophet is welcome in the prophet's hometown" (Luke 4:24 CEB).

Given the staggering abuses of power that the world has witnessed in the last century, it is hard not to recognize the importance of dissent. "Just following orders" is now a cliché representing the inappropriateness of always doing one's "duty" without asking questions. The stunning docudrama *Compliance* (2013) is a disturbing story of what a fast food manager is prepared to do to an employee when an anonymous phone caller poses as a police officer—intimidation, forcible confinement, strip searching, and worse. Watch that film and you can only wonder, "Why did no one speak up?"

Still, prophets must guard against temptations of confusing their own inner drive with God's agenda or of falling for hazards of self-righteousness or of being so hardwired for critiquing that they are entirely defined by patterns of defiance. The *challenge* is to learn both how to *criticize* where

1. Walter Brueggemann, "Prophetic Leadership: Engagement in Counter-Imagination," *Journal of Religious Leadership* 10, no. 1 (Spring 2011): 1–23.

necessary and at the same time "*energize* persons and communities."[2] There is a *pairing* of moves when prophetic responsibilities are outlined. Brueggemann writes of the "urgent" prophetic task as both "to *tell truth* in face of denial" and "to *tell hope* in the face of despair." I have written about this as "denouncing lies" and "modeling truth."[3]

While edgy and on the edge people do not always make our lives easier or comfortable, they are necessary for healthy communities.[4] For change to happen, for justice to come, for the oppressed to be heard, for God to speak, it is important that there be dissenters, protestors, visionaries, and even rebels. While this category serves important functions, Thomas E. Cronin and Michael A. Genovese add that people here "rarely hold public office."[5]

The Bible is filled with examples in this category, including Old Testament prophets, lament psalms, Job, Esther and Mordecai, Stephen, and the faithful of Hebrews 11.

I particularly nominate John the Baptist as a representative of this sphere, standing on the margins of power, literally "a voice crying in the wilderness."

Christian tradition here includes the following: Franciscan orders, the Catholic Worker movement, Desert Fathers and Mothers, Howard Thurman, John Woolman, Dietrich Bonhoeffer, and early abolitionists.

Movement Organizers Sphere

For dreams and visions of prophetic witnesses to coalesce into something more tangible, it is necessary to rally others, educate people, "raise consciousness," and persuade and animate folks to make changes. These

2. Walter Brueggemann, *The Prophetic Imagination*, 2nd ed. (Minneapolis: Augsburg Fortress, 2001), 3.

3. Brueggemann, "Prophetic Leadership," 21; Arthur Paul Boers, "Denouncing Lies, Modeling Truth: Lent and Easter Reflections on Jeremiah and Jesus," in *Peace and Justice Shall Embrace: Power and Theopolitics in the Bible,* ed. Ted Grimsrud and Loren L. Johns (Telford, PA: Pandora, 1999), 86–107.

4. My exploration of spheres here adapts concepts found in Thomas E. Cronin and Michael A. Genovese, *Leadership Matters: Unleashing the Power of Paradox* (Boulder CO: Paradigm, 2012), 185–95. They argue that there are three sequential acts of leadership: first "movement founders" and "idea people" (fifth sphere in my schema), then "movement organizers" and "policy organizers" (sixth sphere), and finally "party leaders," "power brokers," and "office holders" (seventh sphere).

5. Ibid., 187.

"mobilizers, organizers, lobbyists, activist researchers, and educators" are crucial but "seldom run for political office."[6]

Biblically we can think of many examples, including Moses, Joshua, judges, and David leading rebel outlaws before he became king.

An exemplar would be Paul, planter of new churches around the Mediterranean basin.

Christian tradition includes William Wilberforce and abolitionism; Martin Luther King Jr. and the civil rights movement; John Wesley; General Booth and the Salvation Army; the Christian temperance movement; and so on.

Managers and Rulers Sphere

Finally, of course, there are the preeminent and "stereotypical" leaders, those who hold office, are in charge of organizations, wield official power. These are the upper echelons, holders of the highest ranks. They oversee, run, manage, and administer organizations and institutions. They are in charge of governance. From CFOs and CEOs to kings and presidents and prime ministers, these people define issues and set agenda. They have important roles, but there are hazards. Two temptations that faithful rulers must guard against are either thinking they are completely in control and are of primary importance or morally justifying whatever actions they happen to take.[7]

There are many examples in the scriptures, of course, including Daniel and a host of Old Testament kings.

One of my favorite biblical models would be Joseph administering Egypt on behalf of Pharaoh.

In Christian tradition, we can think of church polities and hierarchies (with bishops and archbishops), denominational structures, various kings who profess faith (e.g., Constantine—"even emperors can be disciples"[8]), Casmir of Poland, Margaret of Scotland, and Arrow Leadership programs.

---

6. Cronin and Genovese, *Leadership Matters*, 189.

7. John Howard Yoder wrote: "What I reject is (a) considering the ruler as the primordial mover of history, and (b) modifying the content of moral obligation in order to approve of the ruler's doing things which would be wrong for others" (John Howard Yoder, "Ethics and Eschatology," *Ex Auditu* 6 (1990): 127n12).

8. Craig Hovey, "Is There a Christian Ethic for Emperors?," in *Constantine Revisited: Leithart, Yoder, and the Constantinian Debate*, ed. John D. Roth (Eugene, OR: Wipf and Stock, 2013),161.

Implications of This Spheres Approach

Frequently, Christians fit more than one category. There are varying places and spheres for each of us to act as salt and light on behalf of God's reign.

Some Bible examples cited above work in more than one sphere. (For example, Joseph sought the peace of his country, the place of his exile, and was eventually an administrator.) There is "slippage" between the creative category and the more provocative category of prophets. (E.g., Daniel Berrigan is in both spheres; his poetry, prophetic insight, protests, and activism are deeply intertwined.)

If we were to "scale" the spheres, the first (community) would be the largest, as that is where all Christians belong. The final sphere (rulers) would be the smallest, as only a few people are found there. While the "world" and indeed many Christians prioritize the ruler sphere, the Bible does not share that perspective—all gifts are valued, all faithful disciples are commended.

Frequently in Christian leadership literature, the focus is on the latter two categories: movement organizers and managers/rulers. Yet only a small minority is ever capable of achieving or fulfilling those positions. Besides, there are many other emphases in scripture. Exemplary believers are found in all seven areas. Rather than having anyone fret that he or she is not "really a leader," let us rather encourage all to think about spheres where they are called to act on behalf of God's reign. We can prompt them to consider vital questions: Where do you fit? Where are you called? What are your gifts?

In each sphere, we are invited to step forward, take initiative on behalf of God's reign, and accept responsibility for what we can do. That is always what leadership implies. Christian leadership assumes that *service*—for God's reign and for the good of others—is crucial.

While sometimes certain categories downplay, resent, or even malign each other, Paul's "body" theology reminds us that a diversity of gifts is needed. Walter Brueggemann is on to something important when he insists that we need "an agent of order" (ruler sphere in our schema), "an agent of vision" (prophetic), and even those without power to be in ongoing tension with each other. He gives examples of necessary combinations: king, prophet, and widows/orphans; pharaoh, Moses, and enslaved Israel; Pharisees and chief priests, Jesus, and publicans and sinners.[9]

Cronin and Genovese say change in groups happens in a certain order among the final three spheres: unusual ideas surface with "prophets" (my terminology not theirs), then coalitions and movements are formed by or-

9. Walter Brueggemann, *Peace* (St. Louis, MO: Chalice, 2001), 101–4.

ganizers, and finally action is taken by rulers.[10] Those are three of the most obvious and crucial forms of leadership for bringing about change.

Intriguingly, there are numerous instances of Jesus in the first six spheres. He blessed the wedding at Cana (community sphere). Traditionally, we believe he exercised carpentry and supported his mother for most of his life and made provision for her care at the end (recruiting John for that purpose). He also brought healing to many (support roles sphere). He came alongside others, for example, Zacchaeus and the woman at the well. He was a teacher/rabbi (guides coming alongside sphere). He was a creative and poetic preacher and inventor of parables (creators, innovators, and entrepreneurs sphere). He was a prophet who was ultimately martyred: recall his reception in his hometown synagogue and his clearing of the temple (dissent, prophetic witnesses, and martyrs sphere). He organized followers, particularly disciples, and showed different kinds of attention and ministry, depending on whether he was relating to crowds, the Seventy, the Twelve, or his inner circle of Peter, James, and John (movement organizers sphere).

While Jesus can easily be placed and observed in all of the first six categories, he never was in the seventh sphere of rulership during his on-earth ministry. We only see him as Lord of lords eschatologically; he did not rule during his earthly incarnation. In footwashing and on Palm Sunday, he exemplified subversive leadership understandings. He was mocked with a crown of thorns, undercutting the primacy of earthly rulers. This is intriguing when we think about how Christians may emphasize that category as if it is the highest calling.[11] Furthermore, Jesus's harshest criticisms were reserved for people in that sphere—specifically in confronting leaders, in naming of rulers (Herod "the fox"), and theologically in disparaging remarks made about worldly leaders.

In the Bible, people in this category are particularly prone to the temptations of idolatry and to displacing God (who is the true ruler). Rulers are especially vulnerable to spiritual jeopardy.

---

10. Cronin and Genovese, *Leadership Matters*, 185.

11. See Laurie Beth Jones, *Jesus, CEO: Using Ancient Wisdom for Visionary Leadership* (New York: Hyperion Books, 1995).

Chapter Sixteen

Elusive Measures

What Do Christians Mean When They Call a Leader "Good"?

What Did I Do?

Leadership, I've learned, is not necessarily what it seems, or at least not necessarily what is credited or recognized.

Take my experience with a beloved congregant I'll name as Laura. A frail senior, she had long experienced a progressively debilitating disease. I admired her steady faith and quiet matter-of-factness about her condition. She was always glad to see me, and I felt at ease with her.

One morning, I was phoned and informed that Laura was failing. So I went to the hospital and met with her spouse and some of the middle-aged children, including her oldest daughter Elaine, the family's go-to person. I learned that Laura had an intestinal infection. The hospital staff wanted her on antibiotics to fight the condition. Laura also had stopped eating and staff were hoping to fit her with a stomach tube. "So it's all sorted out," Elaine told me. "Mom's going to have antibiotics, and she might be okay."

It was not my place to give medical advice, but I was uncertain about the antibiotics, and even more about the stomach tube, an uncomfortable way to prolong life (or prolong dying, as my wife puts it). This kind of procedure is emotionally difficult to undo once it is applied. As pastor these were not my questions to raise. But I could ask another: "Have you talked to your family doctor about this? You can explore options with him."

Elaine liked this idea. She learned from the doctor that the staff proposal would likely extend Laura's life but would not bring back her health. The staff were obligated to keep patients alive unless directed otherwise, but the family did not have that obligation. If nothing was done, Laura would likely die a relatively quiet death sooner rather than later. The family conferred and agreed that Laura was prepared to die and that they, too, were at peace with this reality.

So Laura was moved to a quiet room with a single bed. The family gathered around her and invited me along. Various grandchildren gradually drifted in. We were there most of the day. We talked quietly to Laura, who was nonresponsive, and prayed for her. Spouse, children, and grandchildren told her how much they loved her. We read scriptures and sang hymns with hushed voices. Occasionally, I reminded folks that this was a good time to say what still needed to be said to Laura—a blessing, a goodbye.

After a time, Laura's hands grew colder and turned bluish. This suggested that her circulation was shutting down. I alerted the family that death was approaching. I went outside and found Stan, Laura's youngest son. He'd not been able to stay more than a few minutes in the room and was frantically chain-smoking. "Stan," I said, "your mom's time is getting close. Come, it is a good time to be with her." And he did just that.

A little while later, Laura started to breathe more rapidly. All was quiet except for her breathing. And then she was gone. It was a peaceful death, surrounded by loved ones, and had all the holy sensibility of being present when children are born. Nurses had made brief visits throughout the day and now one gently confirmed Laura's death.

People cried quietly and held each other's hands. More scripture was read, a hymn sung, a prayer said. There was no hurry or pressure. "How long can we stay?" Elaine wondered. I told her that the staff said that we could take as long as we needed.

Some time later, Elaine turned to me. "This is all new. What's going to happen to my mother's body?"

I explained that when we left, Laura would be moved to the morgue. From there, the funeral home would pick her up and then prepare her for burial.

Within the hour we were all gone.

The next few days were full as we prepared for the burial of a cherished mother, grandmother, and church member. At the funeral reception, Elaine sought me out. I was glad to check in with her about how she was doing and feeling. After my inquiries, Elaine noted she wanted to thank me for my assistance. "You made a difference," she said.

Yes, I thought. That's true. I helped the family move toward wise end-of-life decisions. Laura was saved from an agonizing, prolonged, unpleasant death. I encouraged people to say necessary final words. I alerted them to when Laura was almost gone. I had been a good pastor.

Elaine's compliment was not on my self-congratulatory list, however. She told me, "Without you we would not have known what would happen to my mother's body after she died."

I tried not to show it, but I was stunned. The work I thought I had done was not recognized. Not all the time I spent with the family. The one thing credited to me was a small tidbit of information that they could just as easily have learned from any of the hospital staff. I smiled and said, "You're welcome."

This good leadership moment reminded me that my work is not to draw attention to myself, even when I feel like I deserve credit. Ministry helps others move to growth and healing for their good. If I am invisible, so much the better. It is not about me, after all. Lao Tzu famous said: "A leader is best when people barely know he exists, not so good when people... acclaim him."[1]

Leadership is notoriously difficult to weigh and evaluate. Pastor André Trocmé offered leadership in LeChambon in Vichy France during World War II. He and fellow villagers dealt with the challenges and crises of hiding and protecting Jews from Nazi persecution. Eugene Peterson, another exemplary pastor in my judgment, offered quite different pastoral care in a suburb of Baltimore for twenty-nine years near the end of the twentieth century. The way I lead in an Anglican context is not the same as when I did so in a Mennonite setting. Can those different contributions be compared or measured?

We may speak of leaders as "good" or "bad" but need to consider what we mean by these terms and to appraise their relevance when we ponder *Christian* leadership and ministry. How do Christians discern "good" leadership? We probably affirm a number of qualities. It is unlikely, however, that anyone can fulfill all our priorities, especially not all of them well. We need clarity about Christian evaluation of leadership.

At Least We Know Where She Stands— Convictions and Policies

When we call a leader "good," we may simply mean that we like his or her convictions, opinions, or policies.

1. Lao Tzu, *Tao Te Ching: A New English Version,* with foreword and notes by Stephen Mitchell (London: Macmillan, 1988), 19, as quoted in Joseph S. Nye Jr., *The Powers to Lead* (New York: Oxford University Press, 2008), ix.

Our Canadian parliament has representation from different political parties (Conservative, New Democratic, Liberal, Bloc Québecois, Green). When I consider which party leader I most commend, my first instinct is to affirm one whose convictions and policy platform most accords with mine. This is the easiest way to evaluate leaders, and possibly the most fun too. Getting together with like-minded friends, I enjoy celebrating with them the achievements of "our" political leader. I also indulge in complaining about those we disagree with, especially if they are the ruling party.

At times we commend politicians just for *having* convictions. In some elections, people complain that we do not know *where* candidates stand. This was an oft-repeated criticism of Mitt Romney in the 2012 presidential election; he was viewed as a "waffler" who formerly as governor supported abortion and socialized medicine but as a presidential candidate opposed them. I frequently heard people compliment George W. Bush, Sarah Palin, and even Toronto's controversial crack-smoking mayor Rob Ford because they were unafraid to express opinions and take unpopular stances. We knew where they stood.

Convictions are important, there is no doubt. Without firm ones, it is unlikely that leaders can help a group move in adaptive directions. Yet opinions are not always and automatically commendable; they may not, for example, be reasonable, consistent, well thought out, virtuous, practical, or, for that matter, even true.

Judging someone by opinions, convictions, and policies is subjective. It is, as I have said, a *fun* category but does not give much depth of analysis. On this basis alone, Democrats will usually not be able to commend any Republican leaders no matter how fine, nor will Republicans be prepared to affirm any Democratic leaders. Christians need additional standards so that you and I can conceivably celebrate the leadership of those whose opinions and ideas are different than yours or mine.

Plays Well with Others—People Skills and Group Dynamics

We can evaluate leaders on how they work with others. A host of priorities could be mentioned here. Does he or she inspire and elicit cooperation and collaboration? Is there an appropriate and empowering delegation of responsibilities? How does he or she function with teams? Does the leader show appropriate compassion and respect? Is he or she genuinely interested in and curious about others? Does he or she prioritize others' needs rather than exploit leadership opportunities for his or her own gain? Can he or she help a group move productively through conflict?

Heifetz and Linsky regard this ability as an important aspect of "thinking politically." By the loaded term "political" they simply mean the capacity of collaborative endeavors, including the following priorities: finding partners and allies, staying close to the opposition, owning responsibility for one's own "piece of the mess," taking seriously the cost and understandable grieving that attends adaptive change and loss, modeling the behavior that one requires of others, and appropriately accepting that not everyone can or will go along with your directions.[2]

The Christian perspective certainly understands the priority and necessity of collaboration. We have only to think of Paul's reflections on what it means for the "body" of Christ to cohere and function well.

Emotional intelligence (EI) says that good leaders have four tasks: self-awareness, self-management, other awareness, and other management. EI suggests that these challenges must occur in that order. Intriguingly, "other management" is frequently what people think of first and primarily when considering leadership. (Weekend workshops on "leadership" focus here.) But collaboration cannot be done well without the prior work of self-awareness, self-management, and other awareness. Without those necessary preliminaries, managing others easily turns into cynical how-to-win-friends-and-influence-people manipulation. Then relationships become a means, something exploited for meeting other objectives. Brueggemann reminds us of God's deep and abiding "commitment to *relationship* (*covenant*) rather than *commodity* (*bricks*)."[3] Relationships are primary, surpassing achievements or products.

Collaborating with others, while obviously important, is not a sufficient criterion for labeling a particular leadership style as "good." After all, even sociopaths are frequently exceptionally able to work well with others.

Getting It Done—Effectiveness

Time and again we commend someone's leadership when we like his or her results, bottom line, or outcomes. Effectiveness is regarded as measurable or manageable. For many this is the first (even the only) criterion for

2. Ronald A. Heifetz and Marty Linsky, *Leadership on the Line: Staying Alive through the Dangers of Leading* (Boston, MA: Harvard Business School Press, 2002), ch. 4.

3. Walter Brueggemann, *Sabbath as Resistance: Saying No to the Culture of Now* (Louisville, KY: Westminster John Knox, 2014), 6.

evaluating leadership. Is the leader competent? Does he or she accomplish and deliver what is needed or promised? Can we see visible, tangible outcomes? Is he or she successful in achieving projected goals? People may employ "metrics" jargon term here. Because of this priority's current prevalence and popularity, Christians need to give it especially careful scrutiny.

This is a common evaluation standard and some might be surprised to realize that it is nevertheless relatively recent. "The obsession with results is a contemporary conceit and one that is partly responsible for eroding the moral dimension of leadership."[4] Much leadership literature—especially *evangelical* leadership literature—has primarily pragmatic emphases. Thus many book titles promise achievable success with a certain number of steps, principles, or "secrets."

It is reasonable to want results and to be able to see and perhaps even count many of them. Measurement can be useful. Churches need to know how many people show up on Sunday from week to week and also how donations during the year line up with disbursements and budgets. While it is not necessarily an easy or particularly pleasant task, as a professor I make no apologies for *grading* students, offering an evaluation of their work with a semblance of (admittedly subjective) measurability. However, questions do need to be raised.

Statistics must not be the final, most important—let alone only—tool. Otherwise the shepherd would not jeopardize ninety-nine sheep to save one young, high-risk lamb. Thoreau made a significant distinction, the difference between measurable "profits" and largely immeasurable (but no less real) "benefits."[5] Frequently the richest goods in life, matters we consider most important, can never be measured. They are good in and of themselves.

One problem is that effectiveness criteria do not necessarily have an underlying ethic. Businesses may have a bottom-line goal of earnings and profits, without regard to externalized costs for local populations or ecologies; they may also disregard the worth of what they produce (making and selling junk can be effectively profitable).

4. Rob Goffee and Gareth Jones, *Why Should Anyone Be Led by You? What It Takes to Be an Authentic Leader* (Boston, MA: Harvard Business Review Press, 2006), 27. They also note that "the classical understanding of leadership is primarily concerned with providing meaning."

5. As explained in Frédéric Gros, *A Philosophy of Walking*, trans. John Howe (New York: Verso, 2014), 89.

There are other concerns. Toxic and evil leaders can be surprisingly effective and may produce worthwhile results.[6] And, further irony perhaps, ethical leadership does not always produce the best or most effective outcomes.[7]

Yet another limitation is that one cannot necessarily predict how actions will turn out. My wife and I thought we raised both children the same way, and yet they are two different people; indeed they even have contrasting memories and interpretations about their upbringings. Ask a seasoned preacher about this: sometimes the best planned and executed sermon lands with a thud; at other times the sermon that seemed to take little time (or that does not fill the preacher with conviction) connects deeply to congregants. In her classic novel about the challenge of overseas missions, Elisabeth Elliot has a long-term missionary explain the following to a new missionary:

> Gradually I came to see that the results which can be called good are few. And they cannot be the criterion for whether or not what we do is worthwhile. It is hopeless to try to weigh up the good, the bad, the futile, and the merely harmless, and hope that there will be enough of the good . . . to justify all the rest.[8]

While potentially useful, prioritizing outcomes too frequently focuses on what is measurable in the short term. Furthermore, measurement risks thinning out the true worth and value of what we do. I once walked five hundred miles on Spain's Camino de Santiago. While the distance traveled sometimes hooks people's attention to my story, that is the least intriguing aspect of the pilgrimage. I wrote two books after my trip that helped me explore and unpack what I *learned* from that experience.

My wife and I once carpooled with a politically active couple to a wedding of mutual friends a hundred miles away. Lorna and I were inspired by the service and sermon and enjoyed reconnecting with friends at the festivities. On the way home, however, our activist acquaintances only compared

6. Thomas E. Cronin and Michael A. Genovese, Leadership Matters: *Unleashing the Power of Paradox* (Boulder, CO: Paradigm, 2012), 262, 266. See also Goffee and Jones, *Why Should Anyone Be Led by You?*, 27; Steven B. Sample, *The Contrarian's Guide to Leadership* (San Francisco: Jossey-Bass, 2002), 107; Aaron Wildavsky, *The Nursing Father: Moses as a Political Leader* (Tuscaloosa, AL: University of Alabama Press, 1984), 189.

7. Goffee and Jones, *Why Should Anyone Be Led by You?*, 27.

8. Elisabeth Elliot, *No Graven Image* (London: Hodder and Stoughton, 1967), 157.

notes about how many people they had "networked with" and tried to win to their cause. Their evaluation reduced an occasion that was rich and good in and of itself into a political recruiting opportunity.

The best events, occurrences, and practices cannot be measured or fathomed. Can worship be quantified? Some would say it can—by the number of people attending and returning. But this measurement, while possibly informative, is ultimately trivial. Worship transcends numbers.

Evangelicals have a predilection for the effectiveness criterion. Guest speakers, alumni awards, and honorary doctorate recipients at a seminary where I taught were regularly introduced with descriptions of the largeness of churches, budgets, or achievements. Size matters after all. I wondered why we did not celebrate the faithful, plodding work of local, small-setting pastors. Most North American churches are not large—thus small church pastors are more directly relevant to the ministry many seminary graduates pursue. Furthermore, it takes increasing amounts of courage and discernment to minister in our post-Christendom era. Overstressing large exceptions can demoralize those who minister in ordinary but challenging circumstances.

Unfortunately, too much attention is focused on "bigger and better," growth and increase. When evangelical ministries expand, it is common to hear the refrain of how "God blessed" the work. Eugene Peterson reminds us that one group of highly successful "growth" agents are malignant tumors; expansion and enlargement are not always and inevitably something to covet.[9]

Happily, Peterson is not the only dissenting minority voice. Gary Hoag, Scott Rodin, and Wesley Willmer are concerned about how we "idolize results," as this inappropriately reflects cultural priorities not our faith.[10] They note that Christian endeavors, typically, are measured according to increases: numbers of "clients or customers," expansion of physical facilities, and financial success—the three *b*'s of bodies, buildings, budgets. They assert that "production-driven leadership" inevitably leads to the following sequence: "expansion-focused strategies," "earthly oriented metrics," "results-based management," and a "utilitarian view of resources." This, they argue,

9. Eugene H. Peterson, *Under the Unpredictable Plant: An Exploration in Vocational Holiness* (Grand Rapids: Eerdmans, 1992), 138.

10. Gary G. Hoag, R. Scott Rodin, and Wesley K. Willmer, *The Choice: The Christ-Centered Pursuit of Kingdom Outcomes* (Winchester, VA: ECFA Press, 2014), x. Other books for alternative perspectives are J. R. Briggs, *Fail: Finding Hope and Grace in the Midst of Ministry Failure* (Downers Grove, IL: InterVarsity, 2014); and C. Christopher Smith and John Pattison, *Slow Church: Cultivating Community in the Patient Way of Jesus* (Downers Grove, IL: InterVarsity, 2014).

is incompatible with the "Kingdom path," a trajectory that leads to the following sequence: "steward leadership," "faithfulness focused strategies," "eternity-oriented metrics" (quality supersedes quantity), "relationship-based management," and "stewardship view of resources."[11]

Christians must be wary of overemphasizing pragmatism. After all, even "God refuses to be useful."[12] An old saw warns: "If you want to make God laugh, tell him your plans." Significant biblical leaders were frequently unsuccessful, as we have seen. Buber speaks of the Bible's "glorification of failure" and notes that it "knows nothing of this intrinsic value of success."[13] The servant in Isaiah 49 not only recognized his own failure but celebrated it: "The claim is that despite failure one is in the right. I trust that God supports me even if events do not... as if the failure were itself a proof of one's integrity."[14] Our falling short need not be a matter of shame but can be one of the most important means through which God works on leaders and their ministries.[15]

Scriptures teach us to realize that we need more than can-do, gung-ho bravado of what we can accomplish. Abraham (impregnating Hagar), Jacob (stealing a blessing), Moses (striking the rock at Meribah), Saul (inappropriately offering a sacrifice), and David (conducting a census) were all judged and condemned for occasions in which they tried to make things happen and force matters to come out right. Control is not a biblical virtue.

This obviously does not mean glorifying ineffectiveness or do-nothing passivity. Rather the issue is whether or not we trust God, whether or not we act in faithfulness to godly priorities.

Measuring accomplishments is generally done over a small time frame. Performance reviews "reward... short-term success and penalize... short-term mistakes."[16] *When* do we "measure" effectiveness? With many Christians, we only see the results of their efforts long after they have lived. The final

11. Hoag, Rodin, and Willmer, *The Choice*, 2, 7–8, 44.

12. Walter Brueggemann, *Hopeful Imagination: Prophetic Voices in Exile* (Philadelphia: Fortress, 1986), 55.

13. Martin Buber, "Biblical Leadership," in *On the Bible: Eighteen Studies*, ed. Nahum N. Glatzer (Syracuse, NY: Syracuse University Press, 2000), 143, 142.

14. John Howard Yoder, *He Came Preaching Peace* (Scottdale, PA: Herald, 1985), 125.

15. See Smith and Pattison, *Slow Church*.

16. Laurence G. Weinzimmer and Jim McConoughey, *The Wisdom of Failure: How to Learn the Tough Leadership Lessons without Paying the Price* (San Francisco: Jossey-Bass, 2013), 9.

judgment means that we cannot weigh works or effectiveness. God sorts out what is straw and what is gold (see 1 Cor 3:12-15).

Christians know that not even the most faithful actions automatically bring about good or hoped-for results. A friend has lived in a decaying inner city for decades. This idealistic committed Christian pastors a small struggling church, and having lived sacrificially, his income is always below taxable levels. He suffered personal tragedies and worked hard, even enduring lengthy stays in jail. I heard him more than once say, with a rueful grin: "We've lost pretty much every battle we've undertaken all these years." The famous investigative reporter I. F. Stone used to assert: "If you expect to see the final results of your work, you have not asked a big enough question."[17]

Weighing effectiveness has usefulness, but it is limited too. God's grace is not a product or outcome. It surprises us and disrupts our lives. And, happily, grace breaks through and good things happen unexpectedly.

The Way of the Righteous—Character

Effectiveness is important but not all-important. Christians can surely agree with Joseph Nye that it is not enough of a priority on its own; we need to have "ethical" goodness.[18]

Jesus had "twofold authority: first, of his moral character with its selfless compassion and unsullied goodness, and second, of the truth of his teaching as the gospel of God."[19] Integrity and truthfulness may be difficult to measure, but any leadership without them ought not be considered *good.*

We may regard a leader as "good" because he or she is a person of virtue, good character, spiritual stature, and acts in ethical and exemplary ways. He or she is a spiritual leader. While these leaders are not necessarily effective, spiritual growth of leaders must be a Christian priority.

Christians value good character, especially in leaders. New Testament epistles spell out character qualifications of those exercising church leadership. For example, 1 Timothy lists the following necessities: "love that comes from a pure heart, a good conscience, and sincere faith" (1 Tim 1:5), being "above reproach, . . . temperate, sensible, respectable, hospitable, . . . not a drunkard, not violent but gentle, not quarrelsome, and not a

17. Cited in Jeff Gates, *Democracy at Risk: Rescuing Main Street From Wall Street* (New York: Basic Books, 2001), 241.

18. Joseph S. Nye Jr., *The Powers to Lead* (New York: Oxford University Press, 2008), 111.

19. Paul D. L. Avis, *Authority, Leadership and Conflict in the Church* (London: Mowbray, 1992), 82–83.

lover of money" (1 Tim 3:2-3), "serious, not double-tongued, not indulging in much wine, not greedy for money" (1 Tim 3:8).

When Christians call a leader "good," we expect that to include good behavior. This we say knowing that virtuous people are not necessarily the most effective; we may call them "unrealistic" or "naive." We commend good virtue, even as we know that unscrupulous individuals can be disconcertingly effective. Nevertheless when we consider Christian leaders in the past, character looms large in our evaluation.

Good leaders should also model and inspire moral and spiritual growth. While personally flawed themselves, Martin Luther King Jr. and Nelson Mandela both motivated many followers to act in a nonviolent, non-retaliatory manner. What was most disappointing and disturbing after September 11 was that so many political leaders (including Christians) and clergy celebrated and fostered fear, anger, and even vengeance.

Although commending character may seem obvious at first glance, in the next chapter we shall see that in many respects character is a diminishing priority in wider culture, a trend that adversely impacts the church.

By Their Fruits—Fruitfulness

When Christians evaluate leadership as "good," we exercise discernment. Jesus said, "You will know them by their fruit" (Matt 7:16 CEB). The most important criterion is also the least tangible: whether or not that person's work is *fruitful*.

Fruitfulness is a biblically rooted concept. Metaphorical uses of "fruit" and "fruitfulness" abound in the New Testament. Jesus used agricultural imagery in parables (e.g., seeds sown in "good soil…bear fruit, in one case a yield of thirty to one, in another case sixty to one, and in another case one hundred to one," Mark 4:20 CEB). Fruitfulness is organic, with no absolutely reliable or predictable cause and effect, as any gardener can tell you. Fruitfulness is not necessarily the same as effectiveness. Fruitfulness cannot be forced, predicted, or quantified. Christians trust that fruitfulness grows from faithfulness, but we cannot prove this. Fruitfulness is decidedly elusive.

Many great Christian leaders, martyrs, and saints were fruitful in spite of tragic failure during their lives or at the time of their deaths. Seventeenth-century Jesuit martyrs in North America did not have much evident success in their lifetimes. Father Jean de Brébeuf worked for six years in Huronia and baptized a grand total of just one adult before being martyred.[20] Nadine

20. Cornelius Michael Buckley, "Foreword," in François Roustang, *Jesuit Missionaries to North America: Spiritual Writings and Biographical Sketches*, trans. M.

Gordimer is supposed to have said: "A serious person should try to write posthumously."[21] What goes for writers is even more true for believers; we concentrate not so much on short-term achievements but on contributing to the advancement of God's reign.

Failure or ineffectiveness need not bother us because we trust in the power of resurrection. And fruitfulness can take a long, long time to unfold. Martyred Jesuit failures nevertheless posthumously inspired French interest in North American missions. Their courageous deaths helped convince a number of Iroquois to convert. Whether you and I assent to all aspects of their seventeenth century Jesuit Roman Catholicism or even support their style of evangelizing missions, surely their courage, passion, sacrifice, steadfastness, and commitment to God deserve respectful affirmation.

Judging faithful Christian actions by effectiveness and *success*, key priorities in our day, can demoralize us. In the face of opposition and great odds, we stress the priority of following God's will and acting on behalf of God's reign. We trust God not only to make good use of small yet faithful efforts but also to weigh the merits and demerits of our deeds.

Let us not think too highly or confidently about our actions or decisions. "We measure our results by abandonment . . . rather than by other outcomes. We humbly let God judge us. We expect mystery and limitations."[22] Christian spiritual traditions emphasize yieldedness to God (medieval mystics spoke of *gelassenheid*) and acknowledge God's judgment.[23] Committing ourselves to fruitfulness means releasing priorities of quantification or control. To use Gerald May's construct, we move from *willfulness* about our

---

Renelle (San Francisco: Ignatius, 2006), 13.

21. Jeffrey Eugenides, "Posthumous," *New Yorker*, December 21, 2012, http://www.newyorker.com/books/page-turner/posthumous.

22. Mary Margaret Funk, *Tools Matter for Practicing the Spiritual Life* (New York: Continuum, 2001), 109.

23. William Stringfellow warned against being a person who claims "that he can second-guess how God will judge him in respect to the decision or course of action which he now undertakes and which he claims is morally right. It is the essence of human sin . . . to boast of the power to discern what is good and what is evil, and thus to be like God. I think men must foreswear such presumption and wait upon the last embarrassing day when all the secrets will be exposed and God judges every act and word of every man" (*A Private and Public Faith* [Eugene, OR: Wipf and Stock, 1999], 25). Later he adds: "the great peril in the notion that a man may intentionally do, and know that he is doing, good . . . is that it preempts the office of God in judging the actions and decisions of men. The man who claims . . . that his action is good is in the arrogant position of asserting that he knows already how God will judge his act or decision" (ibid., 68–69).

agenda, where we try to make or force things to our preference to *willingness* and accepting surrender to God's priorities.[24]

When Jim Forest, a relatively new Christian, was a young social activist, he had the happy fortune to be befriended by Thomas Merton, a Trappist monk. Merton wrote him a letter that speaks to concerns raised here. It is worth quoting at length:

> Do not depend on the hope of results. When you are doing the sort of work you have taken on, . . . you may have to face the fact that your work will be apparently worthless and even achieve no result at all, if not perhaps results opposite to what you expect. As you get used to this idea, you start more and more to concentrate not on the results but on the value, the rightness, the truth of the work itself.
>
> . . . [T]he big results are not in your hands or mine, but they suddenly happen, and we can share in them; . . . there is no point in building our lives on this personal satisfaction, which may be denied us and which after all is not that important. . . . All the good that you will do will come not from you but from the fact that you have allowed yourself, in the obedience of faith, to be used by God's love. Think of this more, and gradually you will be free from the need to prove yourself, and you can be more open to the power that will work through you without your knowing it.
>
> . . . The real hope, then, is not in something we think we can do, but in God who is making something good out of it in some way we cannot see. If we can do His will, we will be helping in this process. But we will not necessarily know all about it beforehand.[25]

The wise contemplative encouraged the young social activist to prioritize working for God by godly means rather than fret or obsess about results. The latter, after all, are in God's hands.

Social activists are frequently overlooked in leadership literature (which is more prone to emphasize businesses, corporations, professional sports, politics). Yet believers easily recognize worthwhile fruit from the abolitionist movement in Britain, say, or the civil rights movement in the United States. Both campaigns heavily involved and relied upon Christian initiatives and participation. Both took a long time, decades or more in fact. Much of that long-drawn-out work does not necessarily show immediate

---

24. This is a major theme in Gerald G. May, *The Awakened Heart: Living Beyond Addiction* (San Francisco: Harper, 1991).

25. Thomas Merton, *The Hidden Ground of Love: The Letters of Thomas Merton on Religious Experience and Social Concerns*, ed. William H. Shannon (New York: Farrar Straus Giroux, 1985), 294–97.

progress, and yet we are grateful for those who take on these thankless tasks and remember the unlikely ways of addressing issues.

> A sit-in or march is not instrumental but it is significant. Even when no immediate change in the social order can be measured, even when persons and organizations have not yet been moved to take a different position, the efficacy of the deed is first of all its efficacy as sign. Since we are not the lord of history there will be times when the only thing we can do is to speak and the only word we can speak is the word clothed in a deed, a word which can command attention from no one and which can coerce no one. But even in this situation the word must be spoken in . . . confidence that it is the Lord of history and His Holy Spirit, not our eloquence or artistic creativity, which will make our sign a message.[26]

These Christian emphases are far from contemporary standards of success, productivity, or effectiveness.

Even achievements in our lifetime are to be questioned. As we have often been reminded, Buber observes: "The Bible knows nothing of this intrinsic value of success." In fact, whenever a success is noted, immediately the Bible also will "announce in complete detail the failure involved in the success."[27]

Sometimes, late in the day, I do two little exercises that have a lot in common and seem similar but are qualitatively different: looking at the day's list of tasks completed and practicing *consciousness examen.*

I love lists and, even more than that, love checking things off my list. (Sometimes I do something not on my list and write it in after it is accomplished, simply for the pleasure of being able to stroke off one more item.) It is useful to review what one achieved in a day and to make plans for days ahead. But I do not want that to be the sole or most important way of reflecting on what has happened.

The *consciousness examen*, a Jesuit discipline, invites us prayerfully to review our day and notice where we have been drawn toward God, where we have been tugged away from God, where God might be nudging us next. Many items that emerge for pondering are never on to-do lists. Frequently they are matters not easily measured or weighed. Usually they are full of intrinsic goods, worthwhile in and of themselves. I am reminded of

---

26. John Howard Yoder, *The Original Revolution: Essays on Christian Pacifism* (Scottdale, PA: Herald, 1971), 161.

27. Buber, "Biblical Leadership," in *On the Bible*, 141, 142.

a quotation attributed to Robert Louis Stevenson: "Don't judge each day by the harvest you reap but by the seeds that you plant."

When Roman Catholics canonize saints, they are discerning fruitfulness. Many saints were exemplary people who died in apparent defeat, not necessarily accomplishing what they set out to achieve. But we do not judge them on this score. Rather we watch whether the seeds they planted in love bore unexpected fruits, perhaps decades or even centuries later. Augustine is reported to have asked: "Why can the dead do such great things?"[28] Oftentimes only in looking back centuries later do we see that people were right in their lonely priorities. We are grateful now for those who opposed slavery early on (a brave and eccentric few). What they stood for seems clear and obvious from the perspective of hindsight. But how do we measure outcomes without the advantage of 20/20 hindsight? We shall return to this matter of saints in our next and final chapter.

Weighing Worship

The ways we weigh worship can parallel how we evaluate leadership. What do we mean when we say that a worship service was "good"?

Sometimes we approve of its aesthetics or taste, similar to affirming the convictions of a leader. But tastes, preferences, and aesthetic sensibilities vary widely.

Sometimes we say worship is good if many people are involved or if there is evidence of leaders collaborating well. (It is always unsettling when key worship leaders compete with one another.) But should teamwork and collegiality be a major means of evaluation? Are there not deeper issues at stake?

At times, worship can be about numbers: offerings collected, people in attendance, altar call responses. We count those who were attracted or stirred. But worship is about the praise of God. God does not necessarily work via majority approval. Instead the Holy Spirit may speak most powerfully through minorities and dissenters.

To my mind one of the most important criteria has to do with *theology* of worship; I regard that as its character. I appreciate and commend the worship of churches I visit when they are theologically grounded, praising God with evident reverence, respect, and care. I do not necessarily agree

---

28. Robert Bartlett, *Why Can the Dead Do Such Great Things? Saints and Worshippers from the Martyrs to the Reformation* (Princeton, NJ: Princeton University Press, 2013), 3.

with every aspect of someone else's theology of worship, but I can recognize and appreciate when others are within Christian theological traditions.

While *fruitfulness* is elusive, difficult to pin down, we should nevertheless expect worship to produce fruit consistent with the justice and righteousness priorities that God calls for throughout scriptures. This was a passionate concern of Old Testament prophets, who denounced affluent worshippers for ignoring the oppression of others. A Nazi-era saying is reputed to have been uttered by Bonhoeffer: "Only those who cry out for the Jews may sing Gregorian Chants."[29] Jesus counseled interrupting worshipful sacrifice in order to be reconciled with others. When worship and rituals are criticized in the scriptures it is because worshippers' lives are not consistent with the just and righteous implications of God's grace.

The same standard applies to good leadership too.

29. Cited by Geffrey B. Kelly and F. Burton Nelson, *The Cost of Moral Leadership: The Spirituality of Dietrich Bonhoeffer* (Grand Rapids: Eerdmans, 2003), 91.

Chapter Seventeen

We Want to Be in That Number

Heroes or Saints?

When Leaders Learn to Cry

The classic spiritual, "When the Saints Go Marching In," has a startling verse:

When our leaders learn to cry
O Lord, I want to be in that number[1]

I am impressed at this matter-of-fact acknowledgement of the reality that leadership may stretch us in uncomfortable and even painful ways. Too many leaders have not learned to cry, to empathize, to suffer.

While in university, I was active in a local congregation that I loved. Several other university students also attended the church. My girlfriend Lorna (later my wife) and I participated in a small group there; we met weekly for prayer, accountability, study, meals, and fun. Church involvement and connections were hugely important for us.

One reason for that was that the pastor—let's call him Robert—was warmly personable. He was attentively present in conversations, asking insightful questions and showing himself to be pastorally supportive. He was well-spoken, eloquent, and persuasive. He had tremendous communication gifts as a teacher and preacher. He shed new light and surprising insights

1. Louis Armstrong, vocal performance of "When the Saints Go Marching In," songwriter unknown, on *The Definitive Collection* (Santa Monica, CA: Universal, 2006).

into Bible passages that might otherwise seem stale and familiar. I took lots of notes when he preached.

In all respects, he seemed to be a natural born leader, with many of the gifts, talents, and capacities that we typically include in that term.

He was also, as it turns out, a sociopath; his personable abilities masked an absence of conscience.

There is no need to belabor all the details of a story that I now realize is all too sadly common. The discovery of his affair with a member was bad enough, but there was more bad news to come. The man that we regarded as an exemplary pastor, father, and husband was a serial adulterer. Robert left our church, moved across the border to pastor another congregation in a different denomination (where he would eventually have an affair with one of the staff).

As this started coming to light, university students active in the church were invited to a small meeting. The gathering was convened by a church elder who explained what had happened. I remember the deep pain that I felt about this news; little was I to know that I would hear many more of these stories in years to come.

I will never forget when the elder, tears falling from his eyes and grief catching at his throat, read from Psalm 55:

> My companion...
> violated a covenant with me
> with speech smoother than butter,
> but with a heart set on war;
> with words that were softer than oil,
> but in fact were drawn swords. (55:20-21)

Robert had significant leadership gifts. He was successful in many respects: thriving congregation, influence in his denomination and among university students, steadily growing numbers at church. Yet those strategic successes were outweighed by his moral lapses and the sorrow that his wrongful behaviors unleashed in many lives and in the congregation for which he was responsible.

I am no longer as surprised or disillusioned by the failures of others, especially knowing how far I myself fall short. But my experience of that wayward pastor, one who seemed to have all the chops of a winning leader, left me permanently wary about how we think about leadership.

Personality and Celebrity

In the last century, wider North American culture has become more and more enamored of celebrities and heroes; this has had an impact on people's attitudes toward leadership.

Leadership genre publications frequently focus on legendarily impressive corporation executives, entrepreneurial business people, national sports figures, military commanders, megachurch ministers, and political power brokers. These luminaries may be stars or celebrities or even heroes, but are they exemplars for Christians who ponder leadership?

As we come to the end of our exploration toward a biblical theology of leadership, we need to pay attention to crucial differences between heroes and saints, between emphasizing personality and stressing character.

The historian Warren Susman notes that in British and English intellectual discourses and publications in the seventeenth through nineteenth centuries, *character* was a high priority. Susman speaks of "the importance of the concept of character." Character was vital to the health of wider culture. It was associated with terms like "citizenship," "duty," "honor," "reputation," "morals," and "integrity."[2] Good character, thought to be worthy of aspiration, was widely promoted. Susan Cain observes about that same era: "In the Culture of Character, the ideal self was serious, disciplined, and honorable. What counted was not so much the impression one made in public as how one behaved in private."[3]

In the late nineteenth and early twentieth century new attitudes emerged. With "objective" psychology and early stages of consumerism, "interest grew in personality, individual idiosyncrasies, personal needs and interests. The vision of self-sacrifice began to yield to that of self-realization."[4] A new term, *personality*, suddenly became important. Along with that, emerging self-help manuals focused on "a very different concept than that of character: *fascinating, stunning, attractive, magnetic, glowing, masterful, creative, dominant, forceful.*"[5] Today, we constantly hear the importance of presentation, image, or (current jargon) "brand."

Popular attention moved from emphasizing *character* to a culture of *personality*. The challenge became how to be "somebody" who stands out,

2. Warren I. Susman, *Culture as History: The Transformation of American Society in the Twentieth Century* (New York: Pantheon, 1984), 273–74.

3. Susan Cain, *Quiet: The Power of Introverts in a World That Can't Stop Talking* (New York: Crown, 2013), 21.

4. Susman, *Culture as History*, 276.

5. Ibid., 277.

who is noticed, attractive, famous (although being infamous can also be admirable). Self-help manuals offered guidance on influencing, impressing, or persuading by developing charm and wit. This was true of Dale Carnegie's emphases in his popular *How to Win Friends and Influence People*, a book that "marked the demotion of certain long-respected virtues. By its teachings, character gave way to personality, self-control to self-fulfillment, industry and thrift to skill at handling people."[6] Books explicitly suggested connections between fostering an attractive personality and business success.[7] Furthermore, the emphasis on personality contributed to the emergence of celebrity culture and movie stars. Individuals, regardless of actual achievements or character, became images for adulatory attention.

Much contemporary leadership literature leans more to the culture of personality than the culture of character. David Brooks notes: "The language of meritocracy (how to succeed) has eclipsed the language of morality (how to be virtuous)."[8] This needs to concern us as Christians.

Portrayals of successful heroes or celebrities in strategically scripted worship services or in books (self-authored or ghostwritten) or on videos are carefully managed images. Incredibly winsome leaders may be depicted in ways that are not necessarily closer to reality than the airbrushed photos of slick pornography magazines. Yet we confuse projected personas with reality: "As often happens in a celebrity culture, the line between public and fictional personas blurs."[9]

This is a major reason why some seminary students are discouraged about regarding themselves as leaders. They are intimidated because they cannot imagine measuring up to the competent, well-oiled, occasionally flashy, charismatic (in the broadest sense), up-front people in large or thriving churches or in the media. They do not perceive themselves as inspirational superstars and therefore feel unqualified for the lofty designation of being a leader. They are undone by exposure to leadership porn.

Nevertheless, every once in a while a mask slips and the public is shocked that a true person is so different from the facade. We realize that a successful media star (interviewer, talk show host) is destructively driven

6. Ian Frazier, "'A New Way of Life,'" review of *Self-Help Messiah: Dale Carnegie and Success in Modern America* by Steven Watts, *New York Review of Books*, October 9, 2014, 38.

7. Susman, *Culture as History*, 281.

8. David Brooks, "The Failed Promise of American Meritocracy," *Seattle Times*, July 14, 2012.

9. Chris Hedges, *Empire of Illusion: The End of Literacy and the Triumph of Spectacle* (Toronto: Knopf, 2009), 4.

and manically controlling. We learn that the grandfatherly comedian sexually abused numerous women over the years. One popular megachurch pastor is revealed to be domineering and manipulative, and another is shown to be involved in drug abuse and sordid extramarital sexual behavior.

If we concentrate on the surface, on appearances of success, on pleasingly projected personas, on the acquisition of skills without attention to integrity, there is no reason to expect actual character in leaders. In her last book, *Dark Age Ahead*, Jane Jacobs argues that the purpose of education has moved from character formation to credentialing. If a student sees education merely as credentialing, then he or she may choose to do whatever it takes to get a particular degree or diploma, jumping through hoops as quickly and easily as possible.[10]

If, however, a student sees education as being about formation, then he or she will be motivated to engage assigned materials. Such students know that deep learning can facilitate character and integrity.

This is of special concern for seminary education. Seminaries move further and further from intense, concentrated, residential programs to dispersed campuses and online learning. Seminary education devolves more and more into credentialing rather than formation. Students are burdened by staggering loans, frequently juggling studies with family life and part-time jobs (perhaps several of them); they are under a lot of pressure.

I saw more than one seminarian who felt so much stress in studies for the ministry (of all things) that he or she engaged in serial, patterned, deliberate plagiarism. The Internet lowers the threshold; it is easy to plagiarize now. Out of time, out of energy, or out of ideas, one can fire up the World Wide Web and purchase a paper or borrow from online articles or blogs.

If seminary education is merely a credentialing hoop, it makes sense to cheat; if education is character formation, then cheating is absurd. Yet, cheaters, it turns out, may prosper.

How can well-motivated Christians break these rules? If they are preparing to be *Christian* leaders, examples of faithfulness and integrity, wouldn't that argue for exemplary behavior?

Well, yes, if students understood seminary as being about character development and formation. Not so much, however, if they see seminary as merely acquiring credentials by any means necessary. One student was in so much of a rush to graduate and to take an offered pastoral position that he plagiarized every one of his assignments in his final seminary class. When I pointed out what seemed to be a moral contradiction, my concern did not

10. Jane Jacobs, *Dark Age Ahead* (New York: Vintage, 2005), ch. 3.

compute for him. He accepted his first pastoral charge a few weeks after our conversation.

A number of years ago, I walked the Camino de Santiago pilgrimage in Spain. Pilgrims who go on foot a certain distance are eligible to receive a cherished *Compostela* certificate from the cathedral office at the end of the pilgrimage. Several pilgrims I met baldly told me that they lied in order to get their certificate. But what meaning does "credentialing" have when based on deception?

Looking for Leaders in the Cloud of Witnesses

As Christians look back on church history, who is it that we celebrate and want to emulate? Celebrities and heroes do not figure so importantly. All Saints' litanies tend to commemorate: the "cloud of witnesses" (Heb 12:1), prophets, apostles, martyrs, pilgrims, missionaries, teachers, pastors, saints or "holy men and women"[11] of course ("whose lives have reflected the light of Christ"[12]), and those "anointed by your Spirit.[13] This is a striking list of exemplary predecessors, people whose examples inspire our faithfulness.

The liturgical year offers many opportunities, not just on All Saints' Day, to reflect on saints and sainthood:

> One of the tasks of the church, in its liturgical life as well as in its formal education, is to recall the history of humanity in a different way than is usual in secular society. History is usually the story of conquerors, where greatness is measured in wars won and peoples subdued. . . . The liturgical year commemorates saints who suffered unjustly, or who alleviated or prevented the suffering of others. . . . Rather than see such people as human-interest sidebar stories in a history focused on the wielders of power, the liturgical calendar puts them in center stage of the history that matters.[14]

11. Howard Galley, ed., *The Prayer Book Office* (New York: Seabury, 1988), 843.

12. "Thanksgiving Litany," in *The Book of Alternative Services of the Anglican Church of Canada* (Toronto: Anglican Book Centre, 1985), 128.

13. The Archbishops' Council of the Church of England, *Common Worship: Daily Prayer* (London: Church House Publishing, 2005), 384.

14. Elaine Ramshaw, *Ritual and Pastoral Care*, ed. Don S. Browning (Philadelphia: Fortress, 1987), 94.

Saints are salutary and impressive, but are they *leaders*? Does this question even matter? Most of the All Saints' litanies' terms—saints, witnesses, apostles, martyrs, prophets—are derived straight from scriptures. Notice that other kinds of leaders mentioned in the Bible—kings, rulers, princes, hierarchs—are *not* named. In fact, Lipman-Blumen warns us not to "look for saints among formal leaders."[15] Saints are more likely to be unsung, behind-the-scenes, salt of the earth.

Saints Aren't All They're Cracked Up to Be

The word *saint* can be contested and controversial terminology.

New Testament Greek employs *hagios*, a word translated as "saints," over sixty times. It has connotations of holiness, being set apart. "Saints" is originally a designation that refers to *all* believers, people we might now just plainly call "Christians." Paul writes, for example, "to all God's beloved in Rome, who are called to be saints" (Rom 1:7). This term carries both affection and an aspirational challenge to grow into holiness. (Paul uses *hagios* frequently but not in his letter to the Galatians, a group about which he had significant reservations and no small anger.)

"Saints" gradually came to be associated with exceptional Christians, no longer all believers. My father (a hard-drinking, chain-smoking businessman with a ferocious temper) once had a friendly argument with our pastor. The pastor had talked about my parents being "saints"; he was right in the original New Testament sense. But my father refused that label, finding it dishonest; English was not his first language, but he knew the connotations of this term. He was in his own way a believer and churchman but was also aware that he did not measure up to some people's pious standards. Perhaps he did not even want to measure up.

One problem with talk about *saints* is that we may celebrate people who behaved in extraordinary ways that appear out of our reach. Who can live up to the joyful sacrificial challenges of Francis of Assisi? Dorothy Day used to growl something to this effect: "Don't call me a saint . . . I don't want to be dismissed that easily."[16] She worried that someone might suggest that her dedicated ascetic lifestyle was unattainable to "regular" Christians. Then

15. Jean Lipman-Blumen, *The Allure of Toxic Leaders: Why We Follow Destructive Bosses and Corrupt Politicians—and How We Can Survive Them* (New York: Oxford University Press, 2005), 5.

16. Quoted in James Martin, *My Life with the Saints* (Chicago: Loyola, 2006), 226.

her commitment could be written off as an anomaly and not in fact a challenge to all.

Yet another issue with saint terminology is that saints can be portrayed in flat, two-dimensional, pious clichés so that most of us do not actually believe the stories about them. *Hagiography* first referred literally to biographies of saints, but the term now may implicitly suggest *whitewash.*

There is understandable suspicion when sainthood gets discussed. In "Reflections on Gandhi," George Orwell wrote: "Saints should always be judged guilty until they are proved innocent." Diarmid MacCulloch reminds us that "one definition of a saint is someone who has not been researched well enough.[17]

I admire how our pastor tried to broaden my parents' understanding of sainthood, but I also believe there is usefulness in acknowledging that some believers are especially exemplary and enduring in their witness and life. Hebrews 12 celebrates the "cloud of witnesses"(CEB) and All Saints' litanies identify key categories of faithfulness. It is also worth admitting that many believers could benefit from setting higher aspirational goals. Our bar is often too low.

Roman Catholicism developed an elaborate method of recognizing and canonizing saints throughout the millennia, including martyrs, prophets, confessors of the faith, miracle workers, teachers, theologians, and liberators. Because of the influence of that approach, many Protestants prefer not to use "saint" terminology at all. Yet the Catholic system, in spite of weaknesses and flaws, does offer good things. Margaret Visser notes: "Sainthood is perhaps the only honor accorded a person without consideration of physical beauty or prowess, wealth, birth, political power, intelligence, fame, or talent; a saint is admired, and considered exemplary, entirely for being good."[18] This is a far cry from the celebrity adulation in our culture of personality.

Several Christian authors helpfully distinguish between heroes and saints. Craig Dykstra writes of the distinctiveness of how Christians read history:

> While human achievement is valued in the Christian story, it has a different place and meaning. The human task is not fundamentally mastery.

---

17. George Orwell, "Reflections on Gandhi," *Partisan Review (London), January 1949, http://www.orwell.ru/library/reviews/gandhi/english/e_gandhi. Diarmaid MacCulloch, Silence: A Christian History* (New York: Penguin, 2013), 203.

18. Margaret Visser, *The Geometry of Love: Space, Time, Mystery, and Meaning in an Ordinary Church* (Toronto: Harper Flamingo Canada, 2000), 88.

> It is rather the right use of gifts graciously bestowed by a loving God for the sake of the good that God intends.... So our basic task is not mastery and control. It is instead trust and grateful receptivity. Our exemplars are not heroes; they are saints. Our epitome is not excellence; our honor is in faithfulness.[19]

Samuel Wells is particularly eloquent in delineating differences between saints and heroes. He notes, for example, that heroes (similar to Dykstra's point about "mastery and control") "make the story come out right." A hero's story is only worth telling once he or she succeeds. Saints, on the other hand, do not have to achieve great things or win amazing victories: "A saint can fail in a way that the hero can't, because the failure of a saint reveals the forgiveness and the new possibilities made in God, and the saint is just a small character in a story that's always fundamentally about God."[20] Wells goes on to contrast heroes and saints in the following ways:[21]

Hero Stories	**Saint Stories**
Central to story of making everything right	Peripheral to story that is always centered on God
Celebrate "strength, courage, wisdom, or great timing"	Saint may be without virtues or valor except faithfulness
Hero fights, does battle, is courageous	Christ has already won, thus saints prioritize "love, joy, peace, faithfulness, gentleness"
Soldier is "icon of heroism"	"The icon of sanctity is the martyr"
Heroes are noble	"The martyr's sanctity makes no sense unless rewarded by God"

19. Craig Dykstra, *Growing in the Life of Faith: Education and Christian Practices* (Louisville: Westminster John Knox, 1999), 76.

20. Rupert Shortt, "Stanley Hauerwas and Samuel Wells: Theological Ethics" (includes an interview with Stanley Hauerwas and Samuel Wells), in *God's Advocates: Christian Thinkers in Conversation*, ed. Rupert Shortt (London: Darton, Longman and Todd, 2005), 180.

21. This schema is summarized from Samuel Wells, *Improvisation: The Drama of Christian Ethics* (Grand Rapids: Brazos, 2004), 43–44.

Heroes succeed; they fear or flee failure	Saints anticipate failure; they open the possibility of a "cycle of repentance, forgiveness, reconciliation, and restoration that is... a new creation"
"The hero stands alone against the world"	Saints depend on God and community: "Of... sixty-four references to saints in the New Testament, every one is in the plural. Saints are never alone"

In speaking of Christian leadership, we set aside glamorous heroic visions and concentrate on creating saints, equipping faithful, fruitful Christ followers. We need to form Mother Teresas, not empower Terry Joneses. In cultivating saints, we focus on priorities not always evident in leadership literature, including humility and surrender. Christian leaders are—or ought to be—averse to triumphalism and self-assurance, boastfulness and self-congratulation.

Just as the scriptures counterculturally and subversively challenge and undermine leadership claims of so many power brokers in both the Old and New Testaments, so we too ought to treat leadership in our day (both our own and that of others) with circumspection.

Here saints have much to teach. Acknowledged and canonized saints were, time after time, *eccentric*. Curtis Almquist oversees the Society of St. John the Evangelist and observed that monks are sometimes seen as *eccentric*, not in the sense of being quirky or odd. He wrote: "I mean eccentric in an etymological sense, as in the Latin *eccentricus*, meaning 'having a different center.'"[22] Christians center and orient their lives alternatively, prioritizing values often not understood or appreciated elsewhere.

Many officially canonized and unofficially recognized saints were deeply countercultural:

> Christian saints attained their exalted status and... recognition in society not by taking the ordinary values of that society to a higher degree, but by inverting them. They rejected... things that most people desire, and

22. Curtis Almquist, "A Letter from the Superior," *Cowley* 31, no. 3 (Pentecost 2005): 3.

> took up a life of self-denial and poverty. This was part of their striving for holiness.[23]

Saintliness is not about success, "irrefutable" principles and secrets, or self-help counsel. It is about cruciformity, being formed and shaped by the costs of faithfulness and discipleship: "Martyrdom of one sort or another, suffering of one sort or another, is what kingdom-bringers must expect."[24]

It is not likely that agenda of sainthood will be featured in MBA programs or on bookstore Business shelves (where leadership books are typically located), unless by accident. More than ever, however, this needs to be the agenda of Christians in church, in seminaries, and elsewhere as we ponder how to form followers of Jesus who lead on his behalf.

When leaders learn to be saints, I want to be in that number.

---

23. Robert Bartlett, *Why Can the Dead Do Such Great Things? Saints and Worshippers from the Martyrs to the Reformation* (Princeton, NJ: Princeton University Press, 2013), 634.

24. N. T. Wright, *How God Became King* (New York: HarperOne, 2012), 241.

CPSIA information can be obtained
at www.ICGtesting.com
Printed in the USA
LVOW03s2105140817
545016LV00013B/171/P